R0459813543

Chapter 11

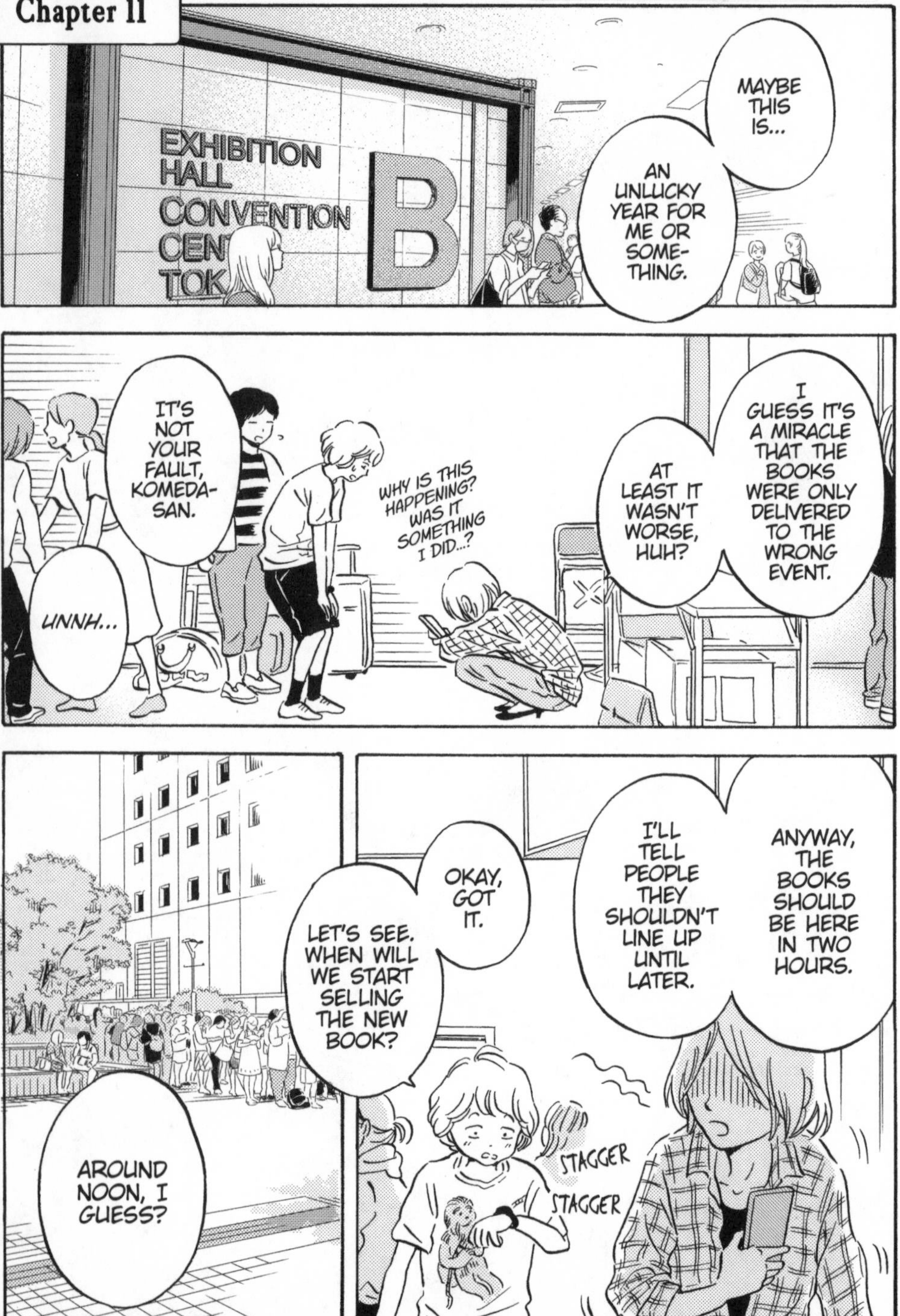
EXHIBITION HALL CONVENTION CENT TOK
B
MAYBE THIS IS...
AN UNLUCKY YEAR FOR ME OR SOME-THING.
I GUESS IT'S A MIRACLE THAT THE BOOKS WERE ONLY DELIVERED TO THE WRONG EVENT.
AT LEAST IT WASN'T WORSE, HUH?
WHY IS THIS HAPPENING? WAS IT SOMETHING I DID...?
IT'S NOT YOUR FAULT, KOMEDA-SAN.
UNNH...
ANYWAY, THE BOOKS SHOULD BE HERE IN TWO HOURS.
I'LL TELL PEOPLE THEY SHOULDN'T LINE UP UNTIL LATER.
OKAY, GOT IT.
LET'S SEE. WHEN WILL WE START SELLING THE NEW BOOK?
STAGGER
STAGGER
AROUND NOON, I GUESS?

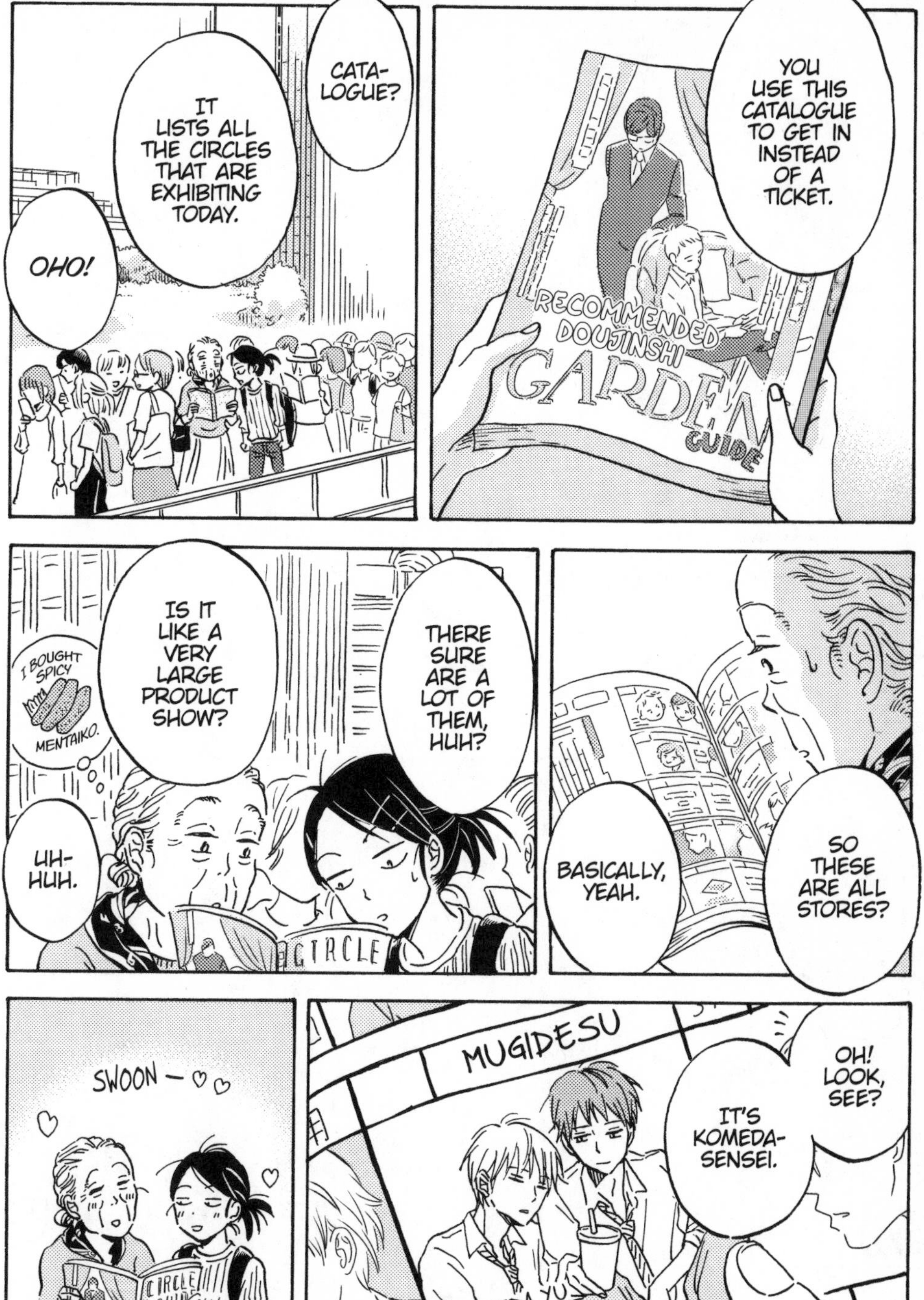
YOU USE THIS CATALOGUE TO GET IN INSTEAD OF A TICKET.
RECOMMENDED DOUJINSHI GARDEN GUIDE
CATA-LOGUE?
IT LISTS ALL THE CIRCLES THAT ARE EXHIBITING TODAY.
OHO!
SO THESE ARE ALL STORES?
BASICALLY, YEAH.
THERE SURE ARE A LOT OF THEM, HUH?
IS IT LIKE A VERY LARGE PRODUCT SHOW?
I BOUGHT SPICY MENTAIKO.
UH-HUH.
CIRCLE
OH! LOOK, SEE?
IT'S KOMEDA-SENSEI.
MUGIDESU
KOMEDA YU
SWOON —
CIRCLE GUIDE

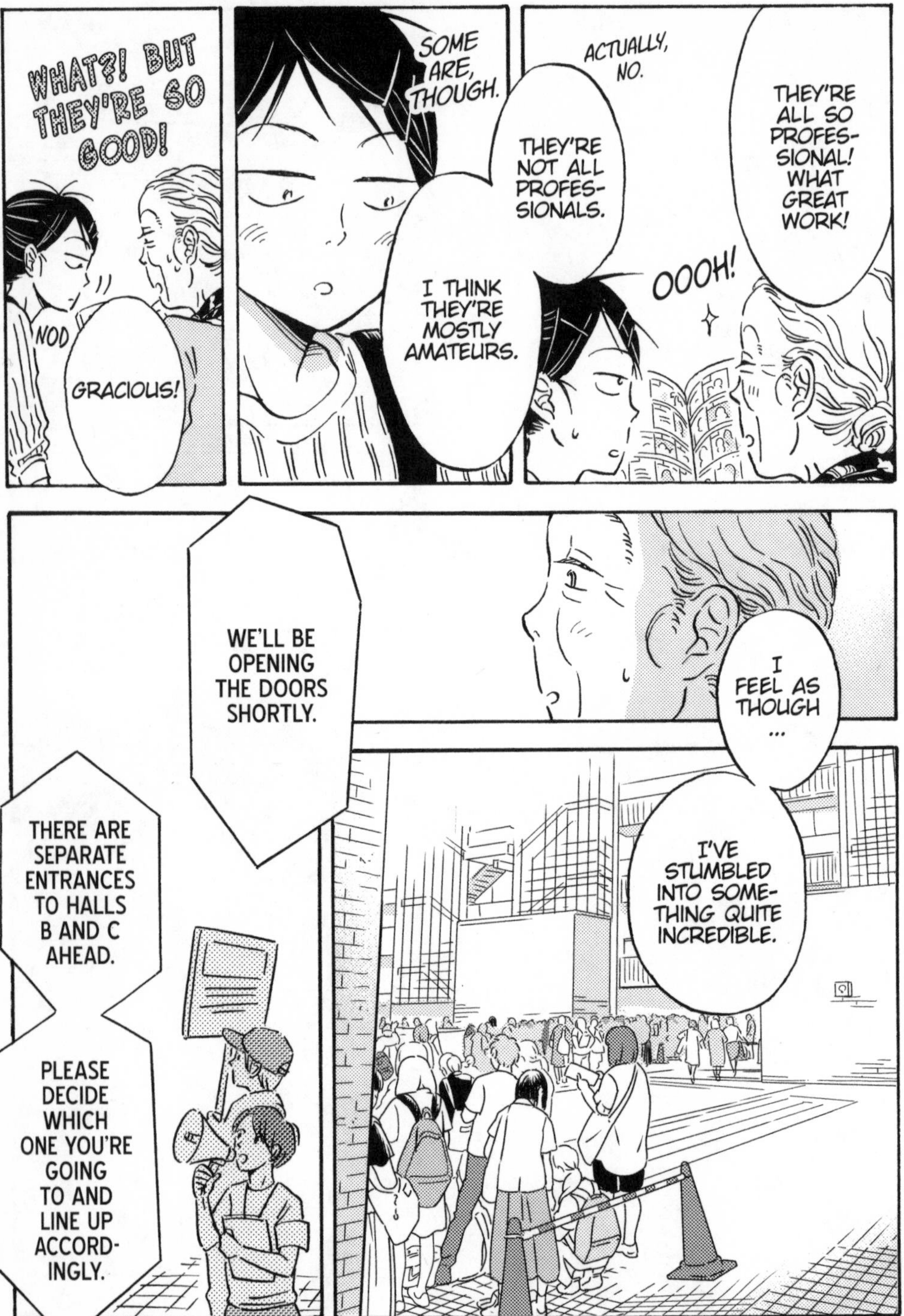
THEY'RE ALL SO PROFES-SIONAL! WHAT GREAT WORK!
OOOH!
ACTUALLY, NO.
THEY'RE NOT ALL PROFES-SIONALS.
I THINK THEY'RE MOSTLY AMATEURS.
SOME ARE, THOUGH.
WHAT?! BUT THEY'RE SO GOOD!
NOD
GRACIOUS!
I FEEL AS THOUGH ...
I'VE STUMBLED INTO SOME-THING QUITE INCREDIBLE.
WE'LL BE OPENING THE DOORS SHORTLY.
THERE ARE SEPARATE ENTRANCES TO HALLS B AND C AHEAD.
PLEASE DECIDE WHICH ONE YOU'RE GOING TO AND LINE UP ACCORD-INGLY.

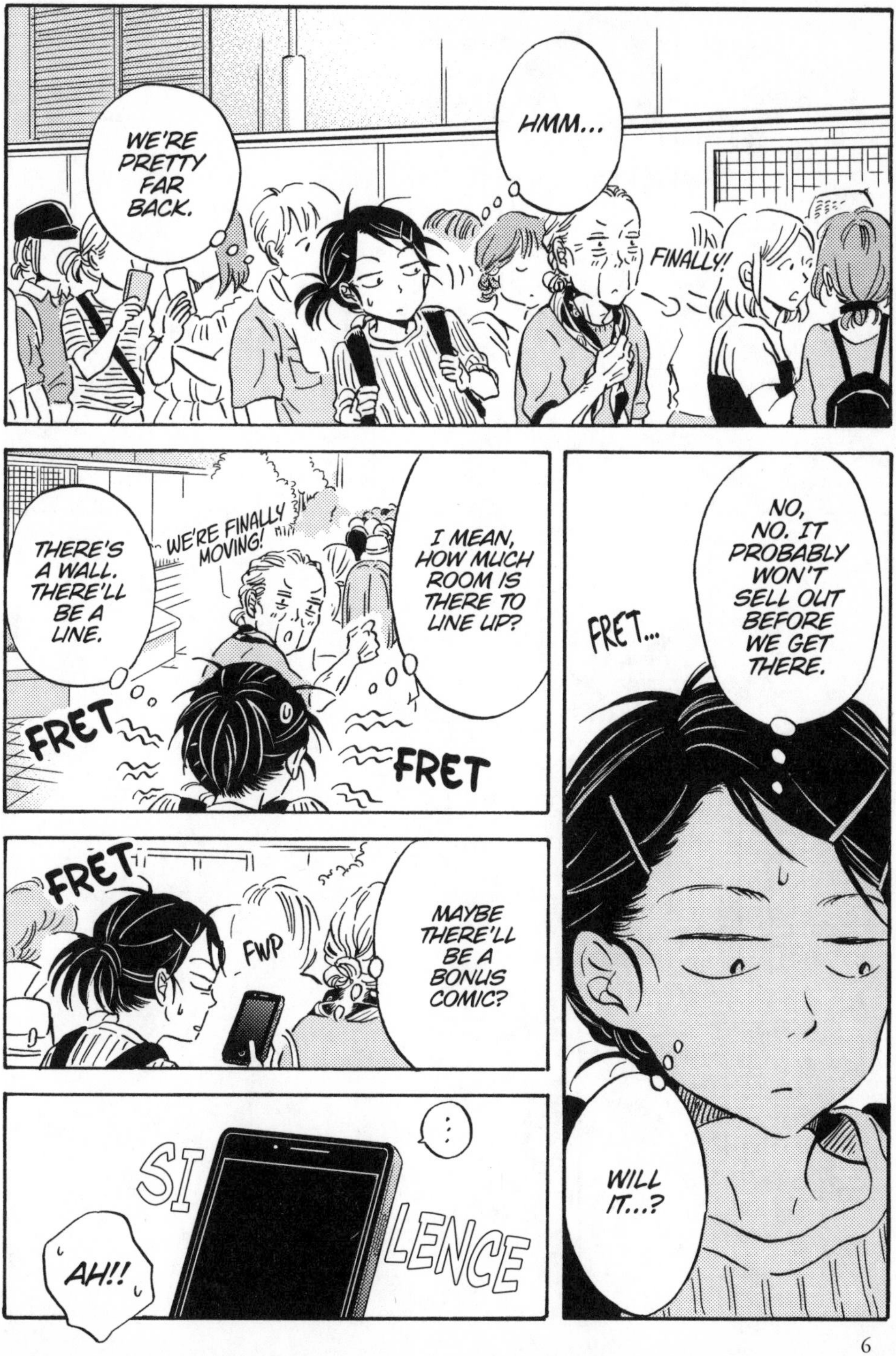
HMM...
FINALLY!
WE'RE PRETTY FAR BACK.
NO, NO. IT PROBABLY WON'T SELL OUT BEFORE WE GET THERE.
FRET...
WILL IT...?
I MEAN, HOW MUCH ROOM IS THERE TO LINE UP?
WE'RE FINALLY MOVING!
THERE'S A WALL. THERE'LL BE A LINE.
FRET
FRET
MAYBE THERE'LL BE A BONUS COMIC?
FWP
FRET
...
SILENCE
AH!!

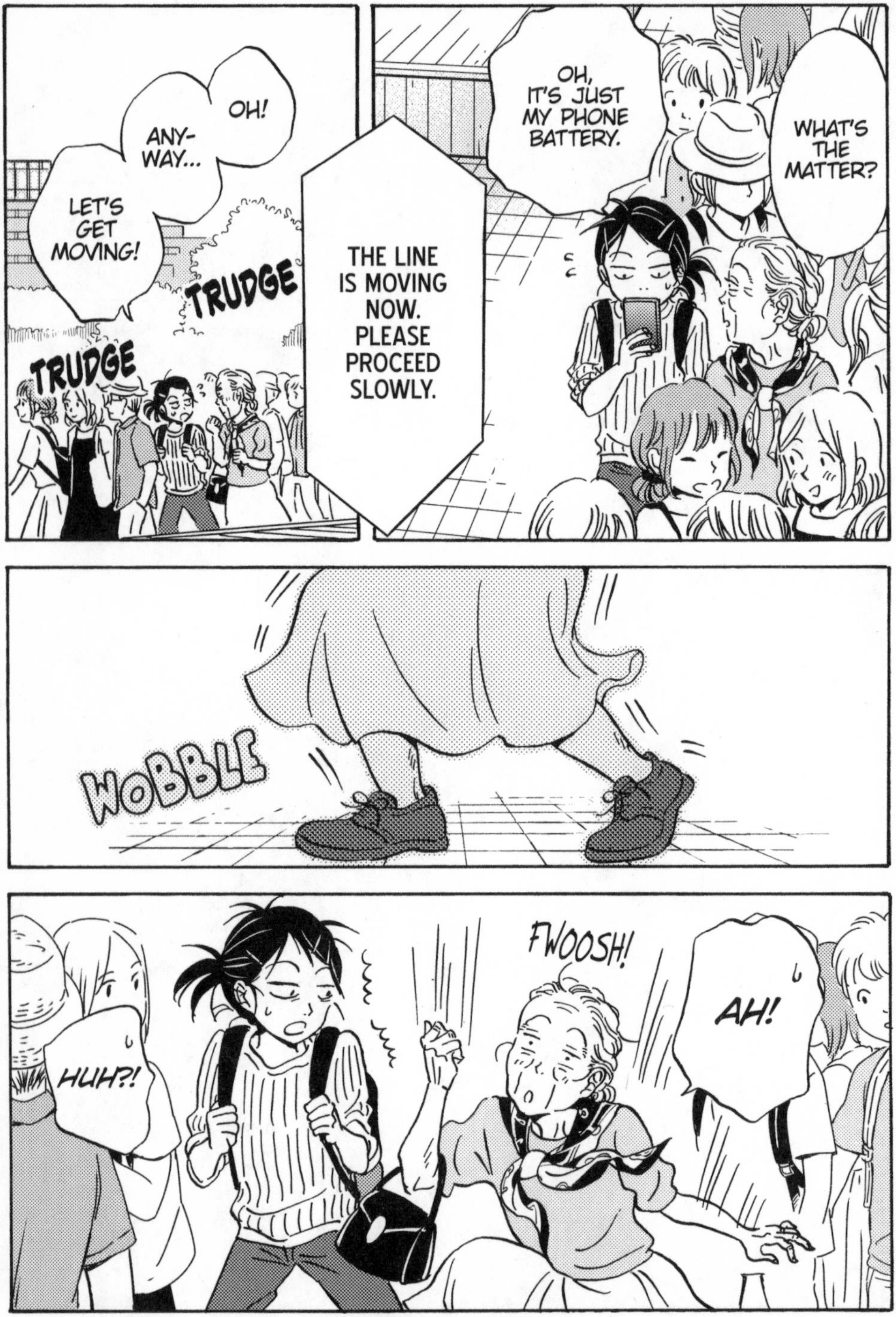
WHAT'S THE MATTER?
OH, IT'S JUST MY PHONE BATTERY.
THE LINE IS MOVING NOW. PLEASE PROCEED SLOWLY.
OH!
ANY-WAY...
LET'S GET MOVING!
TRUDGE
TRUDGE
WOBBLE
AH!
FWOOSH!
HUH?!

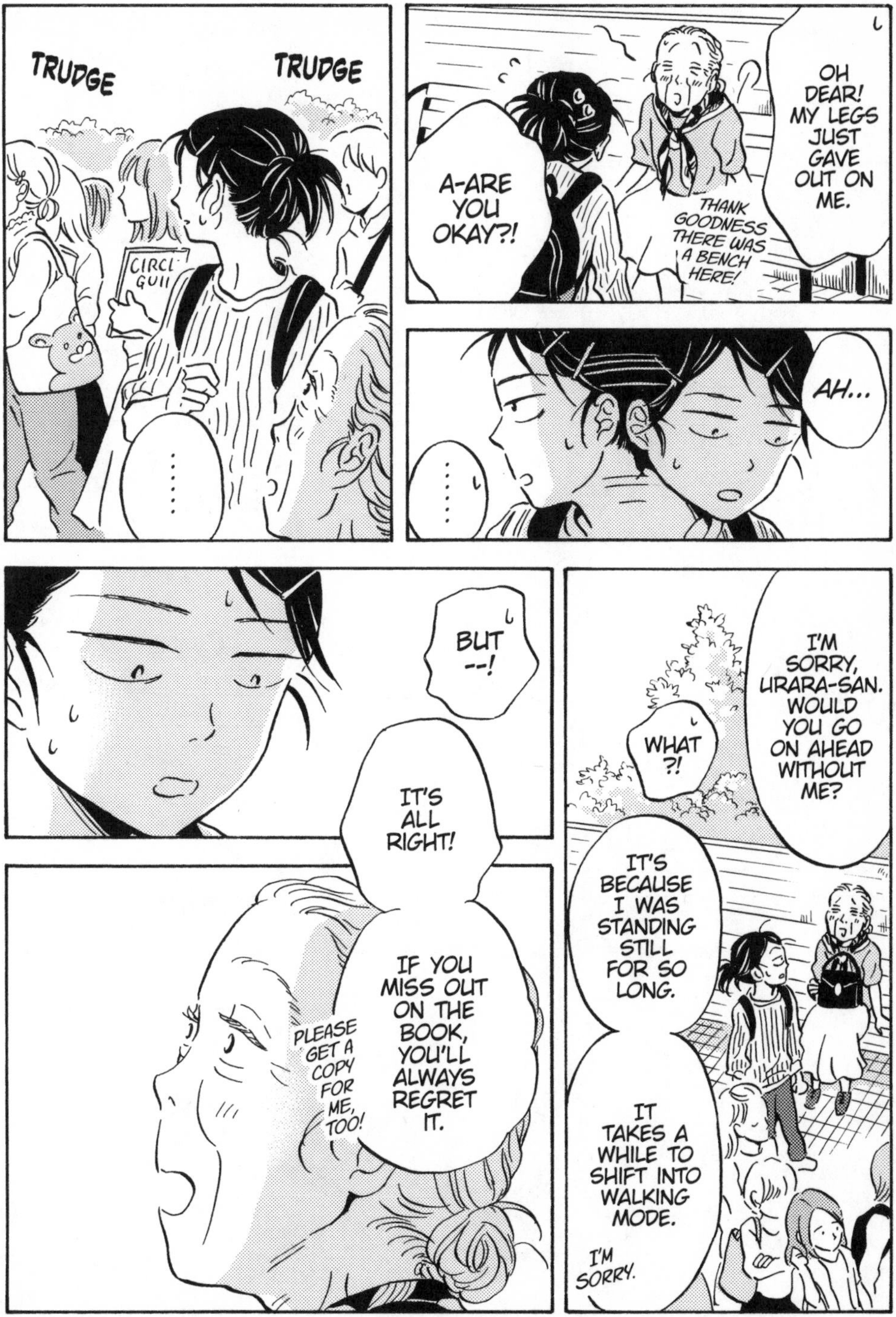
OH DEAR! MY LEGS JUST GAVE OUT ON ME.
THANK GOODNESS THERE WAS A BENCH HERE!
A-ARE YOU OKAY?!
AH...
......
TRUDGE
TRUDGE
......
I'M SORRY, URARA-SAN. WOULD YOU GO ON AHEAD WITHOUT ME?
WHAT?!
IT'S BECAUSE I WAS STANDING STILL FOR SO LONG.
IT TAKES A WHILE TO SHIFT INTO WALKING MODE.
I'M SORRY.
BUT --!
IT'S ALL RIGHT!
IF YOU MISS OUT ON THE BOOK, YOU'LL ALWAYS REGRET IT.
PLEASE GET A COPY FOR ME, TOO!

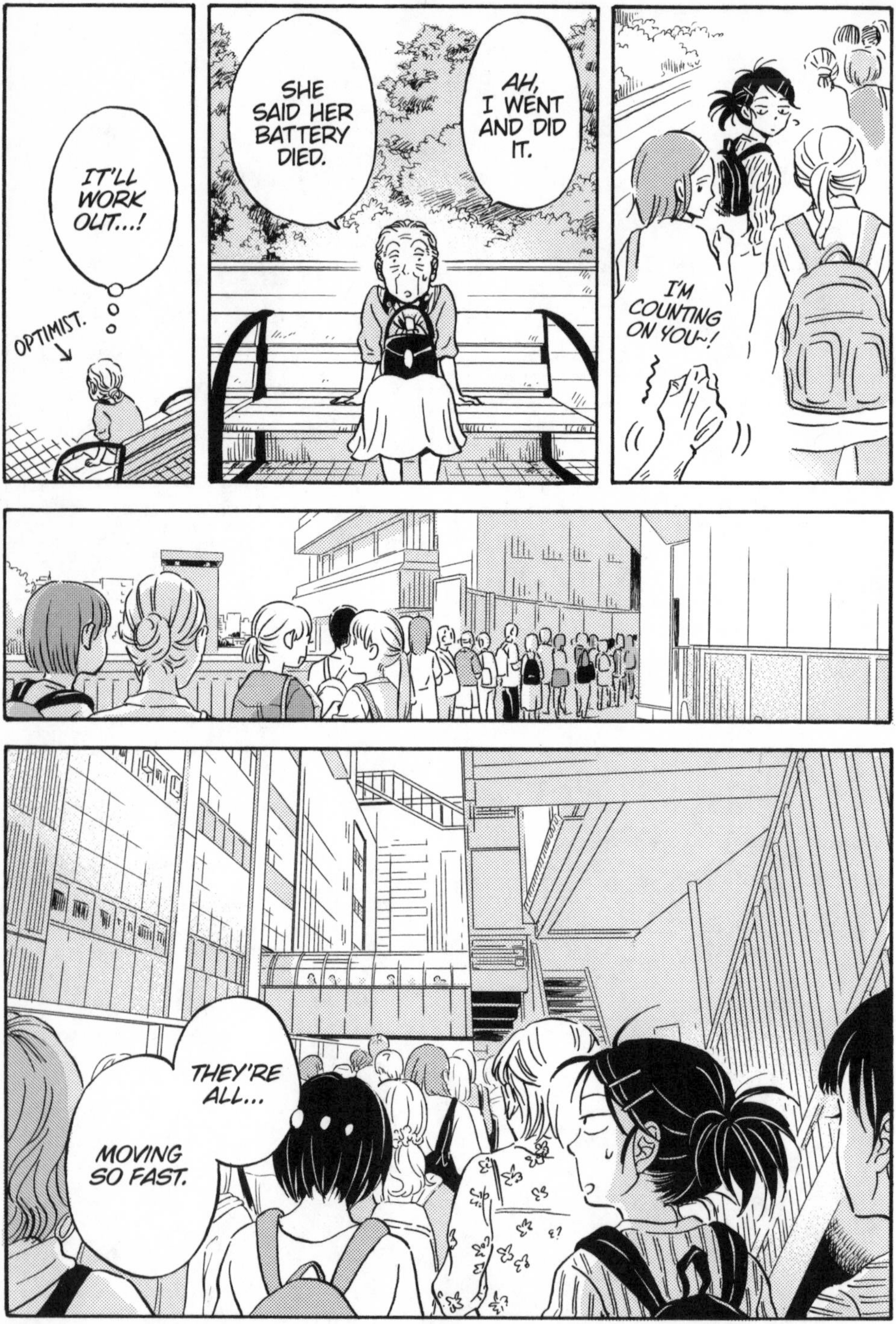
I'M COUNTING ON YOU~!
AH, I WENT AND DID IT.
SHE SAID HER BATTERY DIED.
IT'LL WORK OUT...!
OPTIMIST.
THEY'RE ALL...
MOVING SO FAST.

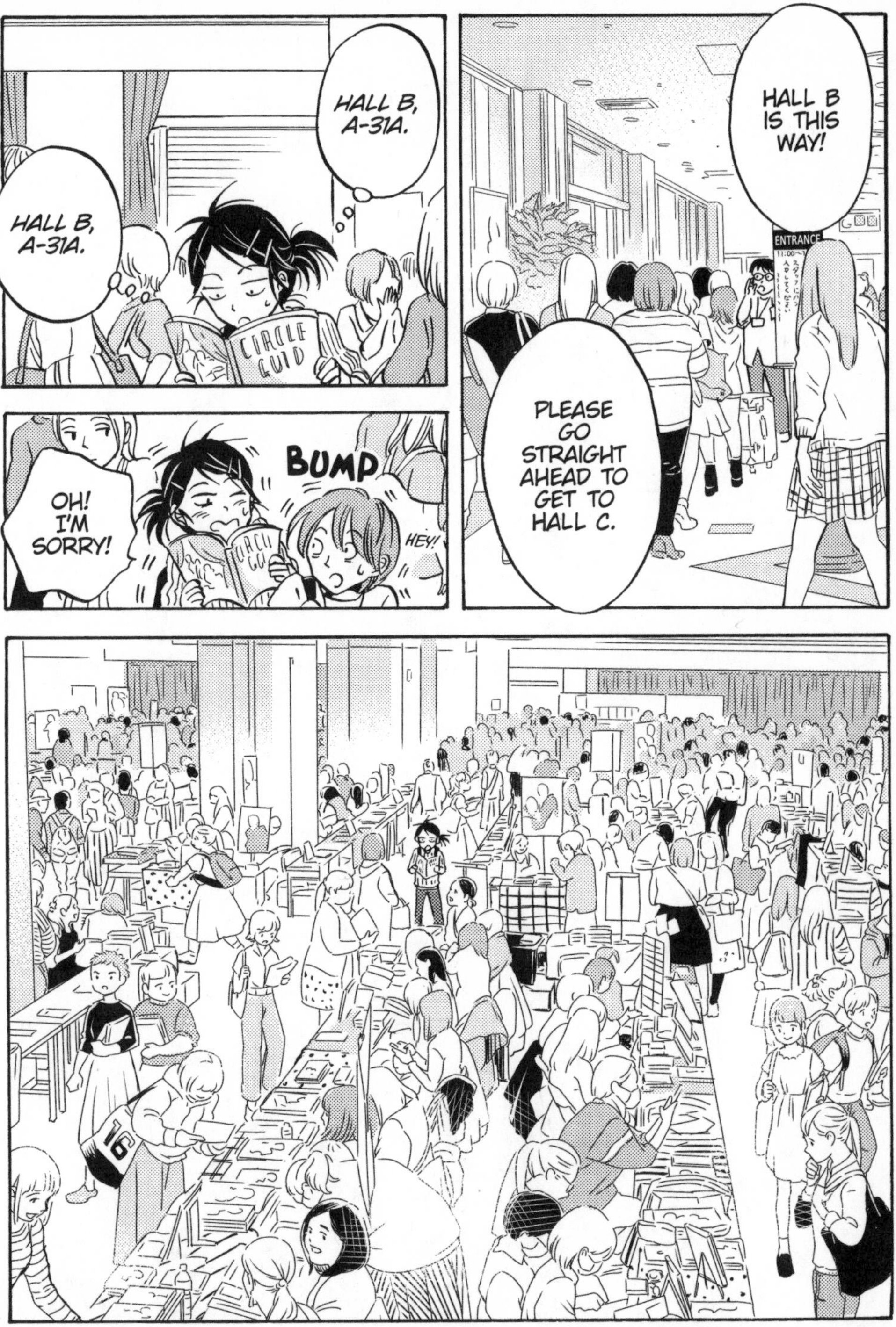
HALL B IS THIS WAY!
ENTRANCE
PLEASE GO STRAIGHT AHEAD TO GET TO HALL C.
HALL B, A-31A.
HALL B, A-31A.
CIRCLE GUID
BUMP
HEY!
OH! I'M SORRY!

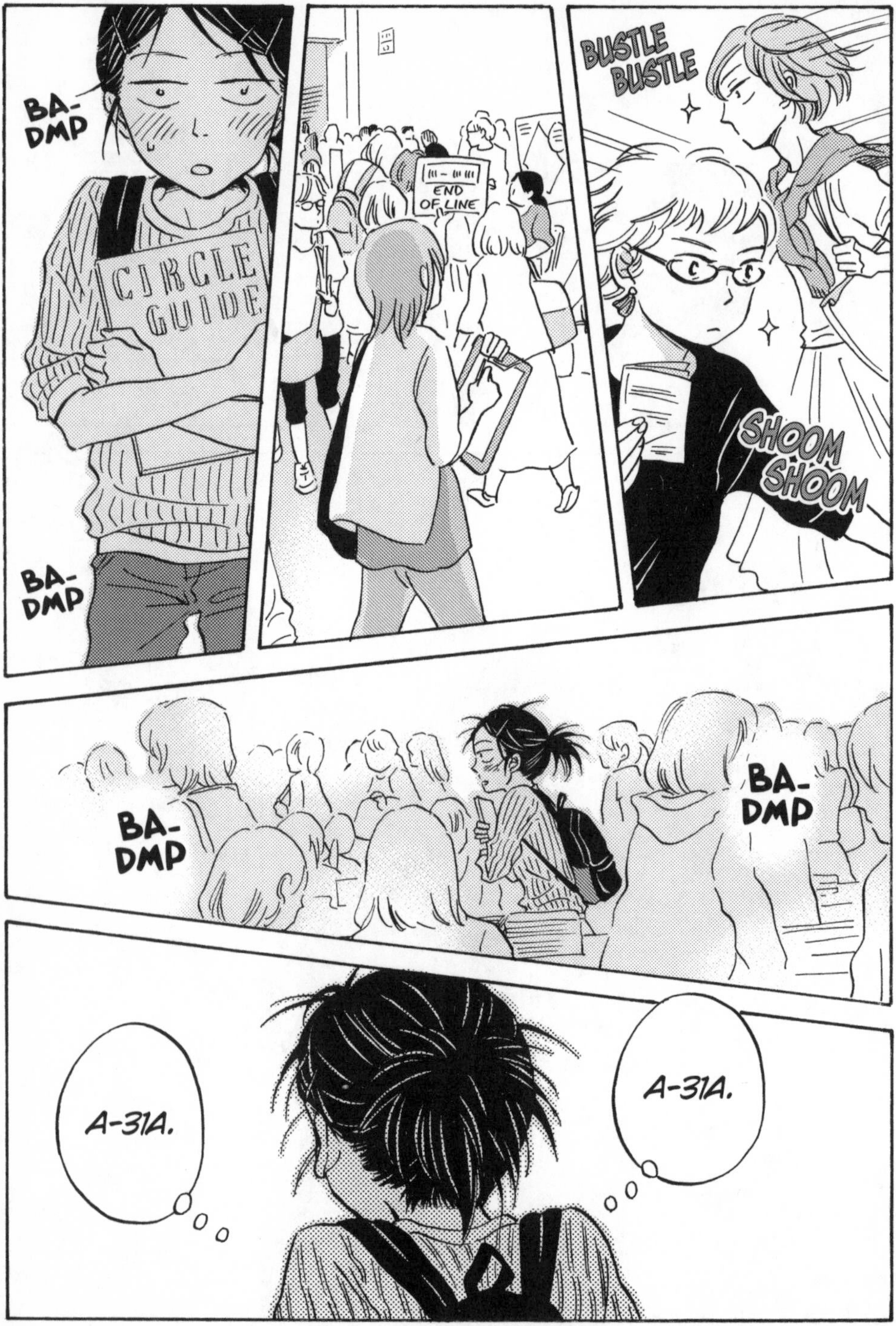
BUSTLE BUSTLE
SHOOM SHOOM
END OF LINE
BA-DMP
CIRCLE GUIDE
BA-DMP
BA-DMP
BA-DMP
A-31A.
A-31A.

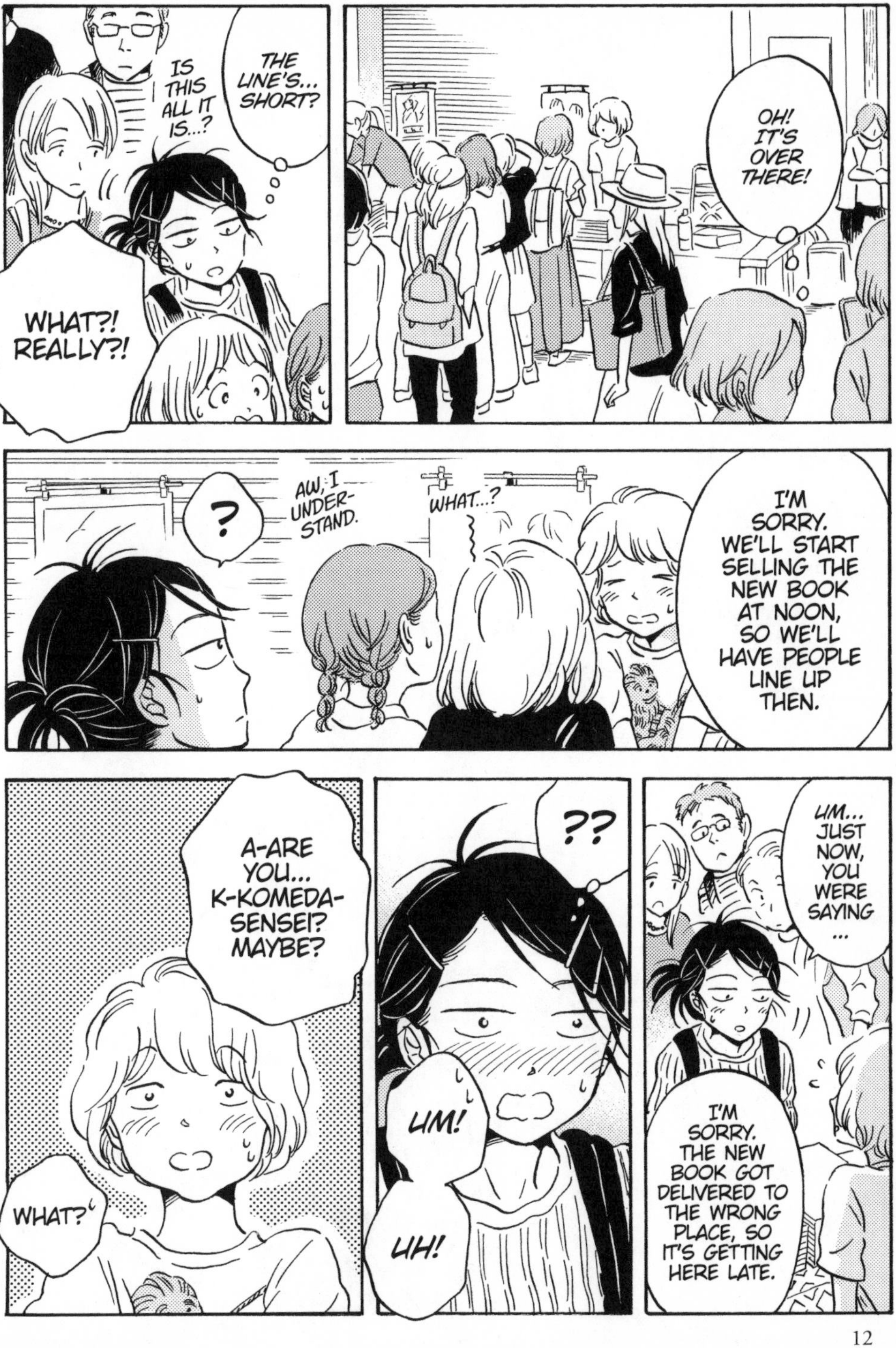
OH! IT'S OVER THERE!
THE LINE'S... SHORT?
IS THIS ALL IT IS...?
WHAT?! REALLY?!
I'M SORRY. WE'LL START SELLING THE NEW BOOK AT NOON, SO WE'LL HAVE PEOPLE LINE UP THEN.
WHAT...?
AW, I UNDERSTAND.
?
UM... JUST NOW, YOU WERE SAYING ...
I'M SORRY. THE NEW BOOK GOT DELIVERED TO THE WRONG PLACE, SO IT'S GETTING HERE LATE.
??
UM!
UH!
A-ARE YOU... K-KOMEDA-SENSEI? MAYBE?
WHAT?

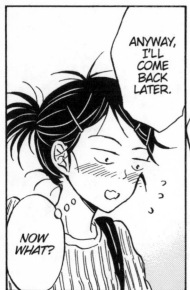

N-NO, I'M SORRY! THAT'S NOT ME.
KOMEDA'S NOT HERE RIGHT NOW. I THINK SHE'LL BE BACK IN A LITTLE WHILE.
WHAT?!
OH!
I-I'M SORRY!
ANYWAY, I'LL COME BACK LATER.
NOW WHAT?
PREVIOUS PUBLICATIONS
MAYBE I SHOULD BUY THE BOOKS THEY DO HAVE WHILE I'M HERE.
I MEAN, I'VE NEVER SEEN THESE ONES BEFORE.
UM, CAN I BUY THESE BOOKS NOW?
OH, YES! OF COURSE.
I JUST NEED TO SEE YOUR ID FIRST!
ADULTSONLY
R 18
成人向け
HUH?!

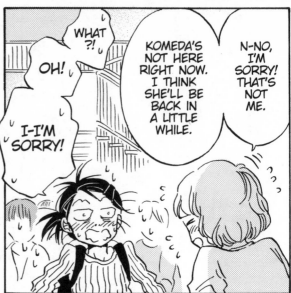

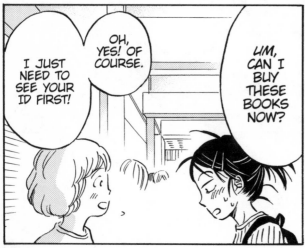

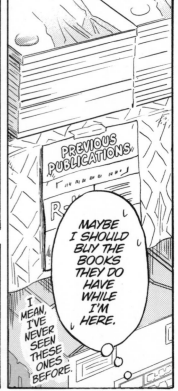

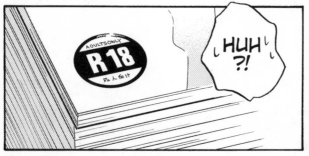

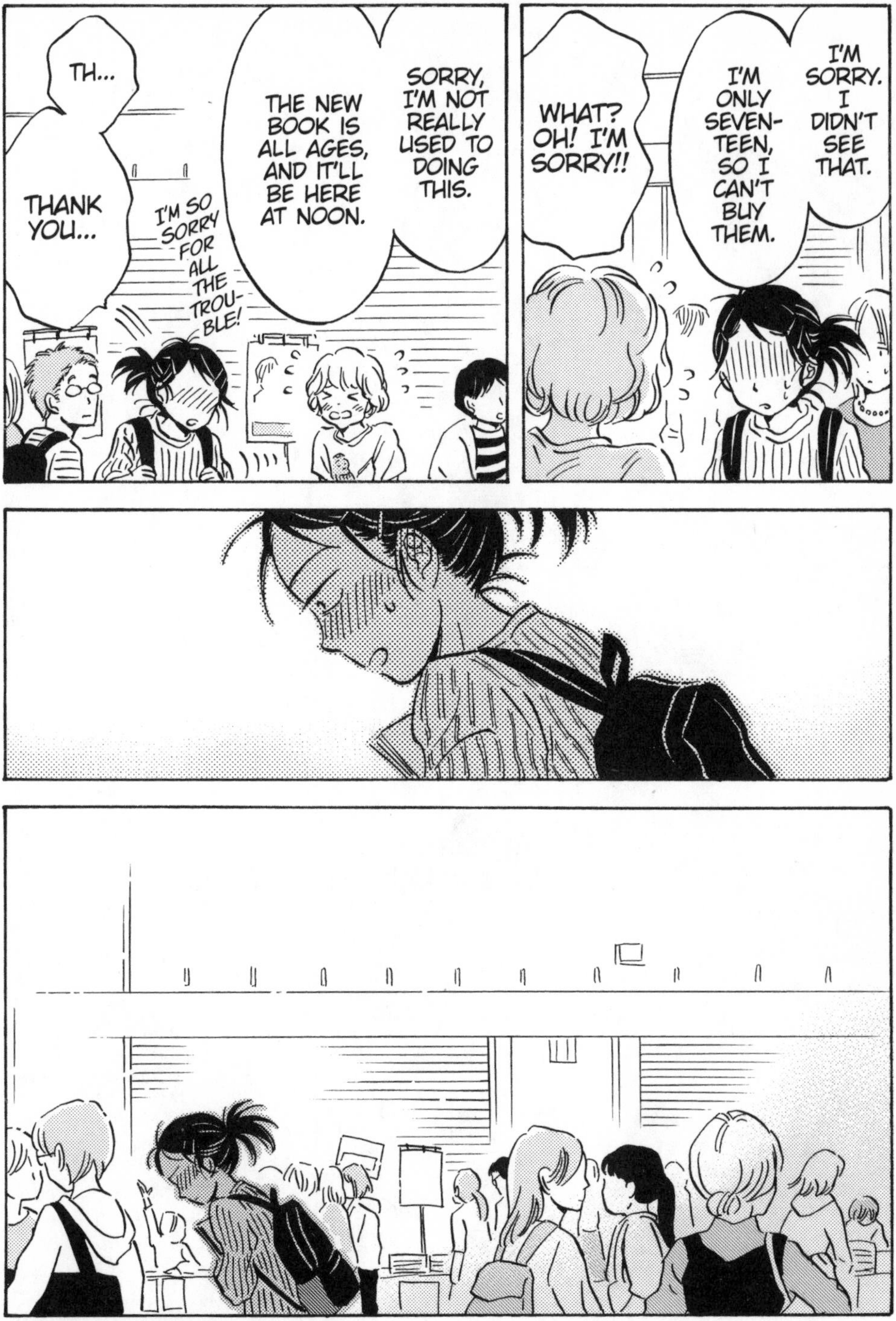
I'M SORRY. I DIDN'T SEE THAT.
I'M ONLY SEVEN-TEEN, SO I CAN'T BUY THEM.
WHAT? OH! I'M SORRY!!
SORRY, I'M NOT REALLY USED TO DOING THIS.
THE NEW BOOK IS ALL AGES, AND IT'LL BE HERE AT NOON.
I'M SO SORRY FOR ALL THE TROU-BLE!
TH...
THANK YOU...

Chapter 11/END

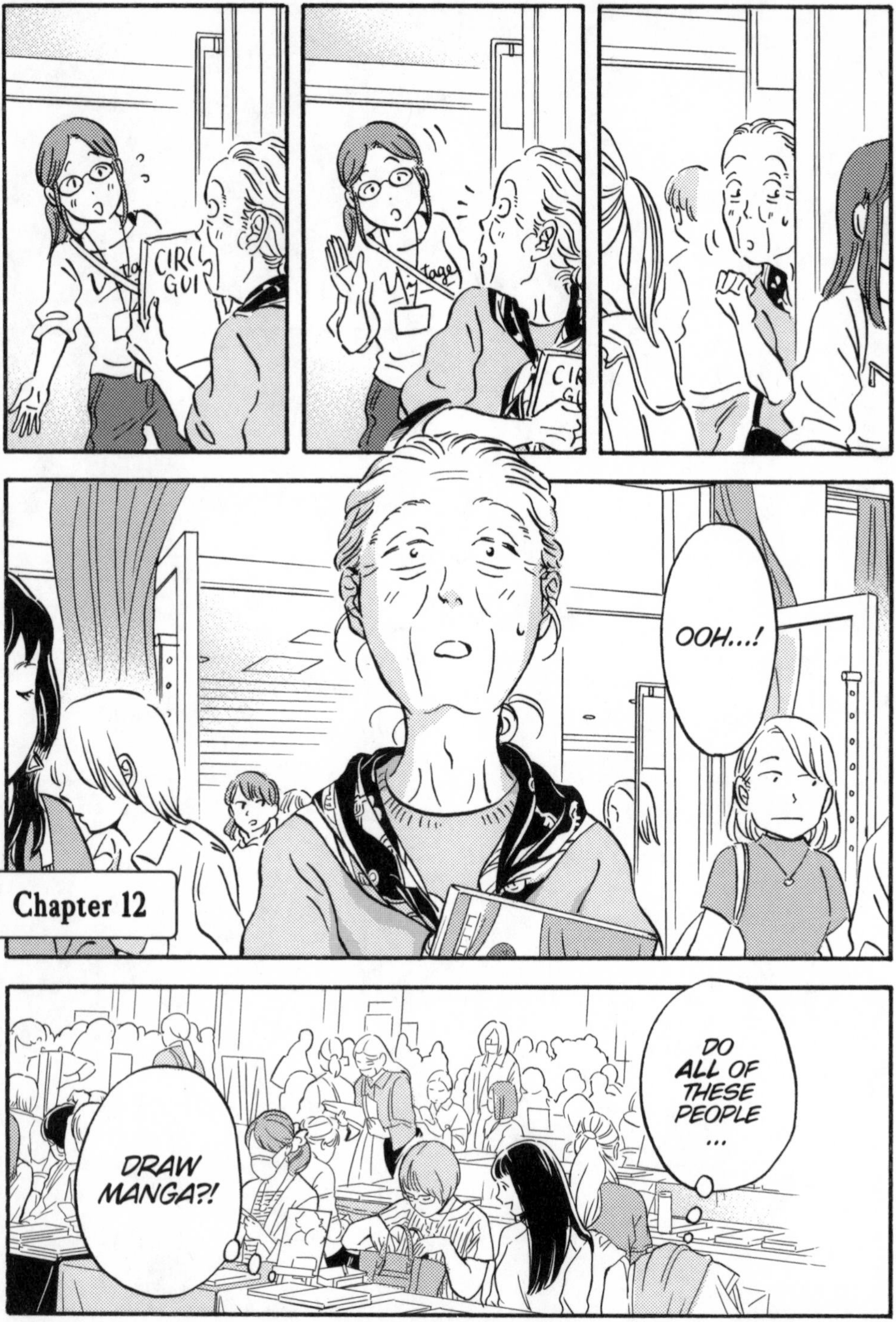
OOH...!
Chapter 12
DO ALL OF THESE PEOPLE ...
DRAW MANGA?!

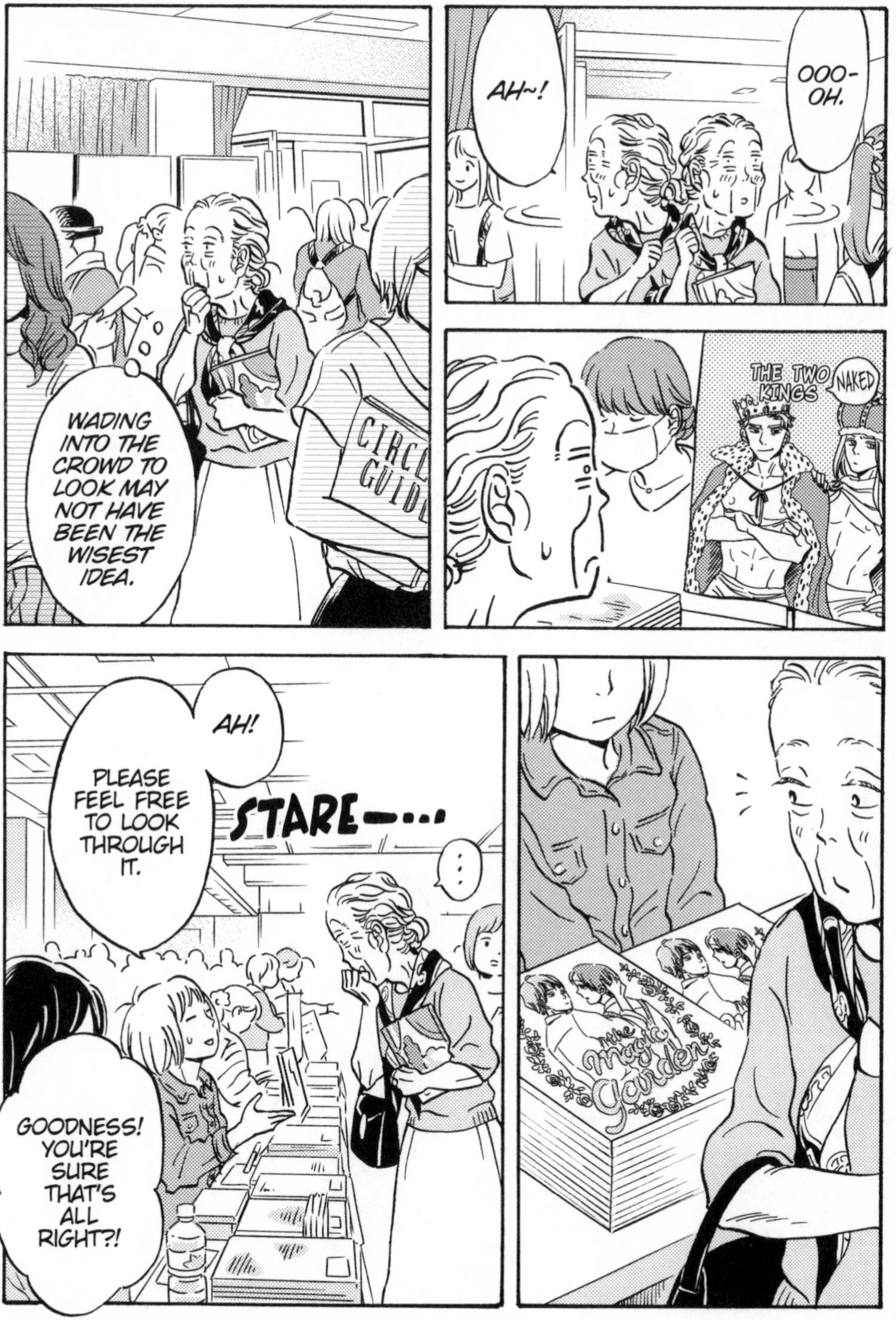
OOO-OH.
AH~!
THE TWO KINGS
NAKED
WADING INTO THE CROWD TO LOOK MAY NOT HAVE BEEN THE WISEST IDEA.
CIRCLE GUIDE
AH!
PLEASE FEEL FREE TO LOOK THROUGH IT.
STARE—...
...
GOODNESS! YOU'RE SURE THAT'S ALL RIGHT?!

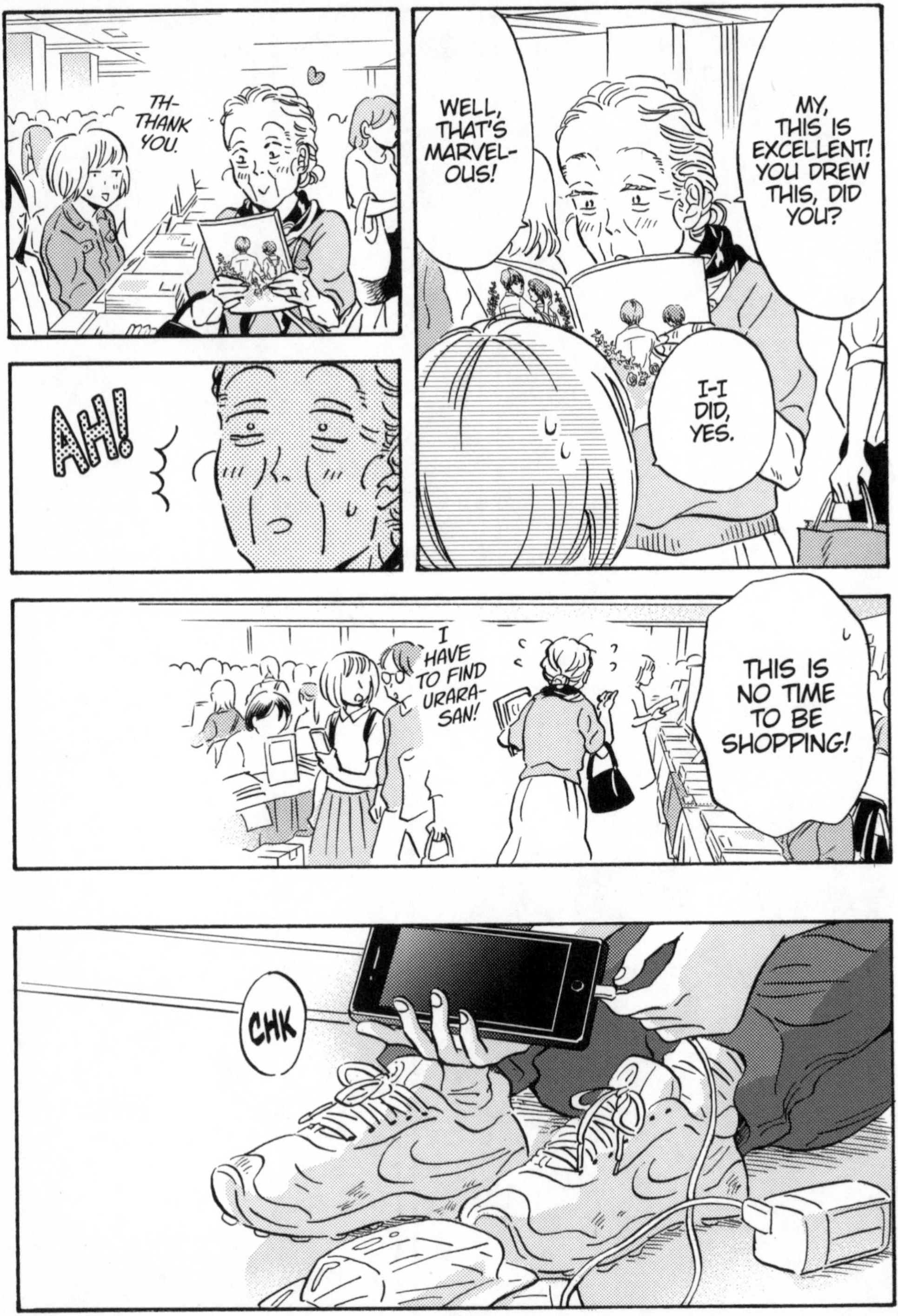
MY, THIS IS EXCELLENT! YOU DREW THIS, DID YOU?
WELL, THAT'S MARVEL-OUS!
I-I DID, YES.
TH-THANK YOU.
AH!
THIS IS NO TIME TO BE SHOPPING!
I HAVE TO FIND URARA-SAN!
CHK

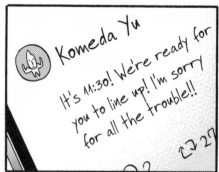

Komeda Yu

It's 11:30! We're ready for you to line up! I'm sorry for all the trouble!!

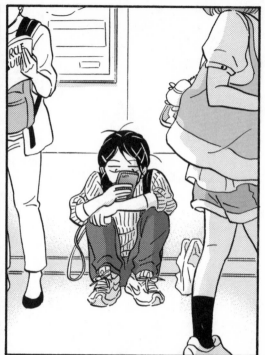

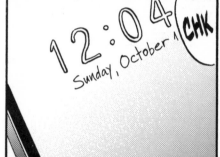

12:04 CHK

Sunday, October

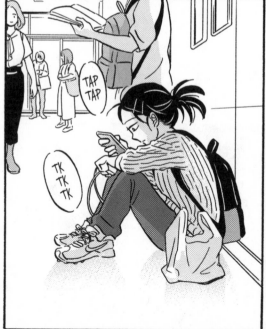

TAP TAP

TK TK TK

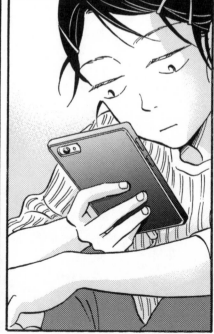

18

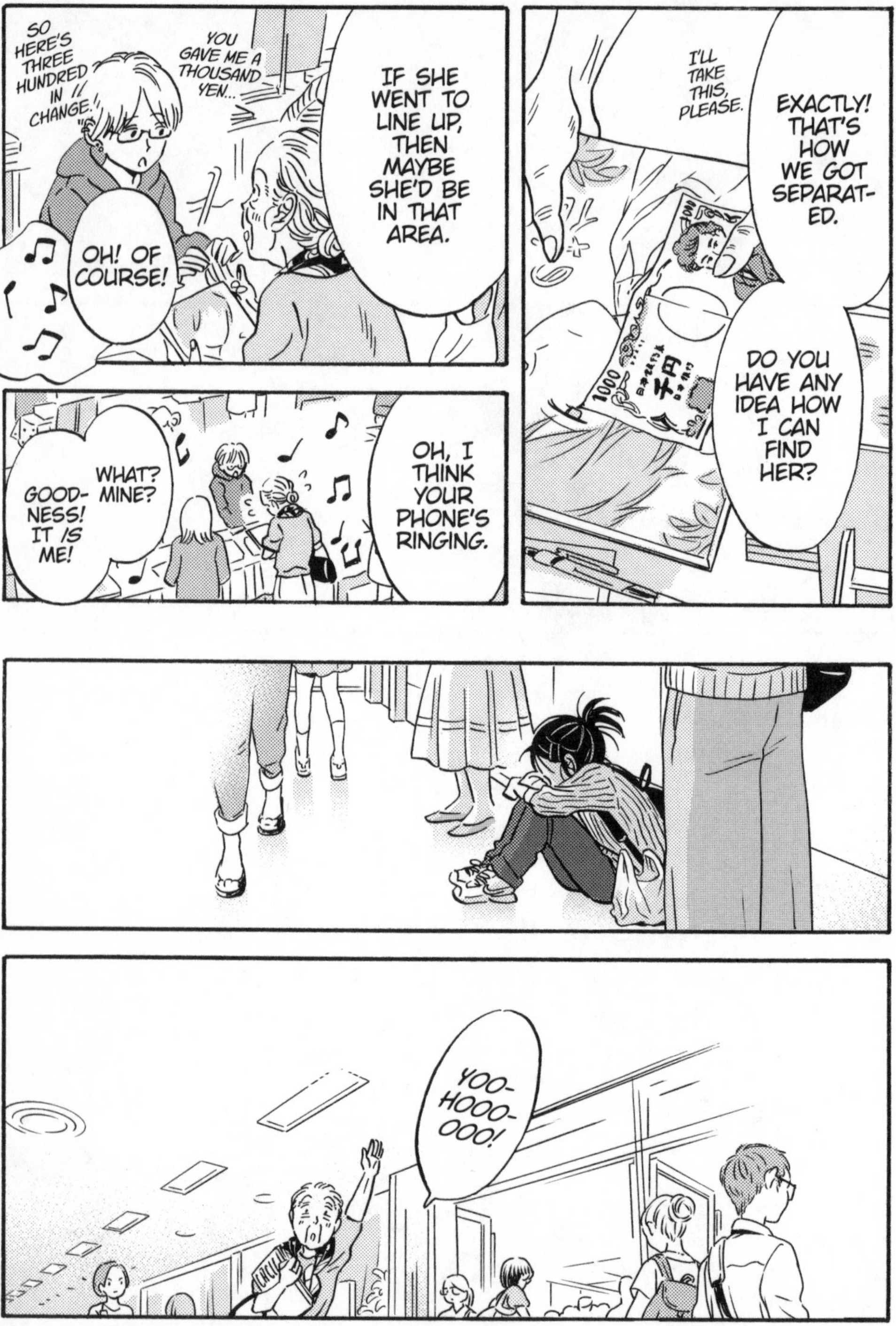
EXACTLY! THAT'S HOW WE GOT SEPARATED.
I'LL TAKE THIS, PLEASE.
DO YOU HAVE ANY IDEA HOW I CAN FIND HER?
IF SHE WENT TO LINE UP, THEN MAYBE SHE'D BE IN THAT AREA.
YOU GAVE ME A THOUSAND YEN...
SO HERE'S THREE HUNDRED IN CHANGE.
OH! OF COURSE!
OH, I THINK YOUR PHONE'S RINGING.
WHAT? MINE?
GOODNESS! IT IS ME!
YOO-HOOOO-OOO!

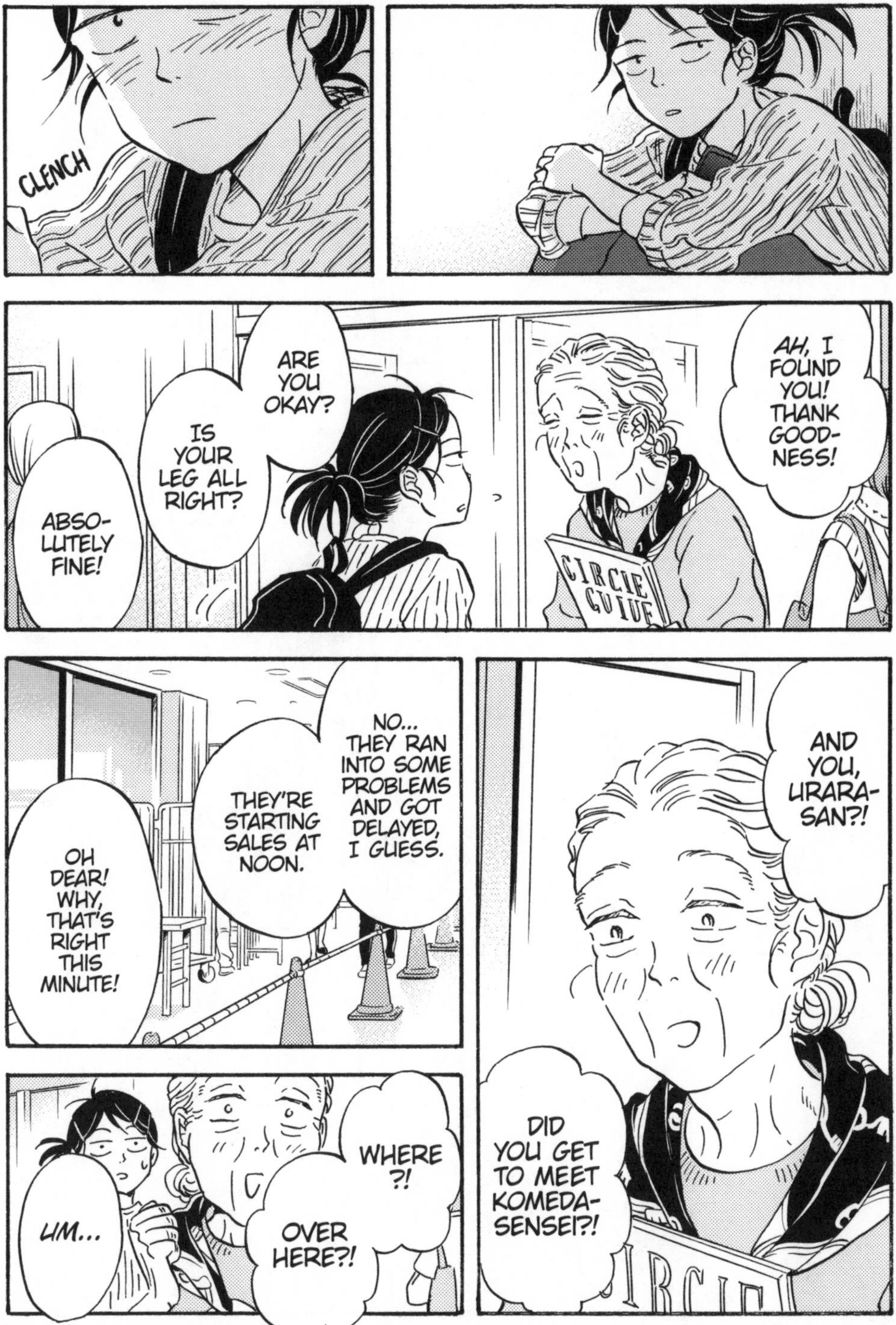
CLENCH
AH, I FOUND YOU! THANK GOODNESS!
ARE YOU OKAY?
IS YOUR LEG ALL RIGHT?
ABSOLUTELY FINE!
AND YOU, URARA-SAN?!
DID YOU GET TO MEET KOMEDA-SENSEI?!
NO... THEY RAN INTO SOME PROBLEMS AND GOT DELAYED, I GUESS.
THEY'RE STARTING SALES AT NOON.
OH DEAR! WHY, THAT'S RIGHT THIS MINUTE!
WHERE?!
OVER HERE?!
UM...

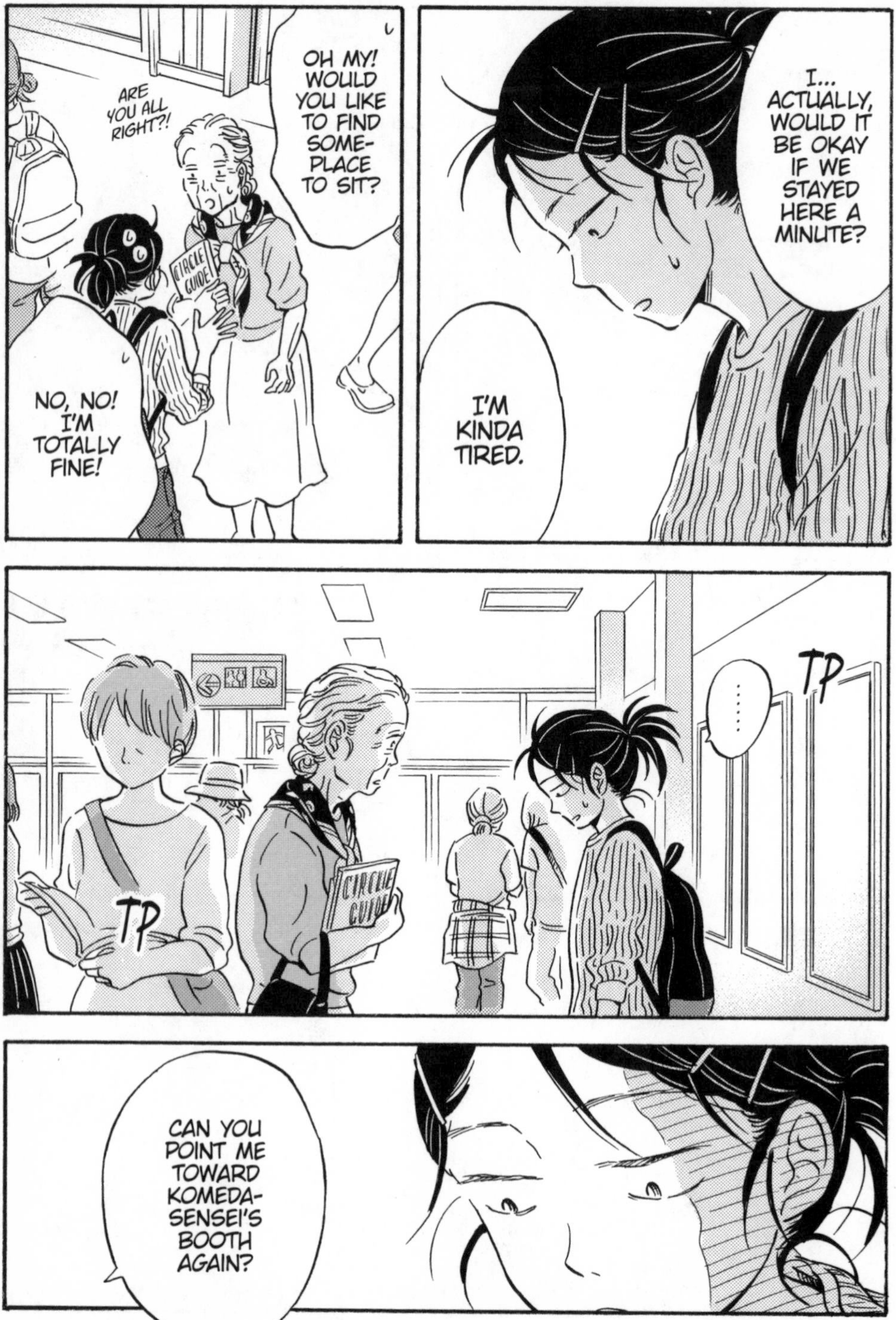

I... ACTUALLY, WOULD IT BE OKAY IF WE STAYED HERE A MINUTE?
I'M KINDA TIRED.
OH MY! WOULD YOU LIKE TO FIND SOME-PLACE TO SIT?
ARE YOU ALL RIGHT?!
CIRCLE GUIDE
NO, NO! I'M TOTALLY FINE!
TP
......
CIRCLE GUIDE
TP
CAN YOU POINT ME TOWARD KOMEDA-SENSEI'S BOOTH AGAIN?

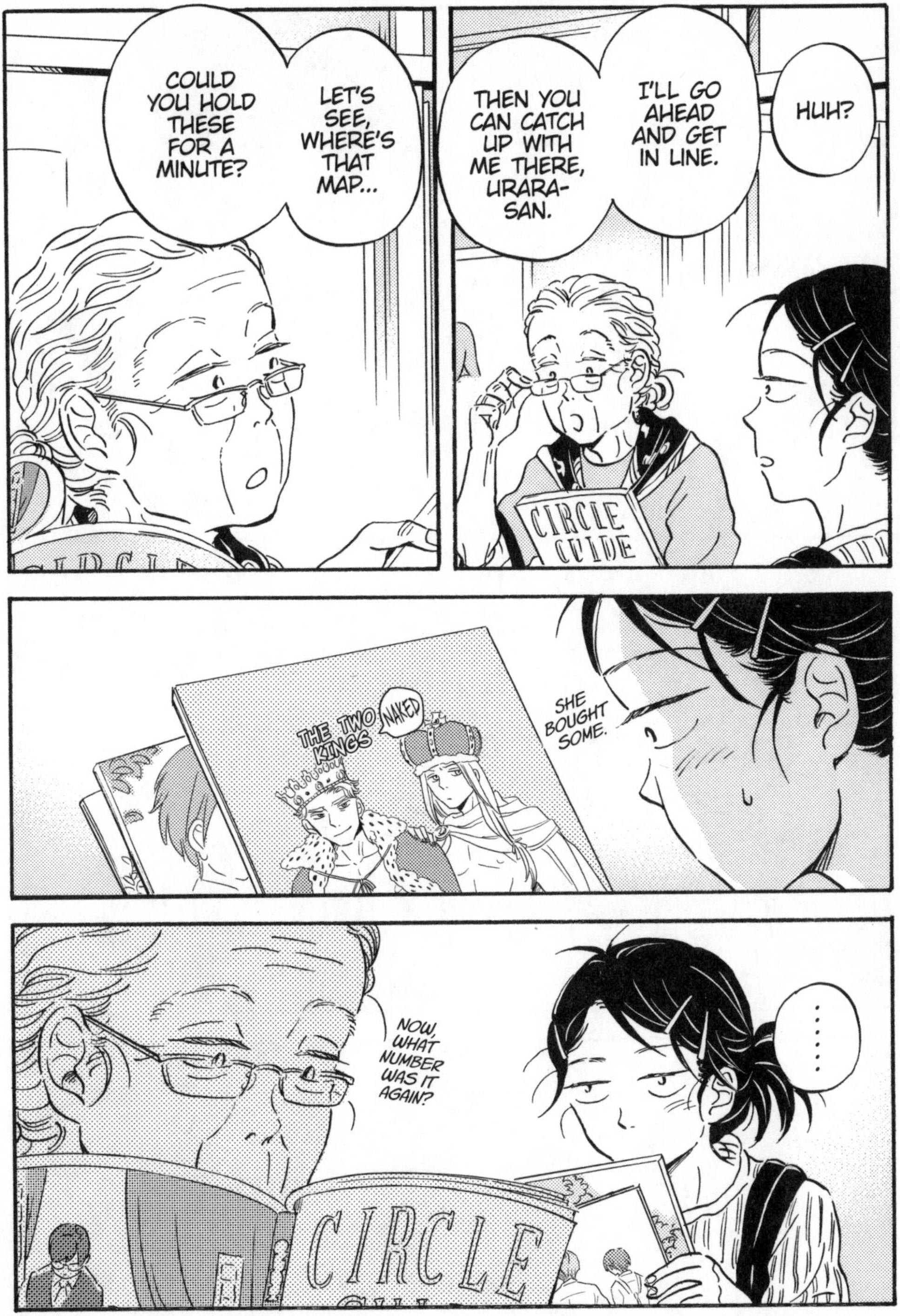
HUH?
I'LL GO AHEAD AND GET IN LINE.
THEN YOU CAN CATCH UP WITH ME THERE, URARA-SAN.
CIRCLE GUIDE
LET'S SEE, WHERE'S THAT MAP...
COULD YOU HOLD THESE FOR A MINUTE?
SHE BOUGHT SOME.
THE TWO NAKED KINGS
......
NOW, WHAT NUMBER WAS IT AGAIN?
CIRCLE

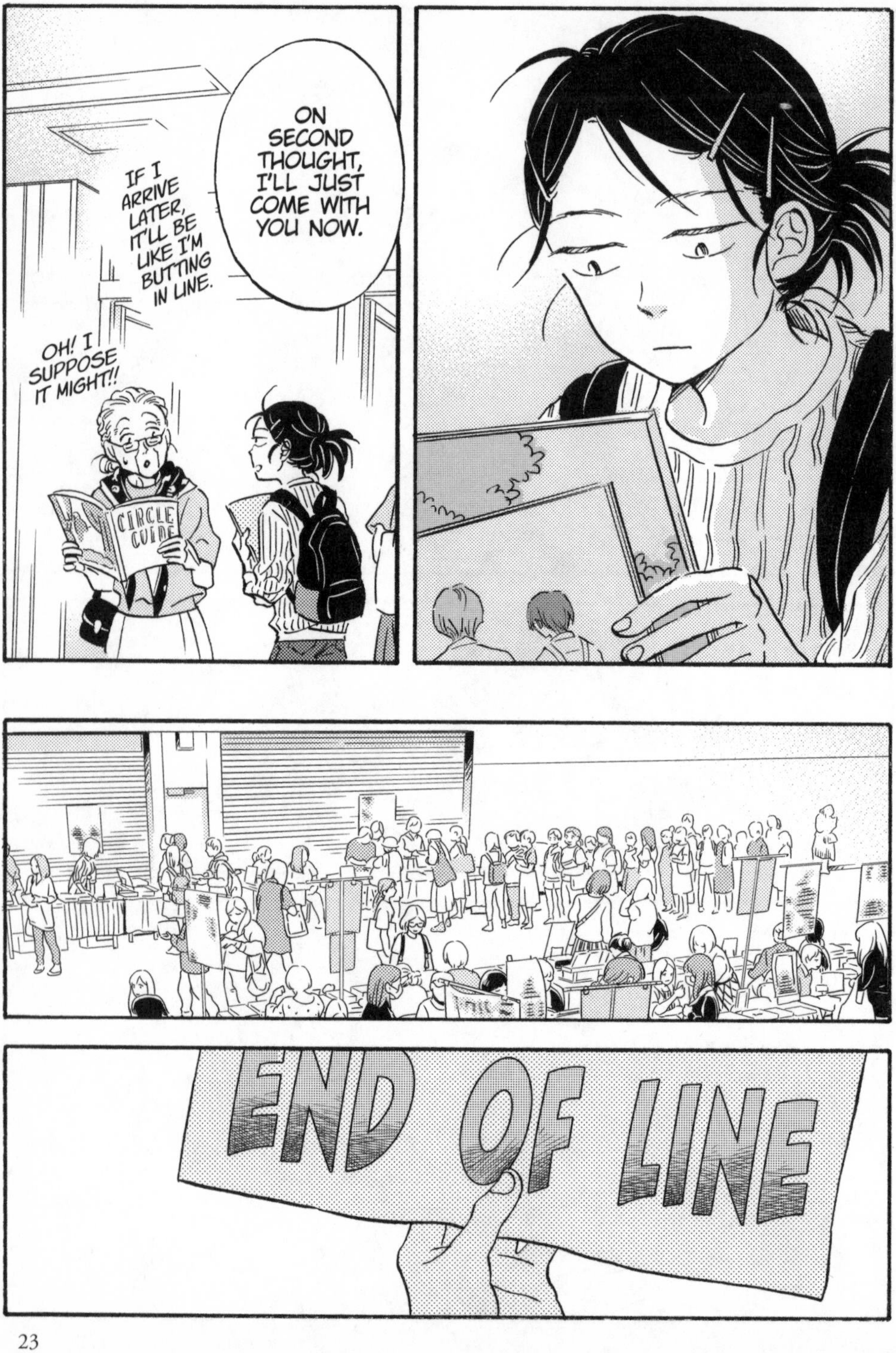
ON SECOND THOUGHT, I'LL JUST COME WITH YOU NOW.
IF I ARRIVE LATER, IT'LL BE LIKE I'M BUTTING IN LINE.
OH! I SUPPOSE IT MIGHT!!
CIRCLE GUIDE
END OF LINE

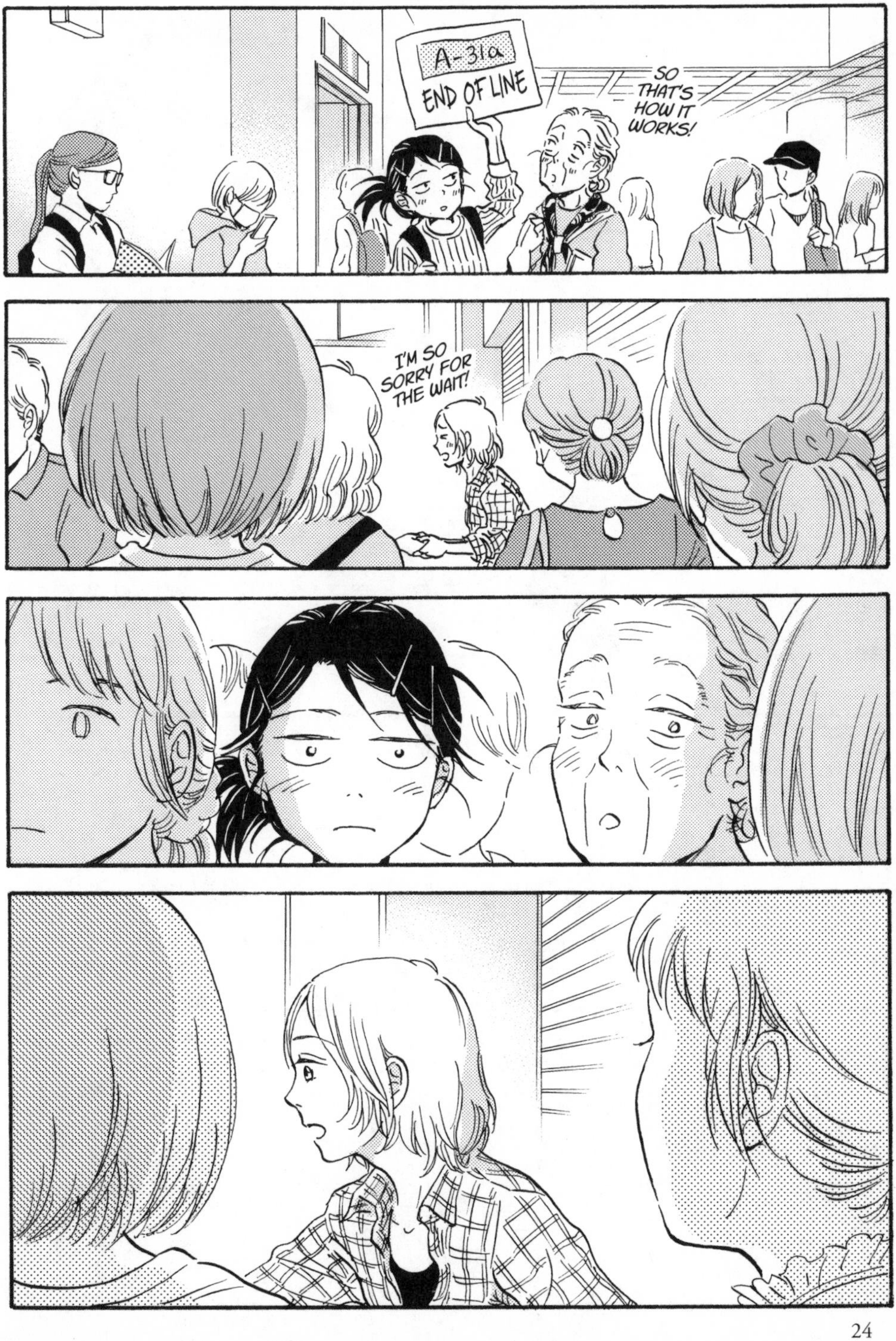
A-31a
END OF LINE
SO THAT'S HOW IT WORKS!
I'M SO SORRY FOR THE WAIT!

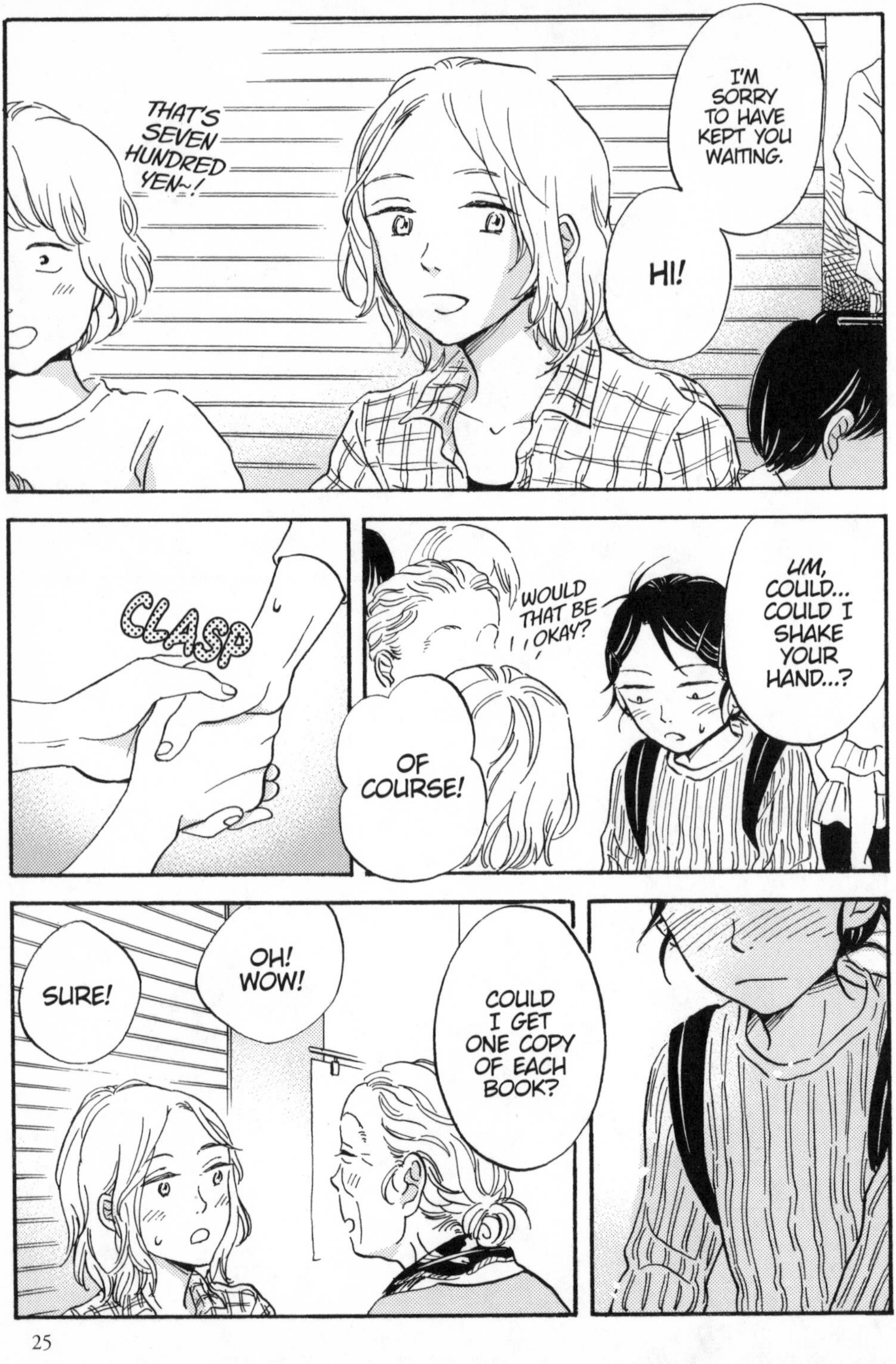
I'M SORRY TO HAVE KEPT YOU WAITING.
HI!
THAT'S SEVEN HUNDRED YEN~!
UM, COULD... COULD I SHAKE YOUR HAND...?
WOULD THAT BE OKAY?
OF COURSE!
CLASP
COULD I GET ONE COPY OF EACH BOOK?
OH! WOW!
SURE!

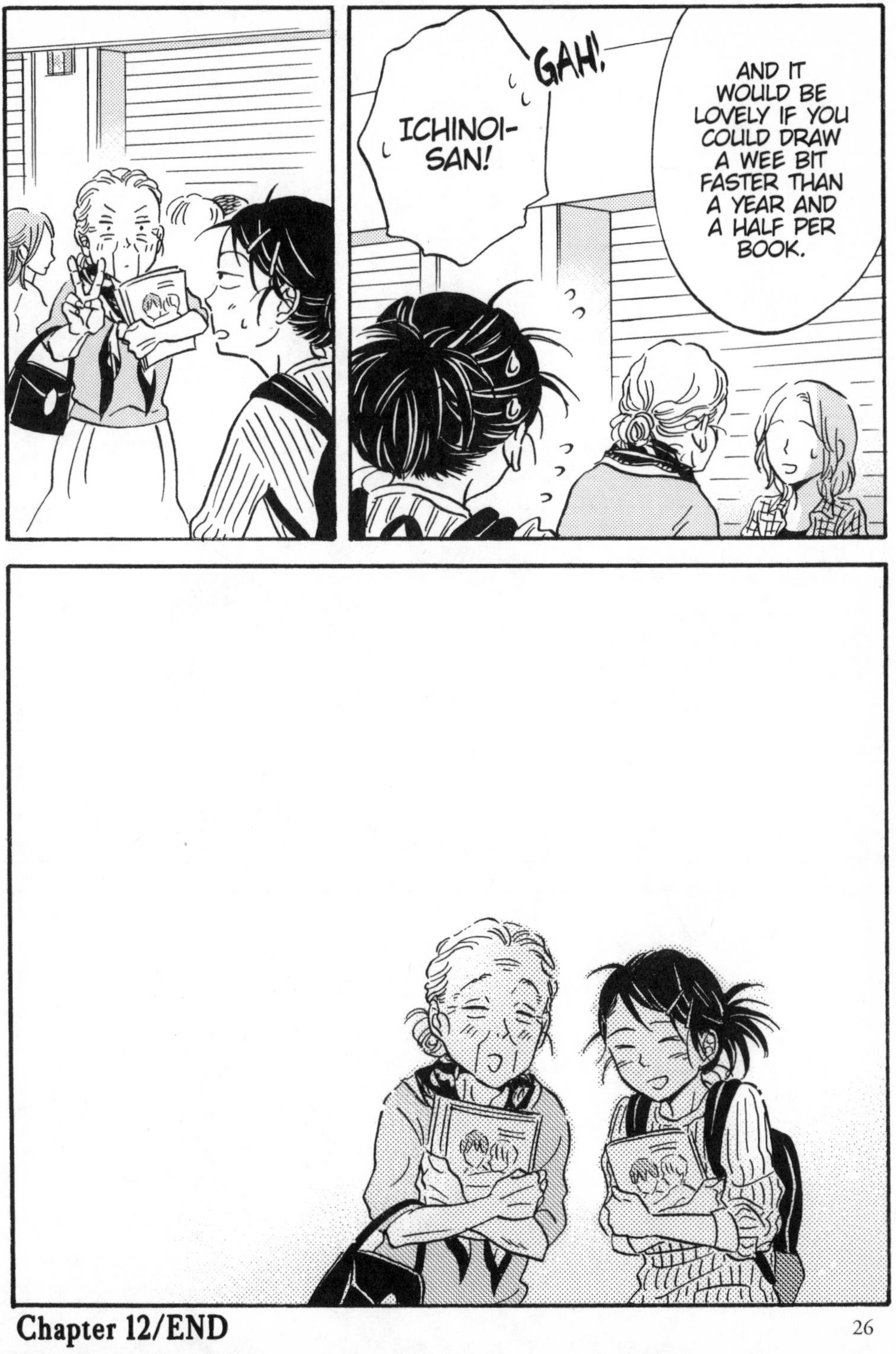
AND IT WOULD BE LOVELY IF YOU COULD DRAW A WEE BIT FASTER THAN A YEAR AND A HALF PER BOOK.
GAH!
ICHINOI-SAN!

Chapter 12/END

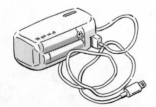

metamorphosis

Chapter 13

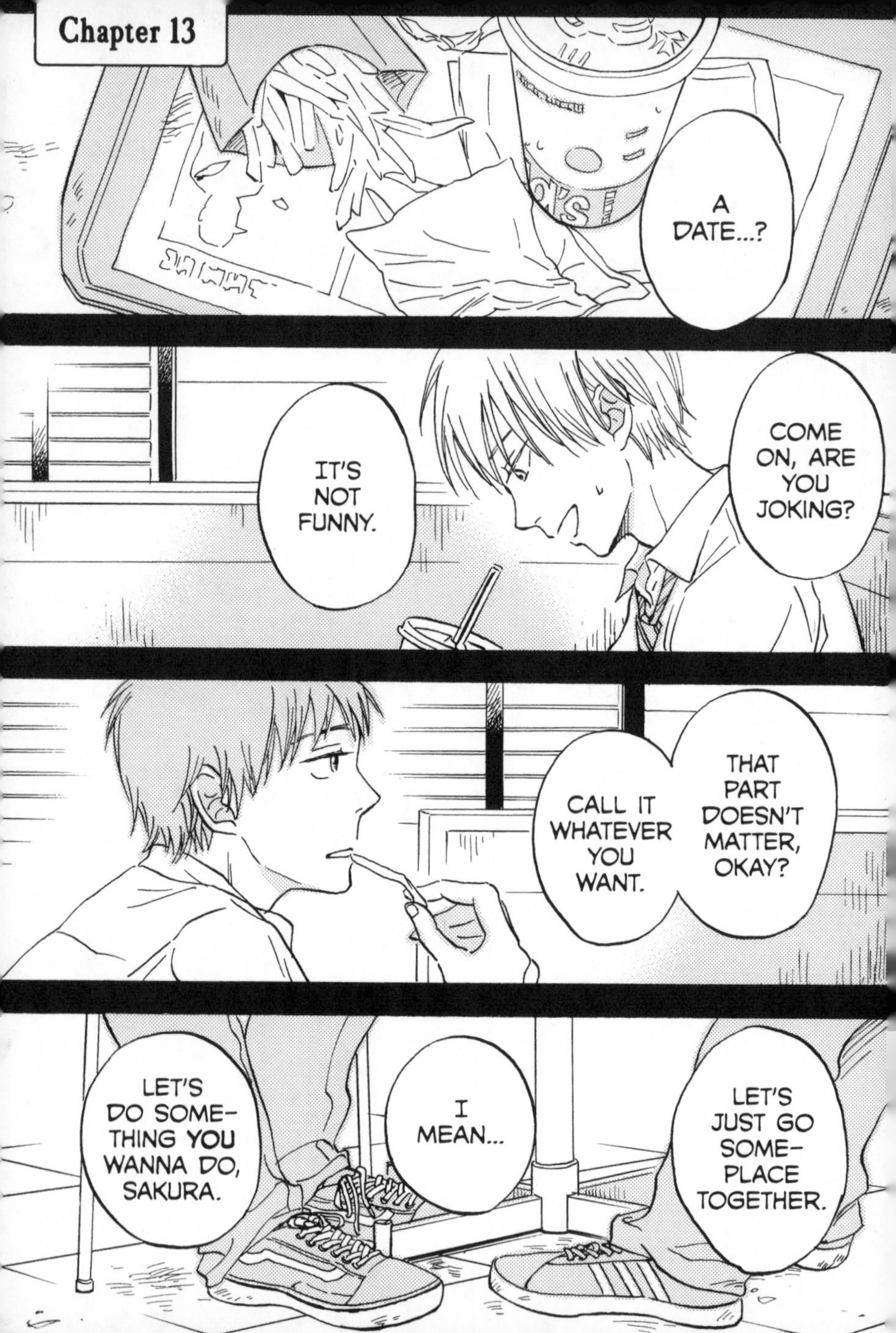
A DATE...?
COME ON, ARE YOU JOKING?
IT'S NOT FUNNY.
THAT PART DOESN'T MATTER, OKAY?
CALL IT WHATEVER YOU WANT.
LET'S JUST GO SOME-PLACE TOGETHER.
I MEAN...
LET'S DO SOME-THING YOU WANNA DO, SAKURA.

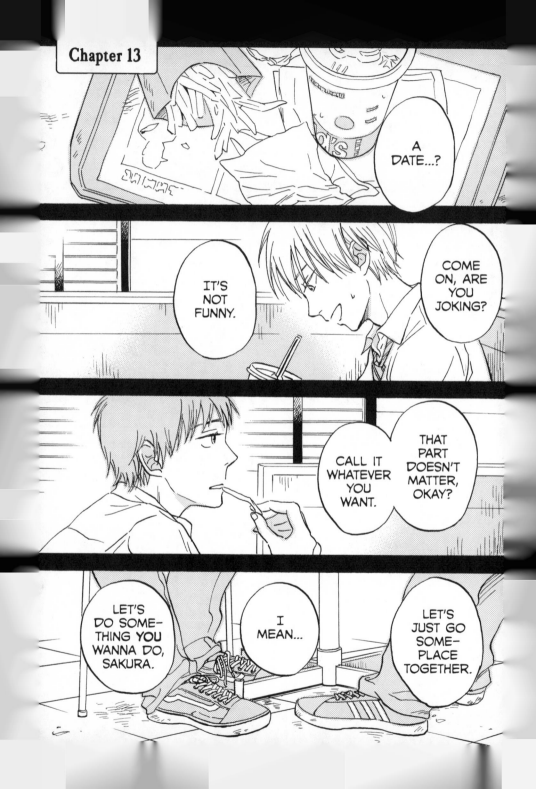

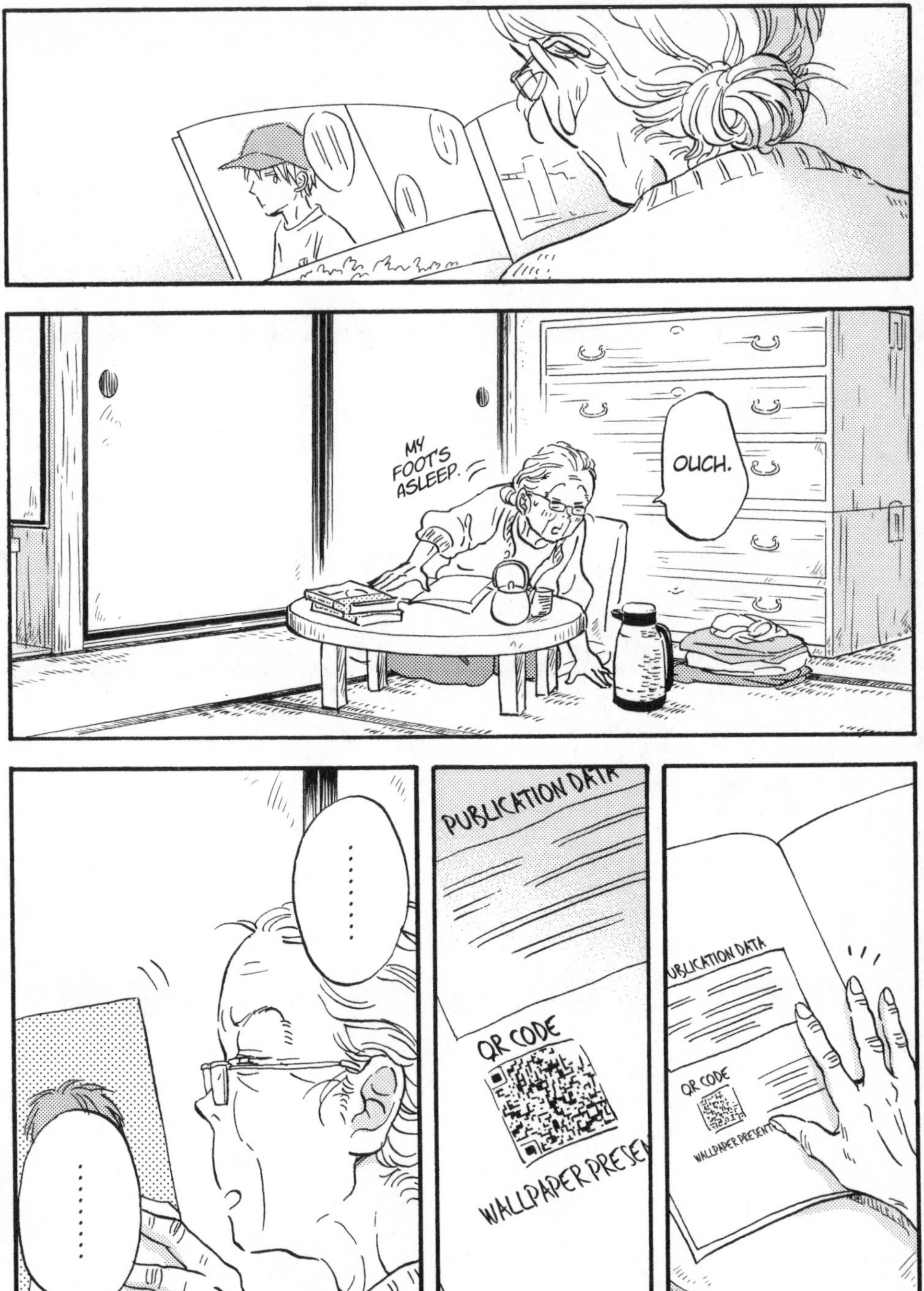
OUCH.
MY FOOT'S ASLEEP.
UBLICATION DATA
QR CODE
WALLPAPER PRESENT
PUBLICATION DATA
QR CODE
WALLPAPER PRESEN
......
......

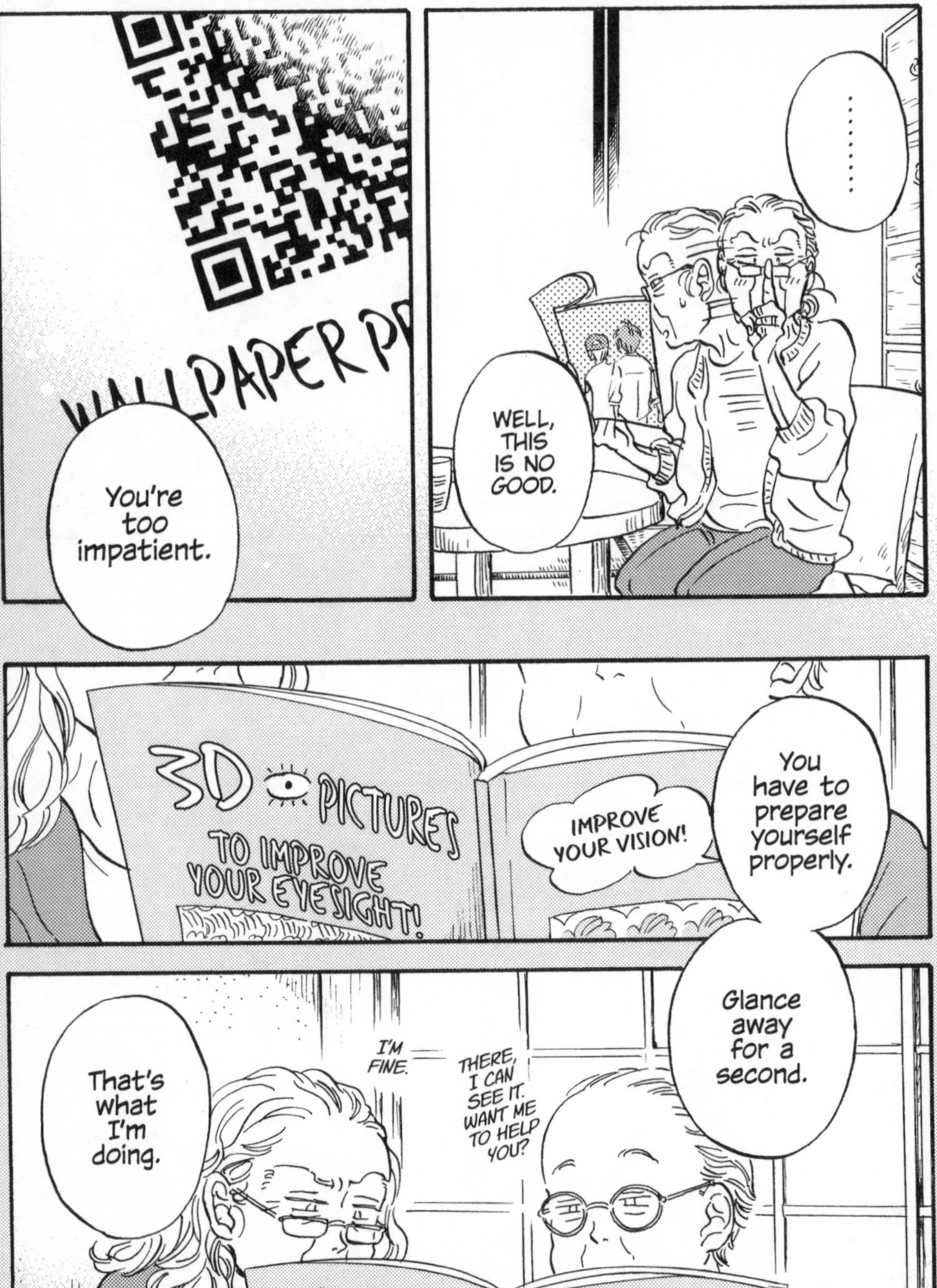
......
WELL, THIS IS NO GOOD.
WALLPAPER
You're too impatient.
You have to prepare yourself properly.
IMPROVE YOUR VISION!
3D PICTURES TO IMPROVE YOUR EYESIGHT!
Glance away for a second.
THERE, I CAN SEE IT. WANT ME TO HELP YOU?
I'M FINE.
That's what I'm doing.
IN JUST ONE MINUTE
IMPROVE YOUR VISION!
3D PICTURES
TO IMPROVE

All right, here! Start by looking at my finger.
CROSS YOUR EYES.
Now keep your eyes like that and look!
It's no use. I can't see it.
You're approaching it half-heartedly.
I bet you think it doesn't matter either way.
He got me.
3D PICTURES
YOU MAY THINK IT'S INSIGNIFI-CANT,
BUT YOU ALWAYS GO HALF-WAY ON THINGS.
YOU HAVE NO FOCUS.
THAT'S THE SORT OF THING BLAH BLAH YADDA YADDA.
YES, DEAR.
UTTERLY INDIFFERENT.
WHEW!
ICHINOI

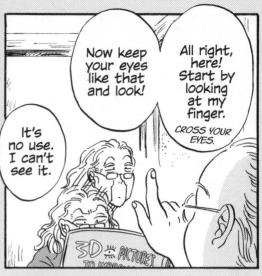

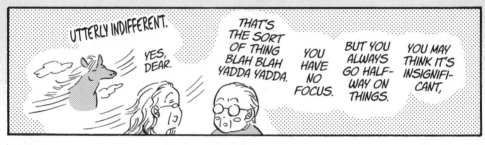

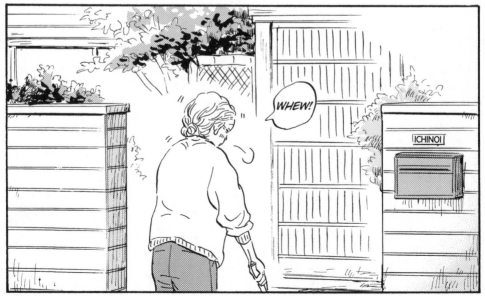

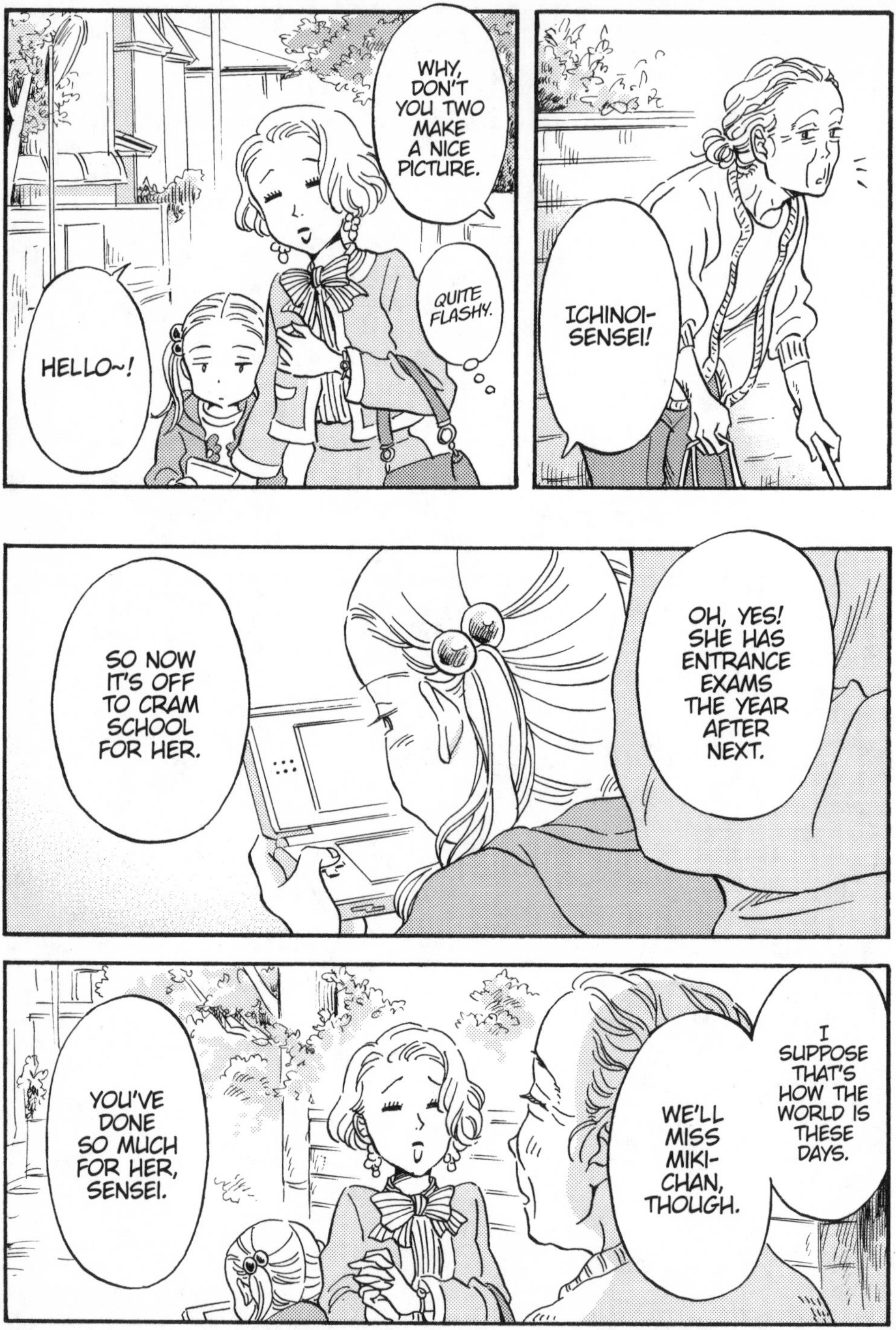
ICHINOI-SENSEI!
WHY, DON'T YOU TWO MAKE A NICE PICTURE.
QUITE FLASHY.
HELLO~!
OH, YES! SHE HAS ENTRANCE EXAMS THE YEAR AFTER NEXT.
SO NOW IT'S OFF TO CRAM SCHOOL FOR HER.
I SUPPOSE THAT'S HOW THE WORLD IS THESE DAYS.
WE'LL MISS MIKI-CHAN, THOUGH.
YOU'VE DONE SO MUCH FOR HER, SENSEI.

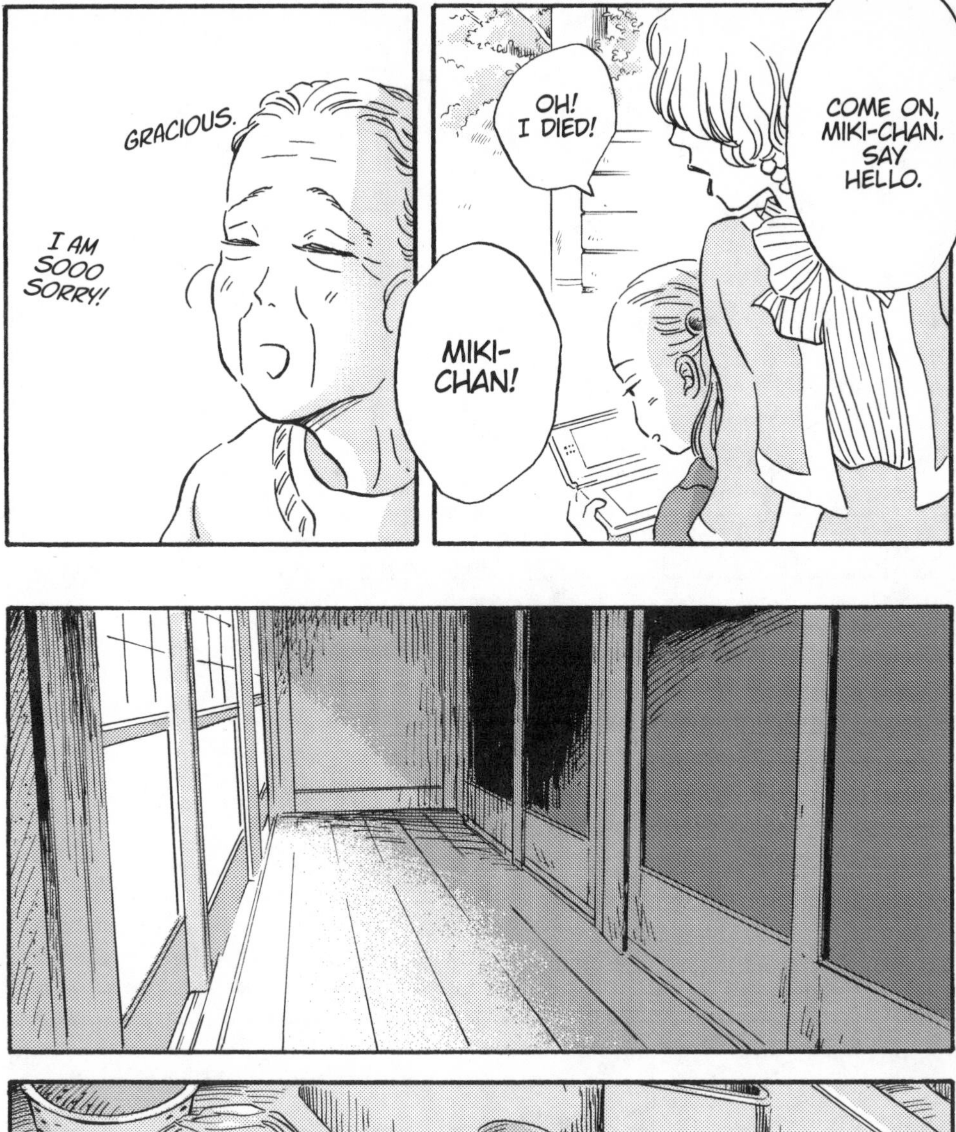
COME ON, MIKI-CHAN. SAY HELLO.
OH! I DIED!
MIKI-CHAN!
GRACIOUS.
I AM SOOO SORRY!

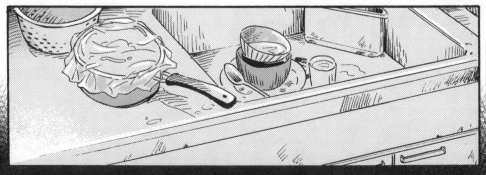

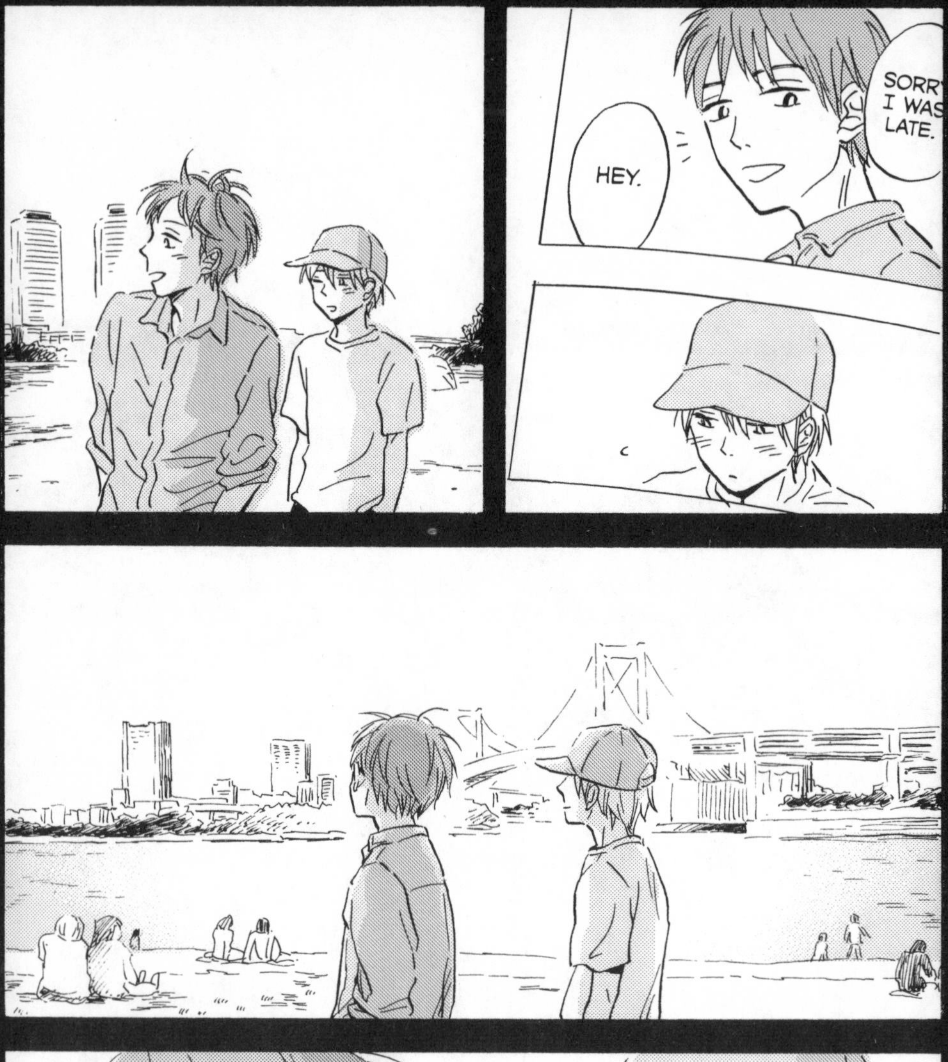
SORRY I WAS LATE.
HEY.

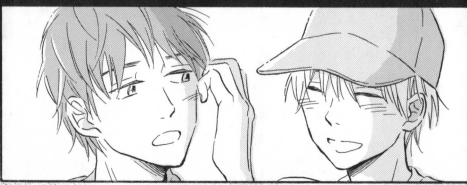

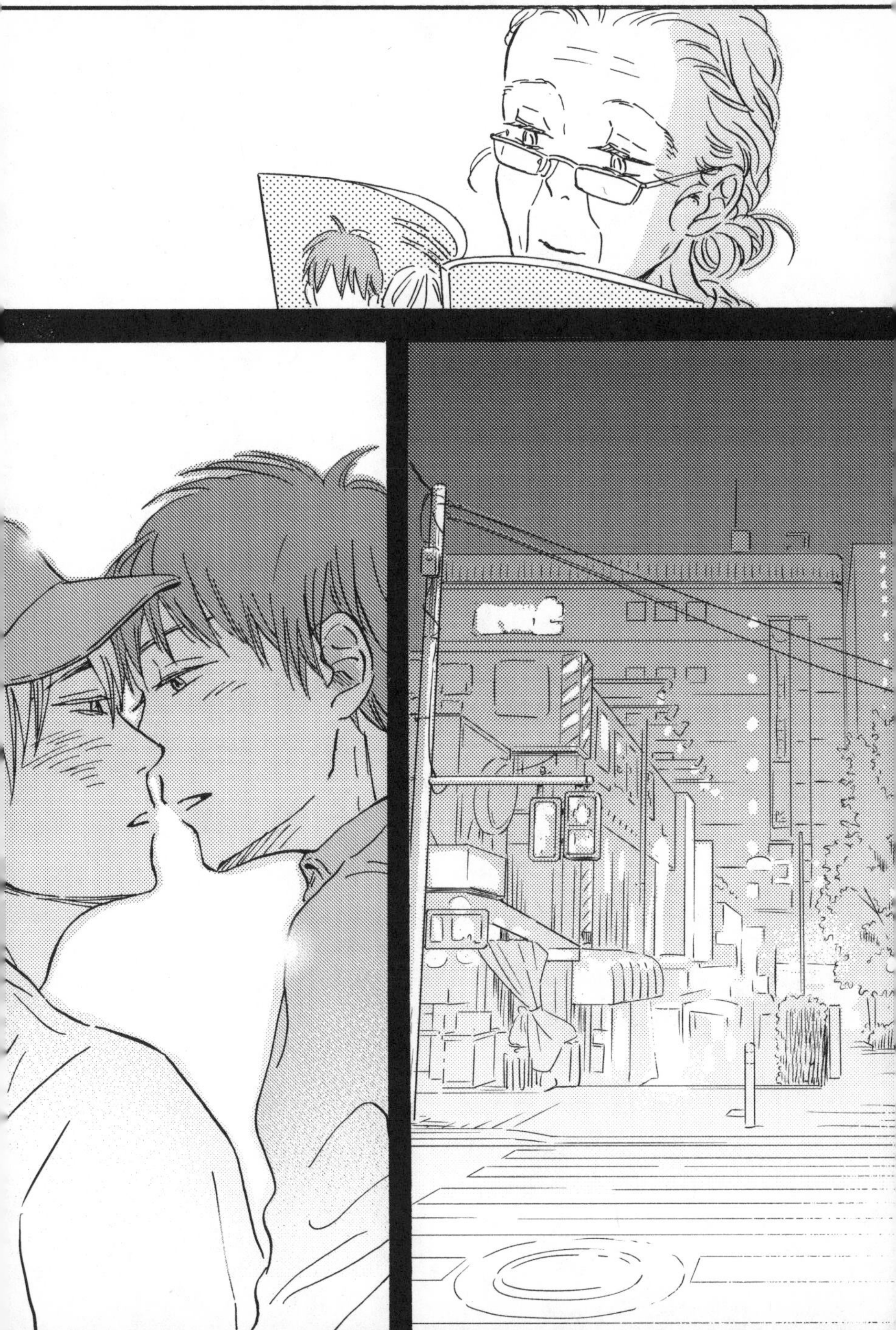

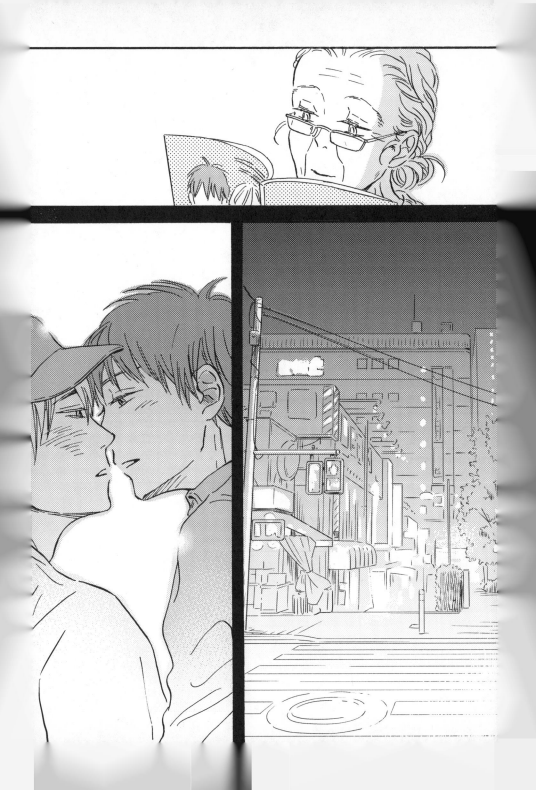

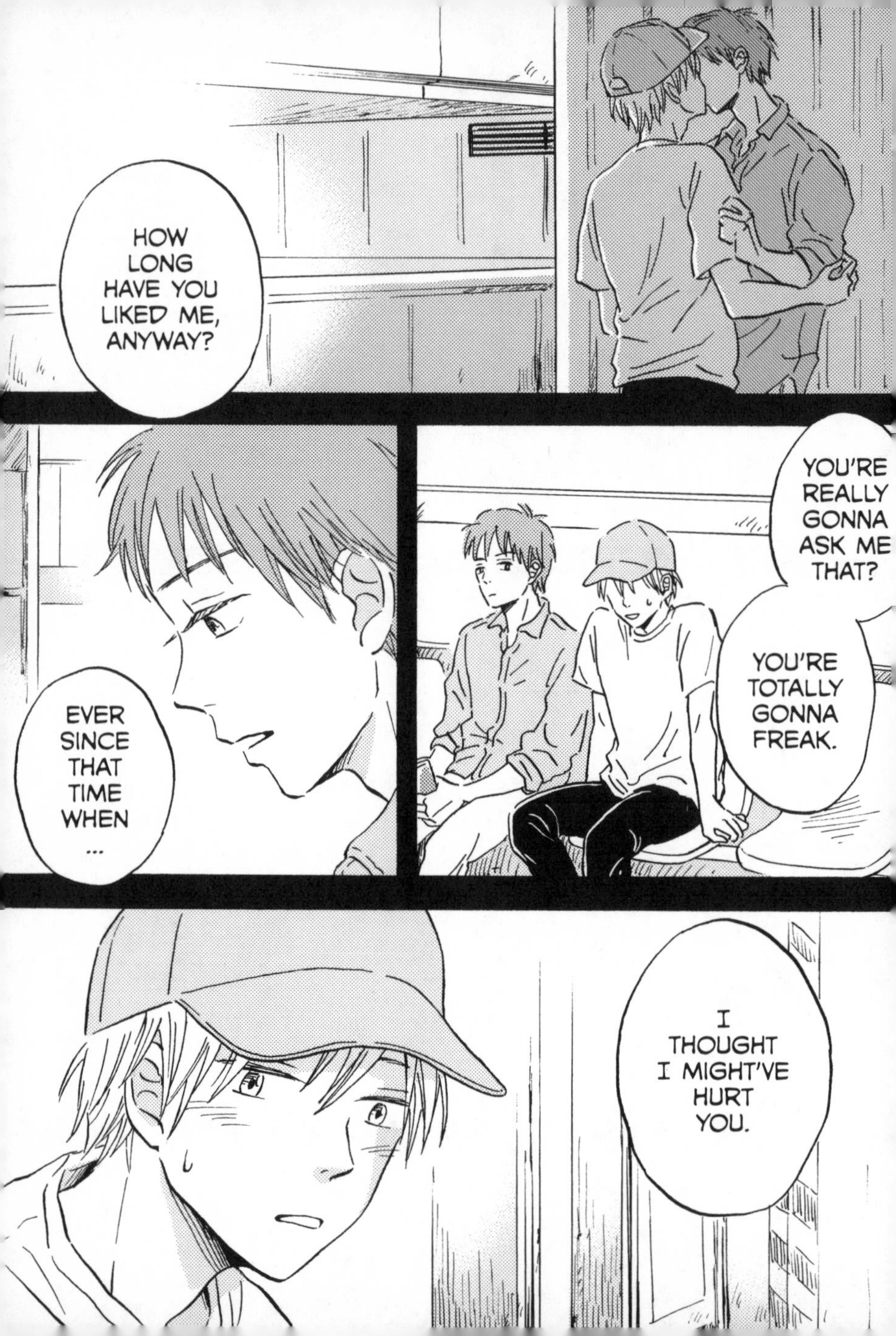
HOW LONG HAVE YOU LIKED ME, ANYWAY?
YOU'RE REALLY GONNA ASK ME THAT?
YOU'RE TOTALLY GONNA FREAK.
EVER SINCE THAT TIME WHEN ...
I THOUGHT I MIGHT'VE HURT YOU.

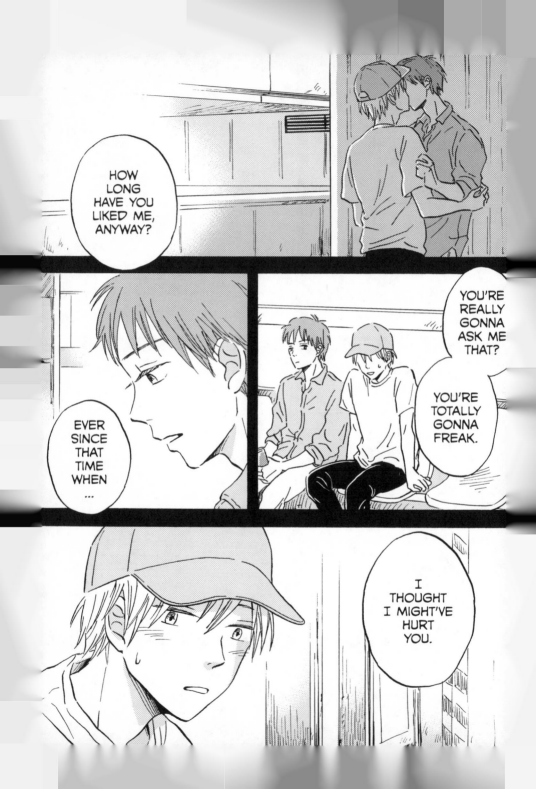

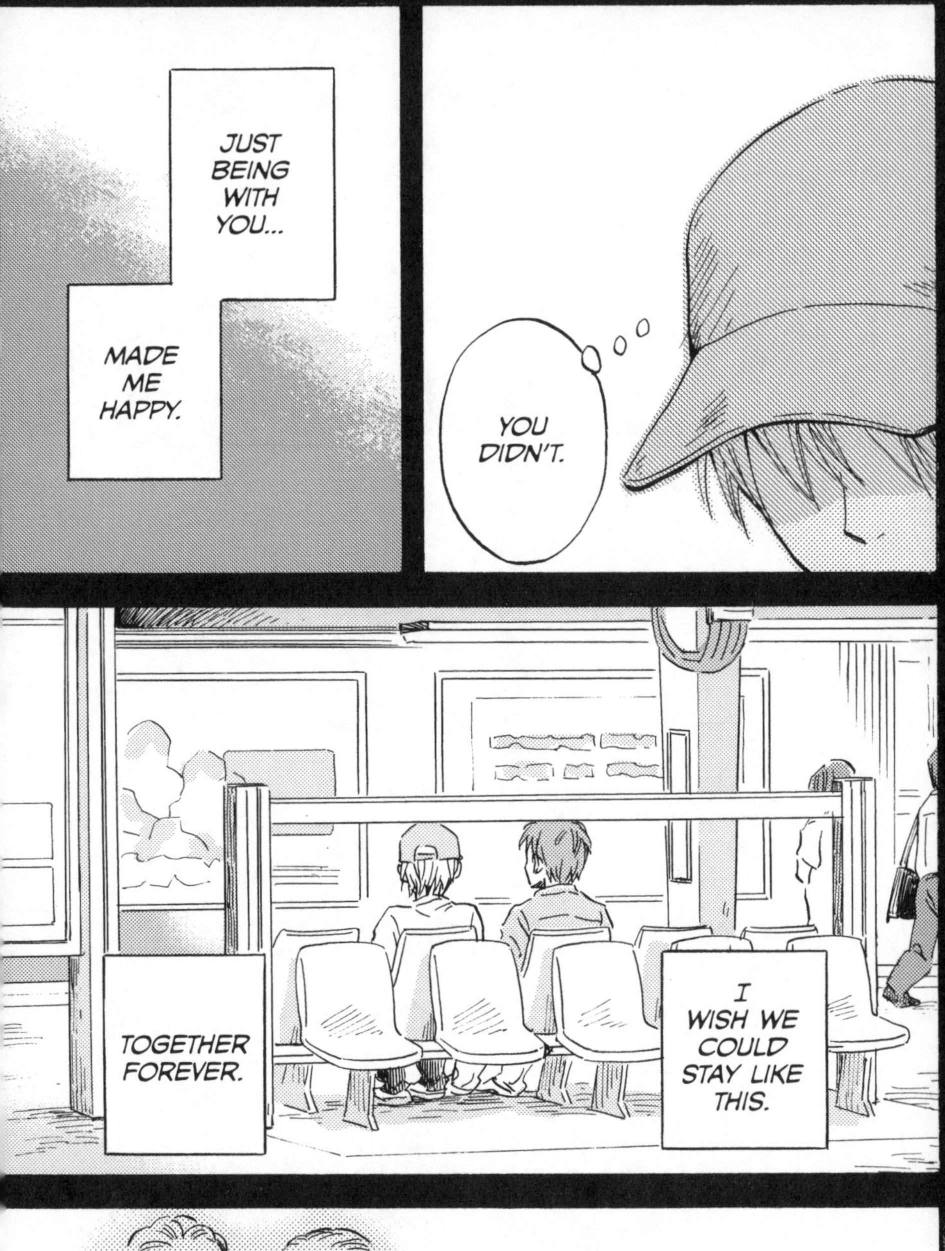
YOU DIDN'T.
JUST BEING WITH YOU...
MADE ME HAPPY.
I WISH WE COULD STAY LIKE THIS.
TOGETHER FOREVER.

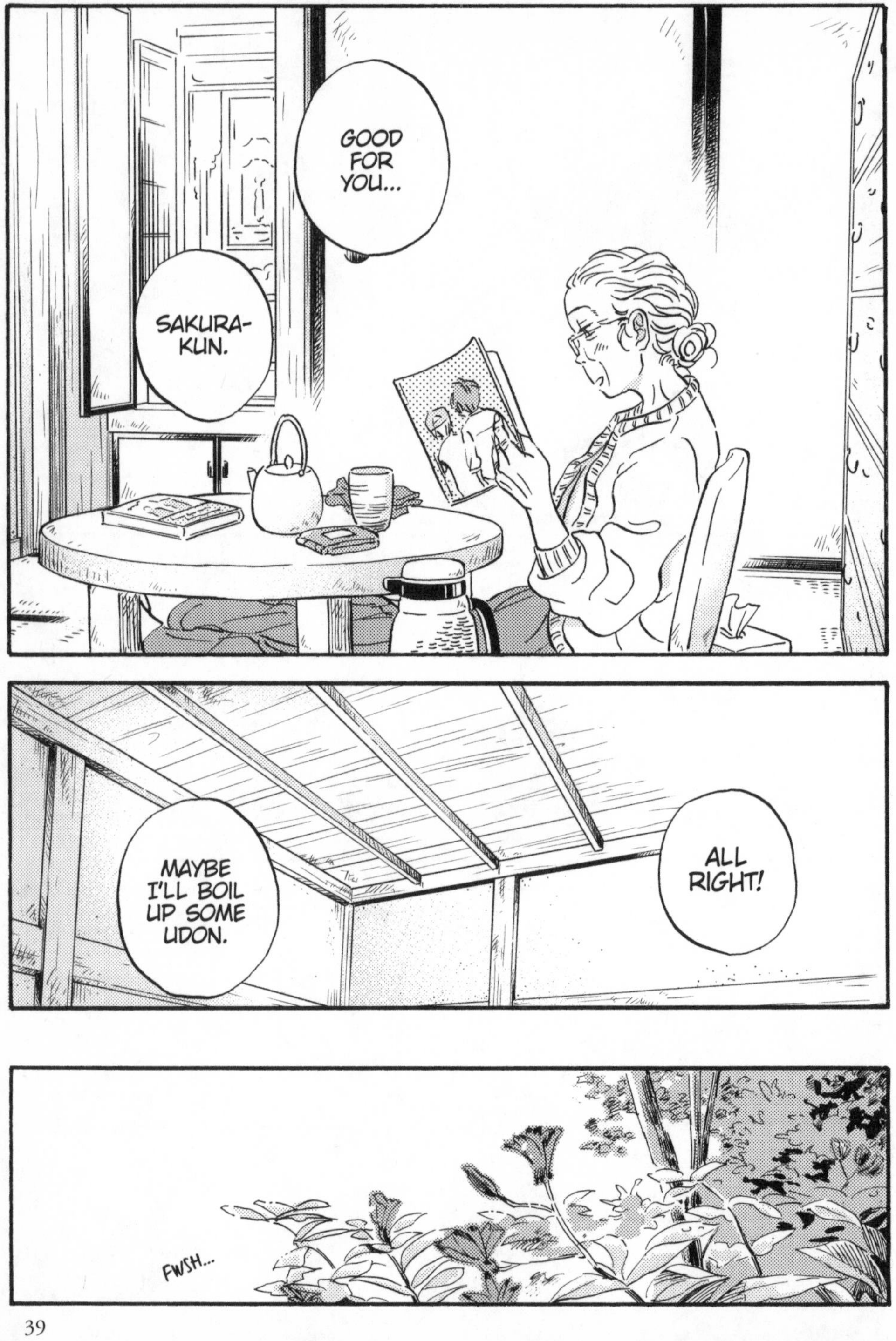
GOOD FOR YOU...
SAKURA-KUN.
ALL RIGHT!
MAYBE I'LL BOIL UP SOME UDON.
FWSH...

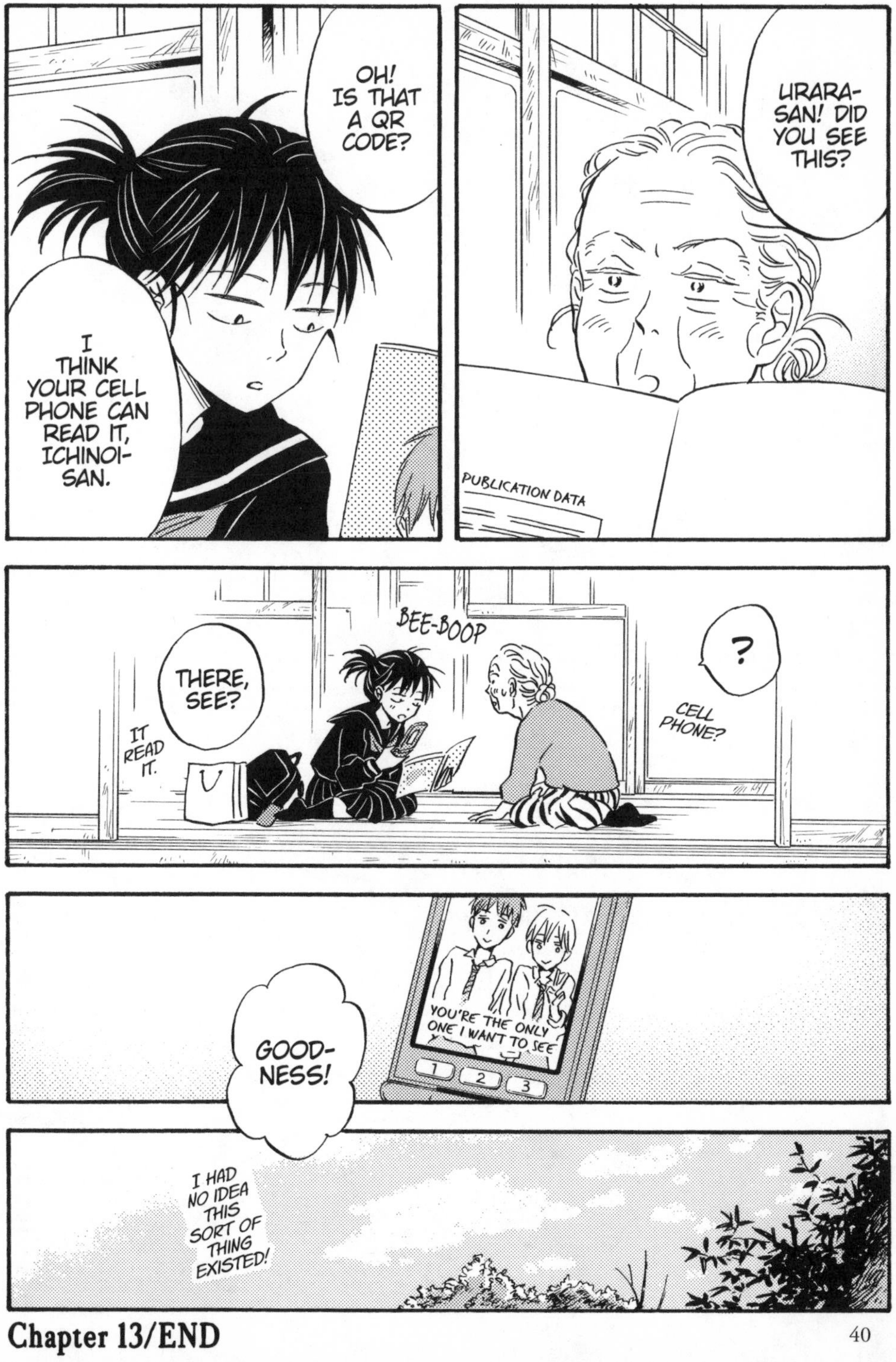
URARA-SAN! DID YOU SEE THIS?
PUBLICATION DATA
OH! IS THAT A QR CODE?
I THINK YOUR CELL PHONE CAN READ IT, ICHINOI-SAN.
?
CELL PHONE?
BEE-BOOP
THERE, SEE?
IT READ IT.
YOU'RE THE ONLY ONE I WANT TO SEE
GOOD-NESS!
1 2 3
I HAD NO IDEA THIS SORT OF THING EXISTED!

Chapter 13/END

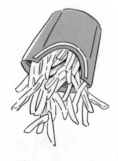

BL Metamorphosis

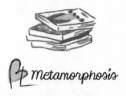

Chapter 14

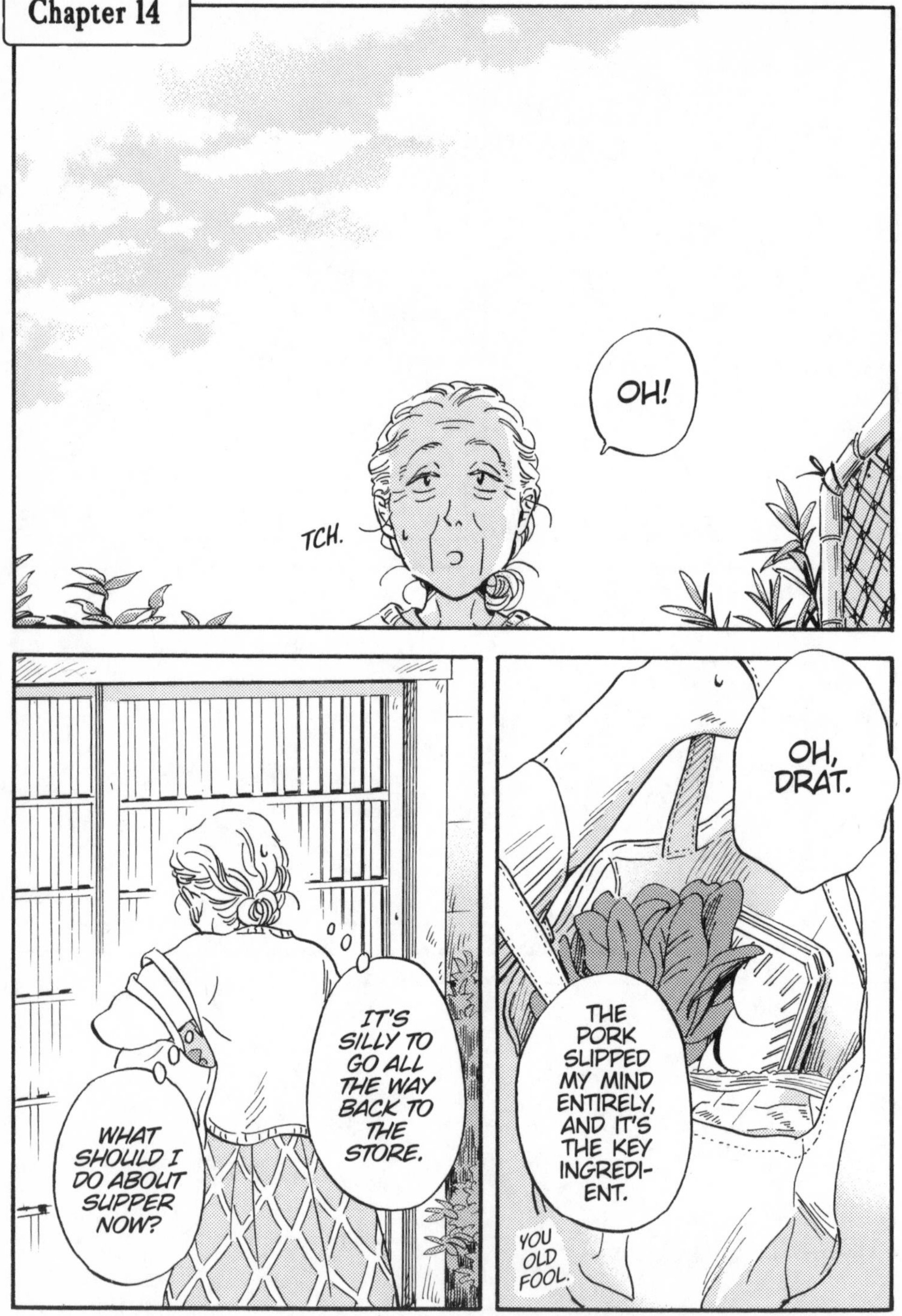

OH!
TCH.
OH, DRAT.
THE PORK SLIPPED MY MIND ENTIRELY, AND IT'S THE KEY INGREDI-ENT.
YOU OLD FOOL.
IT'S SILLY TO GO ALL THE WAY BACK TO THE STORE.
WHAT SHOULD I DO ABOUT SUPPER NOW?

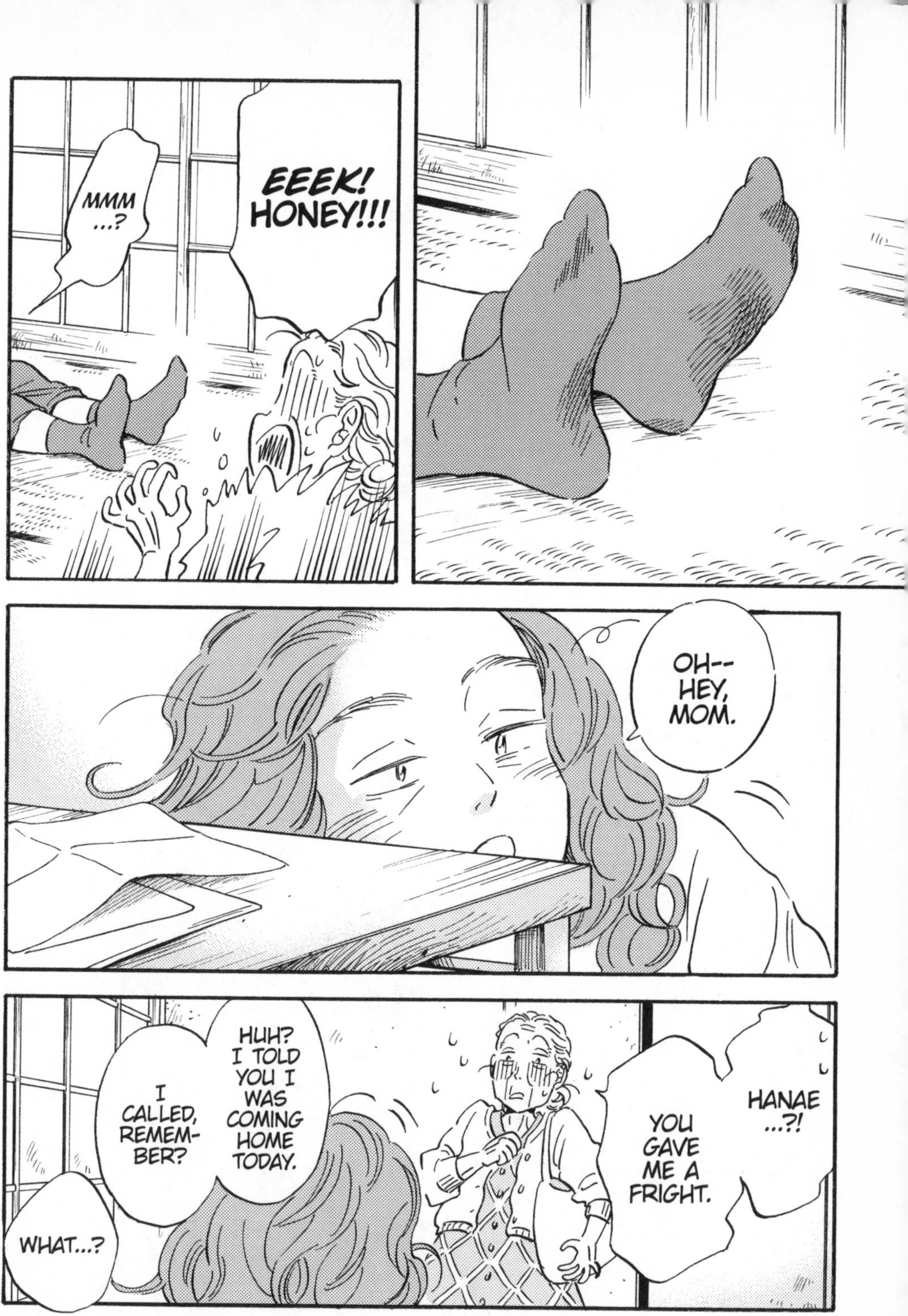
EEEK! HONEY!!!
MMM ...?
OH-- HEY, MOM.
HANAE ...?!
YOU GAVE ME A FRIGHT.
HUH? I TOLD YOU I WAS COMING HOME TODAY.
I CALLED, REMEMBER?
WHAT...?

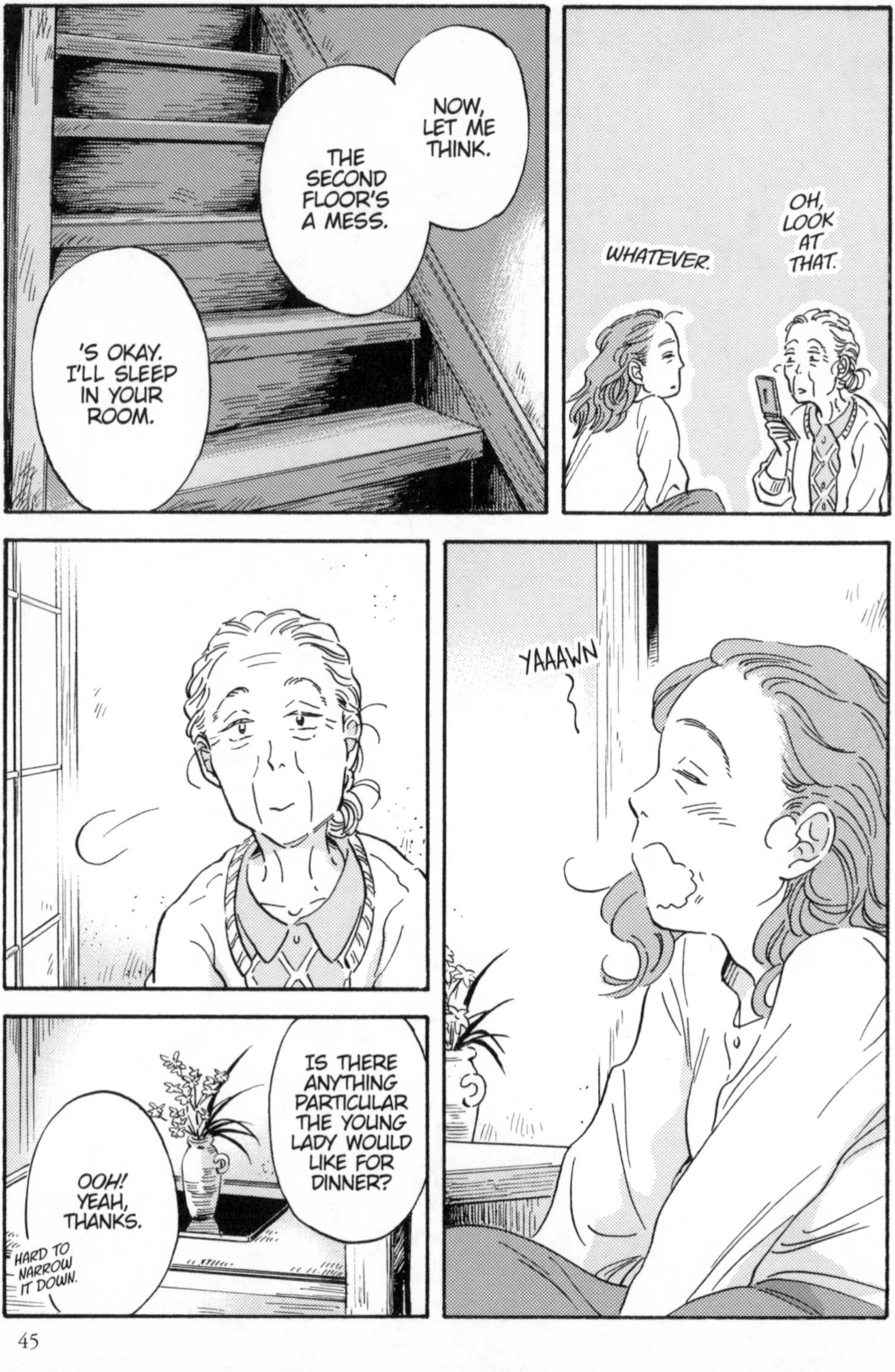
OH, LOOK AT THAT.
WHATEVER.
NOW, LET ME THINK.
THE SECOND FLOOR'S A MESS.
'S OKAY. I'LL SLEEP IN YOUR ROOM.
YAAAWN
IS THERE ANYTHING PARTICULAR THE YOUNG LADY WOULD LIKE FOR DINNER?
OOH! YEAH, THANKS.
HARD TO NARROW IT DOWN.

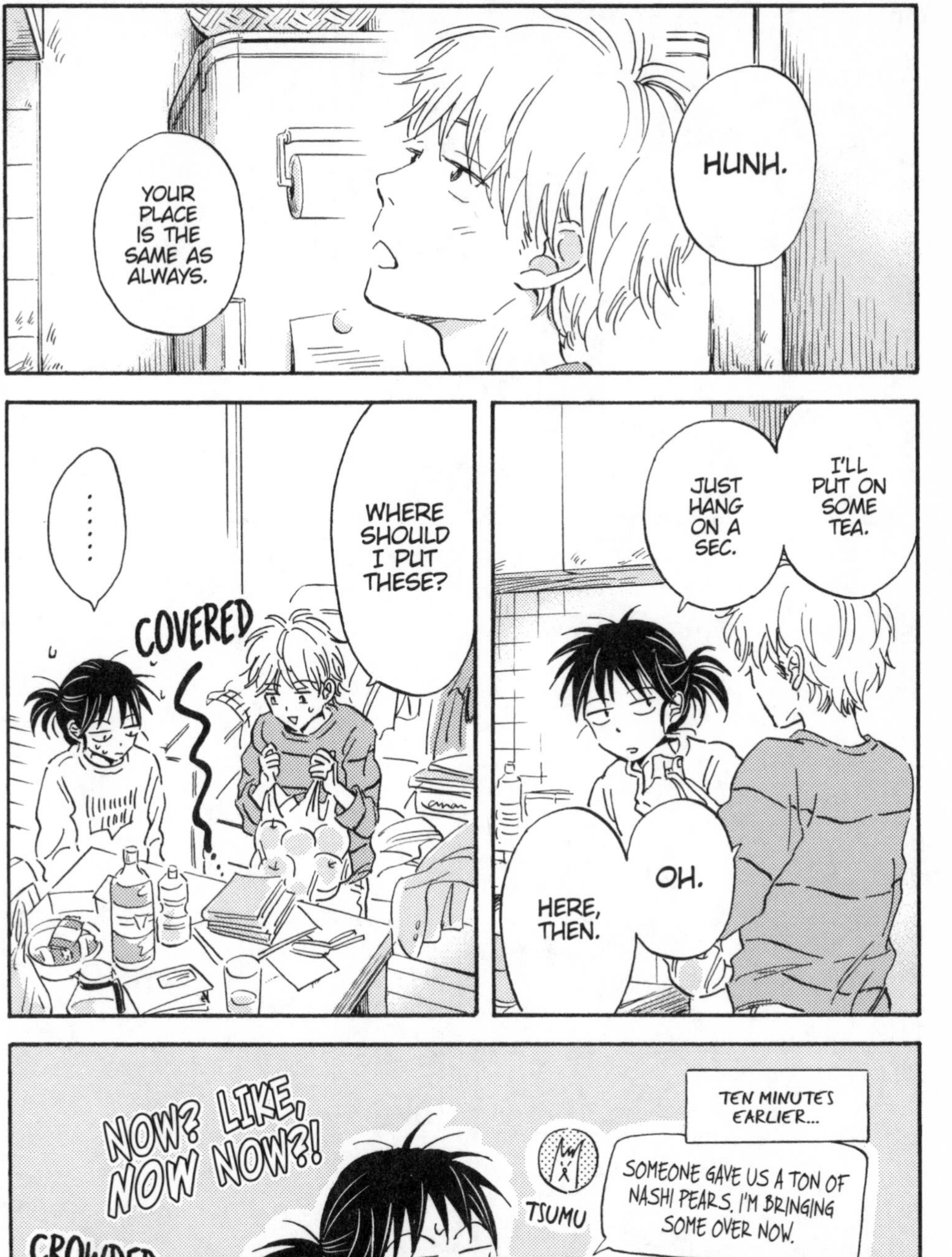
HUNH.
YOUR PLACE IS THE SAME AS ALWAYS.
I'LL PUT ON SOME TEA.
JUST HANG ON A SEC.
OH.
HERE, THEN.
WHERE SHOULD I PUT THESE?
......
COVERED
TEN MINUTES EARLIER...
SOMEONE GAVE US A TON OF NASHI PEARS. I'M BRINGING SOME OVER NOW.
TSUMU
NOW? LIKE, NOW NOW?!
CROWDED~

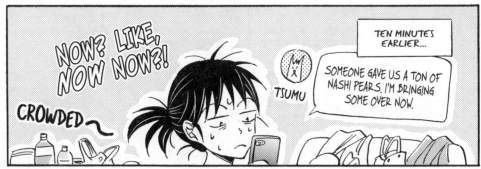

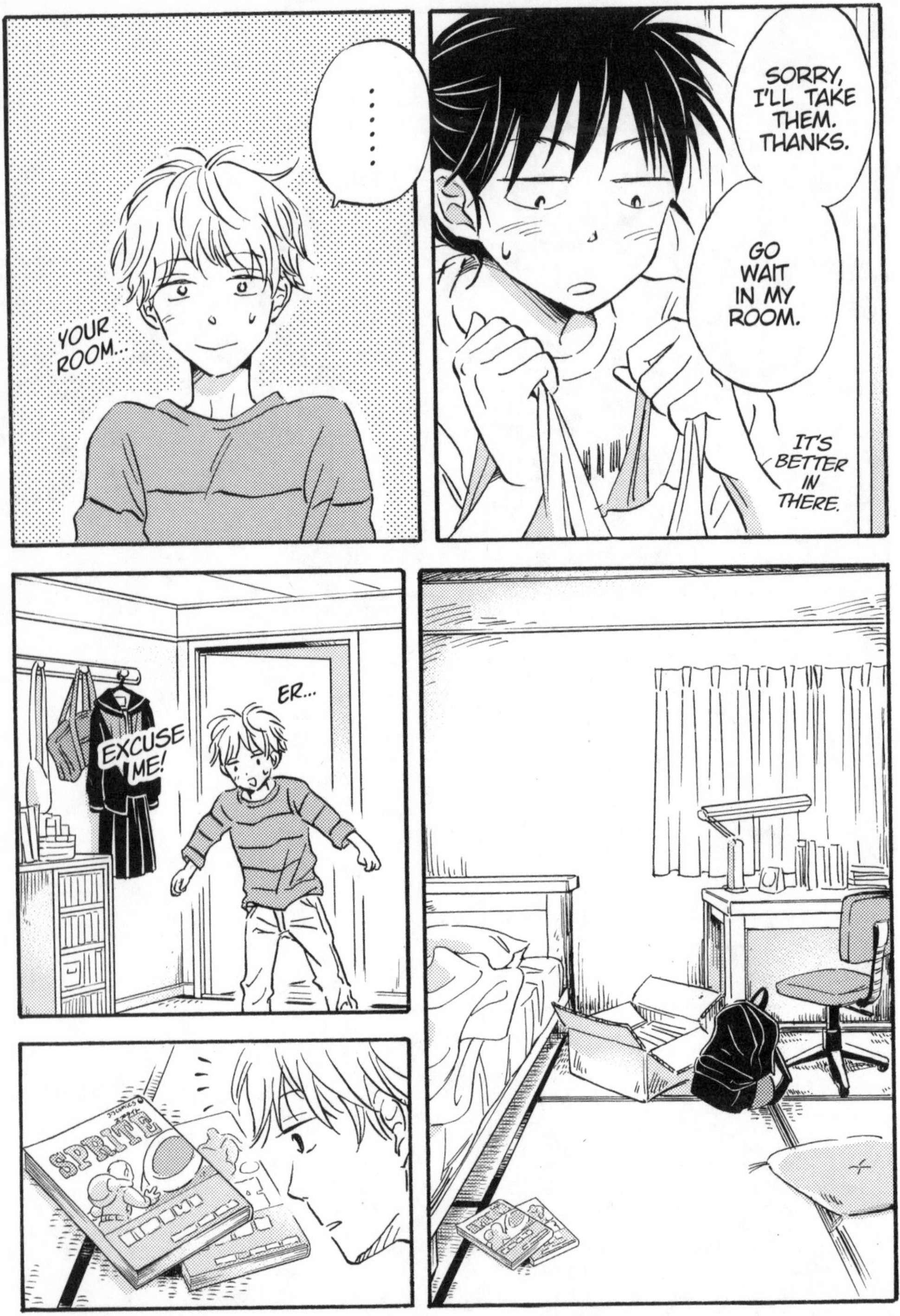
SORRY, I'LL TAKE THEM. THANKS.
GO WAIT IN MY ROOM.
IT'S BETTER IN THERE.
......
YOUR ROOM...
ER...
EXCUSE ME!
SPRITE

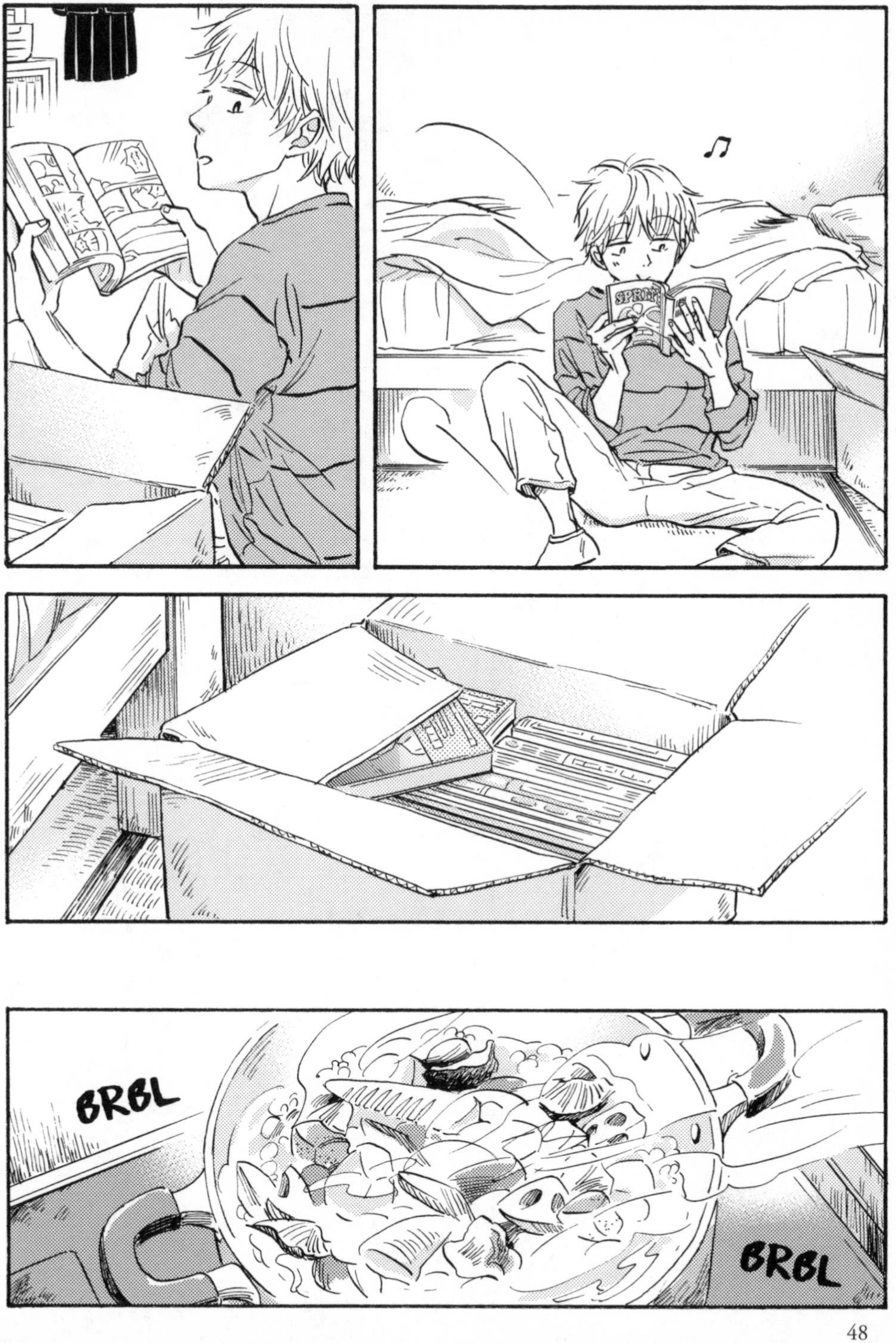
BRBL
BRBL

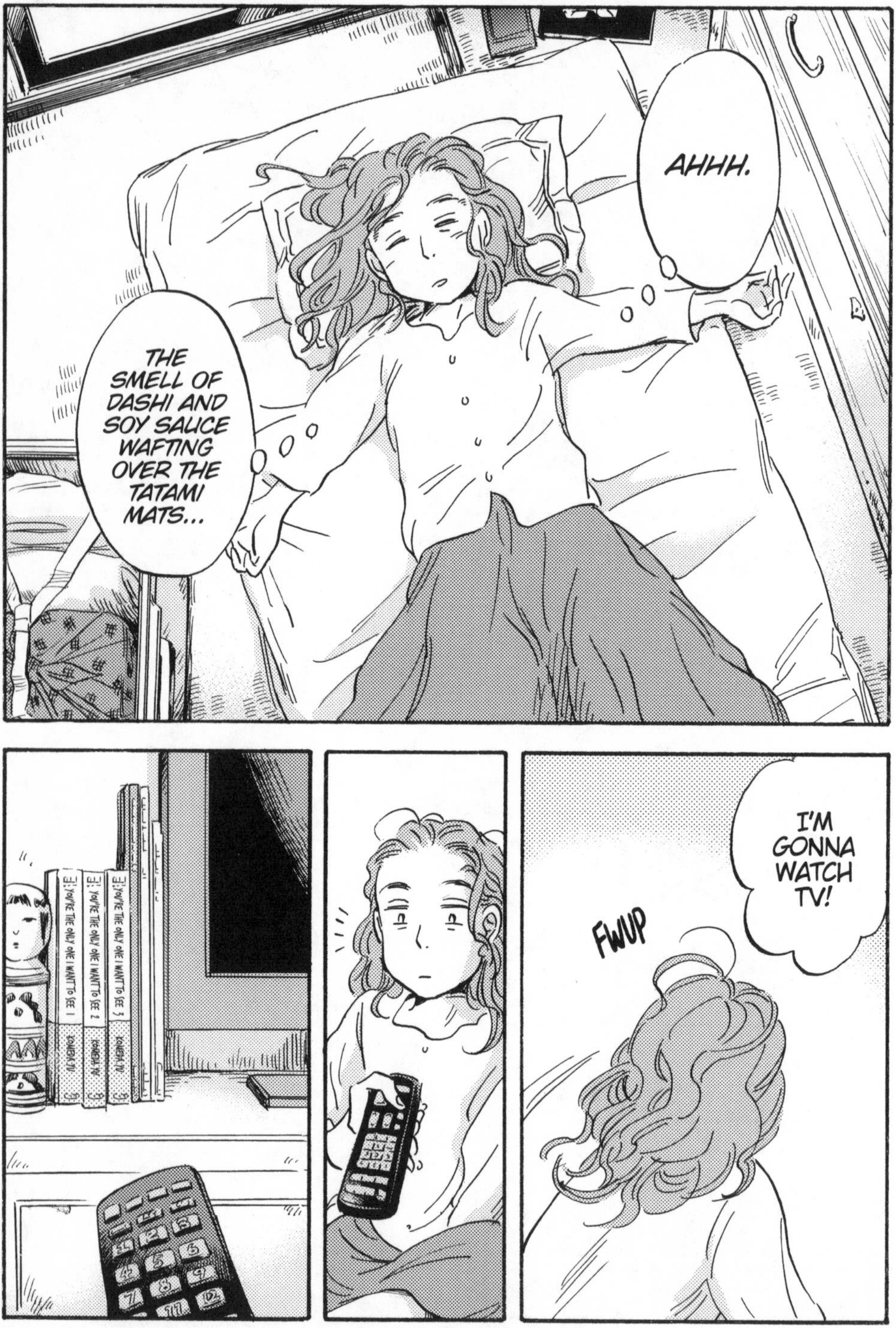
AHHH.
THE SMELL OF DASHI AND SOY SAUCE WAFTING OVER THE TATAMI MATS...
I'M GONNA WATCH TV!
FWUP
YOU'RE THE ONLY ONE I WANT TO SEE 1
YOU'RE THE ONLY ONE I WANT TO SEE 2
YOU'RE THE ONLY ONE I WANT TO SEE 3

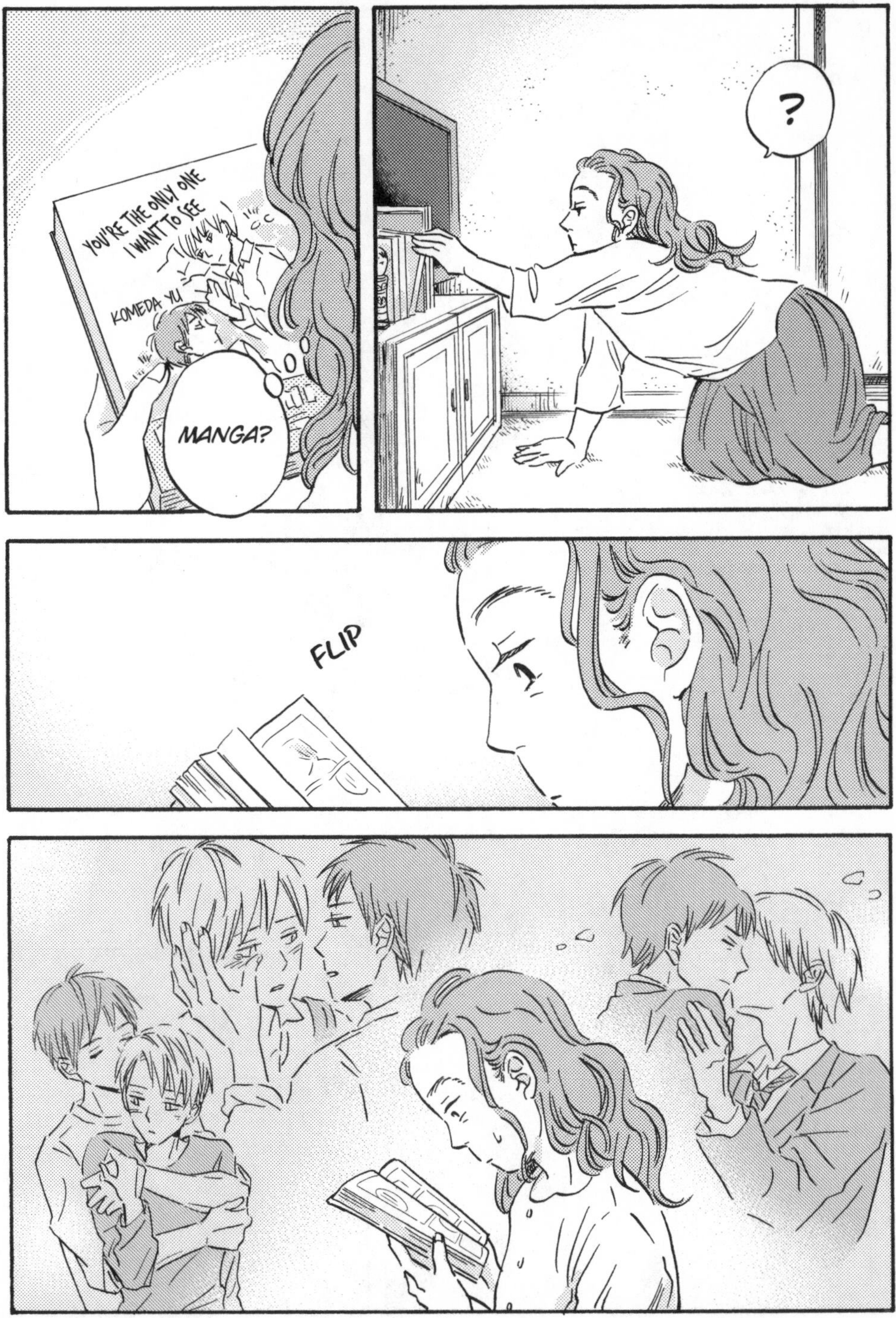
?
YOU'RE THE ONLY ONE I WANT TO SEE
KOMEDA YU
MANGA?
FLIP

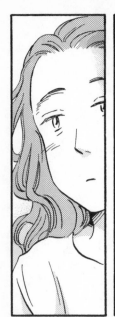

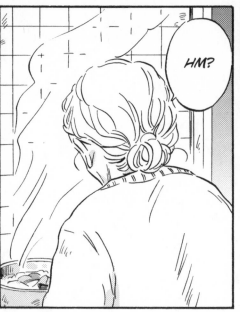

HM?

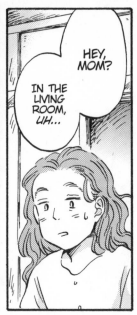

HEY, MOM?

IN THE LIVING ROOM, UH...

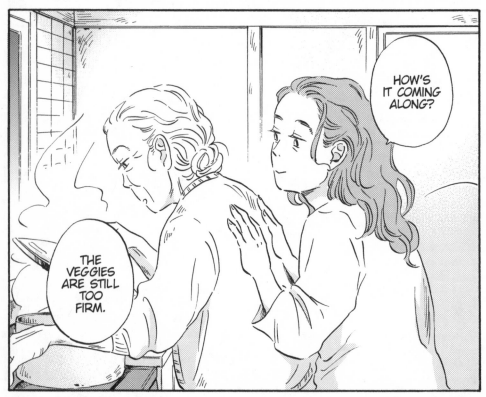

HOW'S IT COMING ALONG?

THE VEGGIES ARE STILL TOO FIRM.

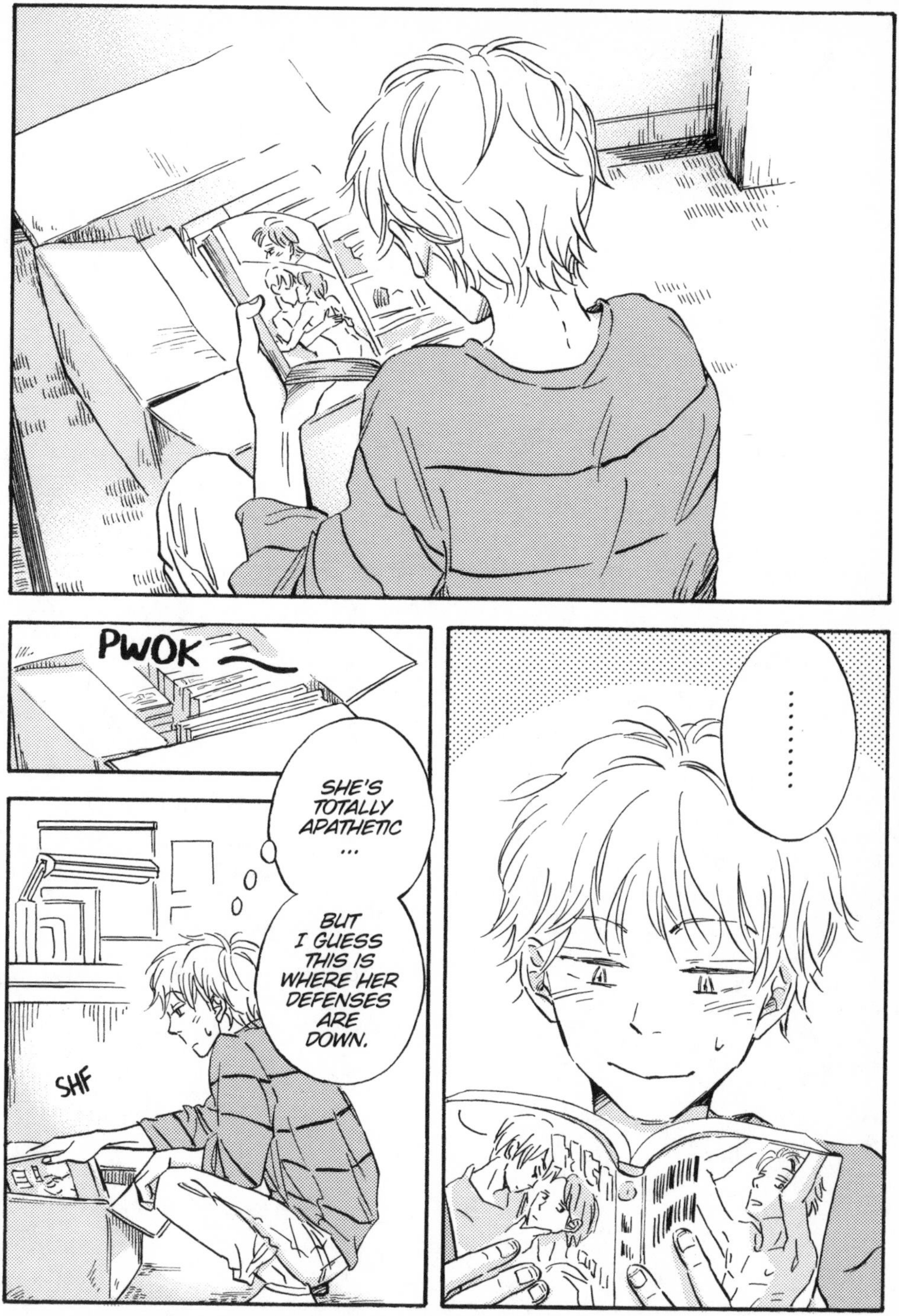
......
PWOK
SHE'S TOTALLY APATHETIC ...
BUT I GUESS THIS IS WHERE HER DEFENSES ARE DOWN.
SHF

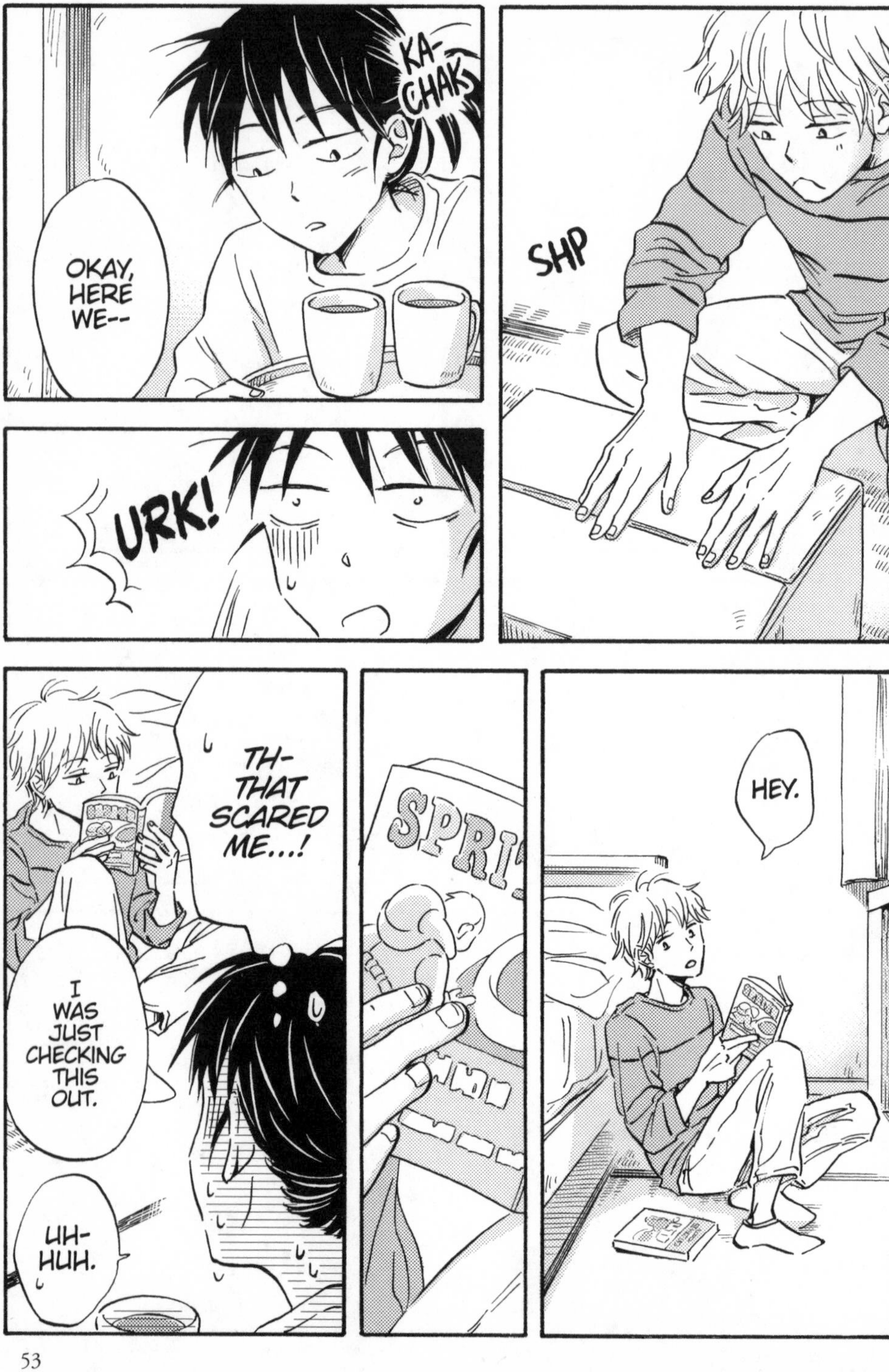
SHP
KA-CHAK
OKAY, HERE WE--
URK!
HEY.
TH-THAT SCARED ME...!
I WAS JUST CHECKING THIS OUT.
UH-HUH.

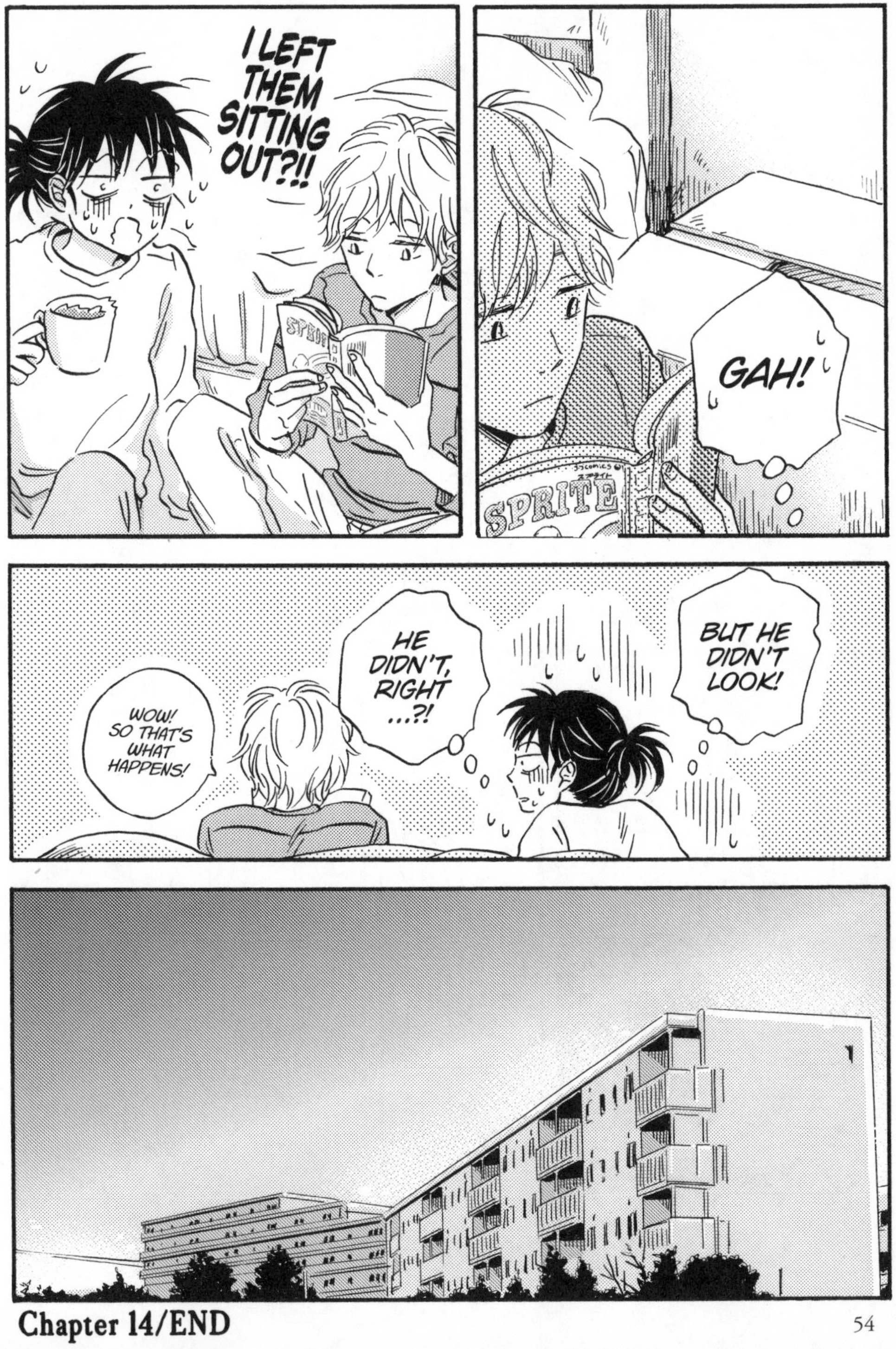
SPRITE
GAH!
I LEFT THEM SITTING OUT?!!
BUT HE DIDN'T LOOK!
HE DIDN'T, RIGHT ...?!
WOW! SO THAT'S WHAT HAPPENS!

Chapter 14/END

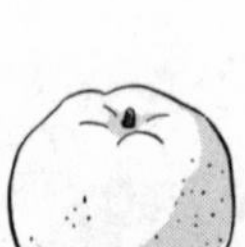

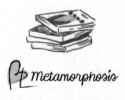
metamorphosis

Chapter 15

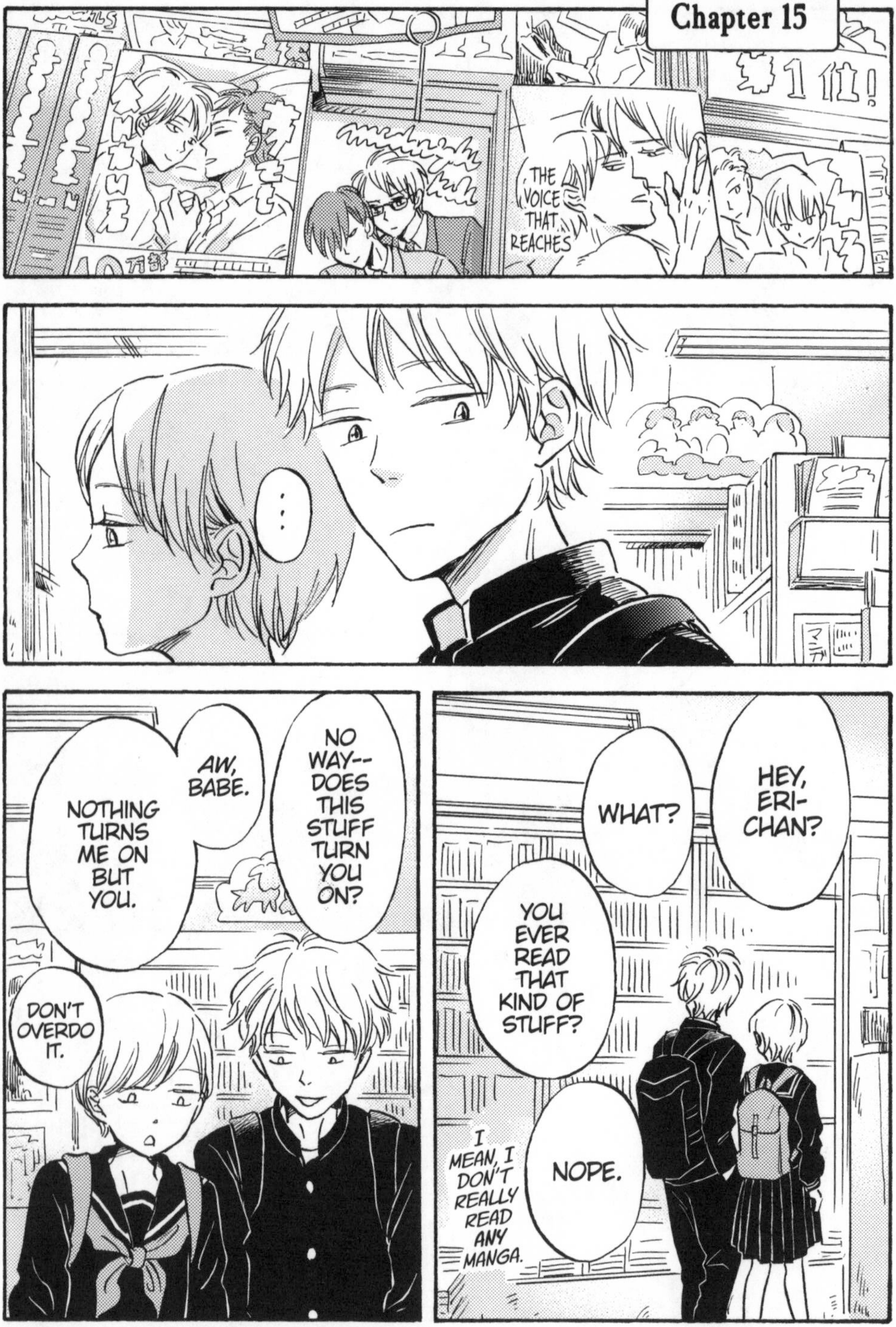
第1位!
THE VOICE THAT REACHES
...
HEY, ERI-CHAN?
WHAT?
YOU EVER READ THAT KIND OF STUFF?
NOPE.
I MEAN, I DON'T REALLY READ ANY MANGA.
NO WAY-- DOES THIS STUFF TURN YOU ON?
AW, BABE.
NOTHING TURNS ME ON BUT YOU.
DON'T OVERDO IT.

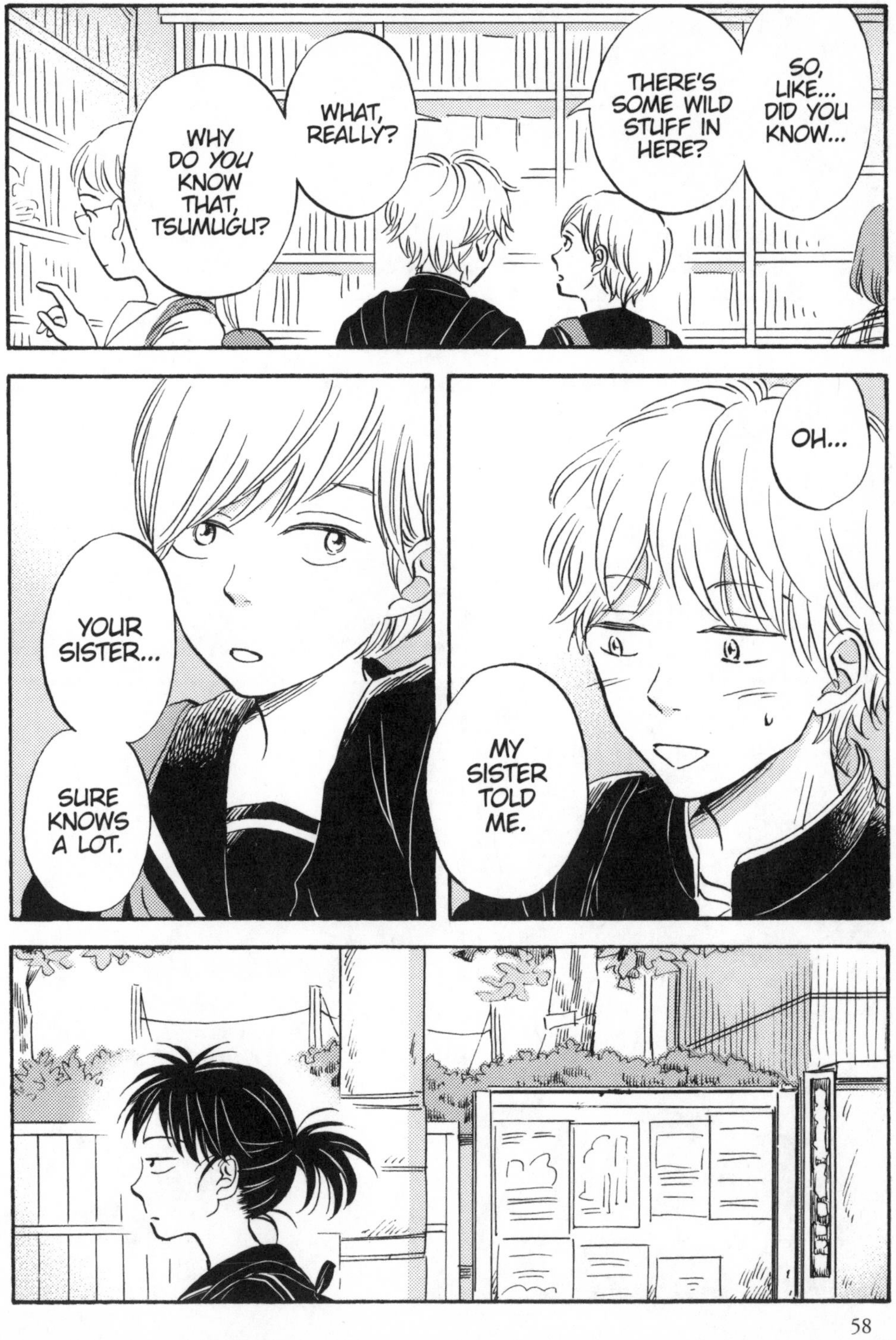
SO, LIKE... DID YOU KNOW...
THERE'S SOME WILD STUFF IN HERE?
WHAT, REALLY?
WHY DO *YOU* KNOW THAT, TSUMUGU?
OH...
MY SISTER TOLD ME.
YOUR SISTER...
SURE KNOWS A LOT.

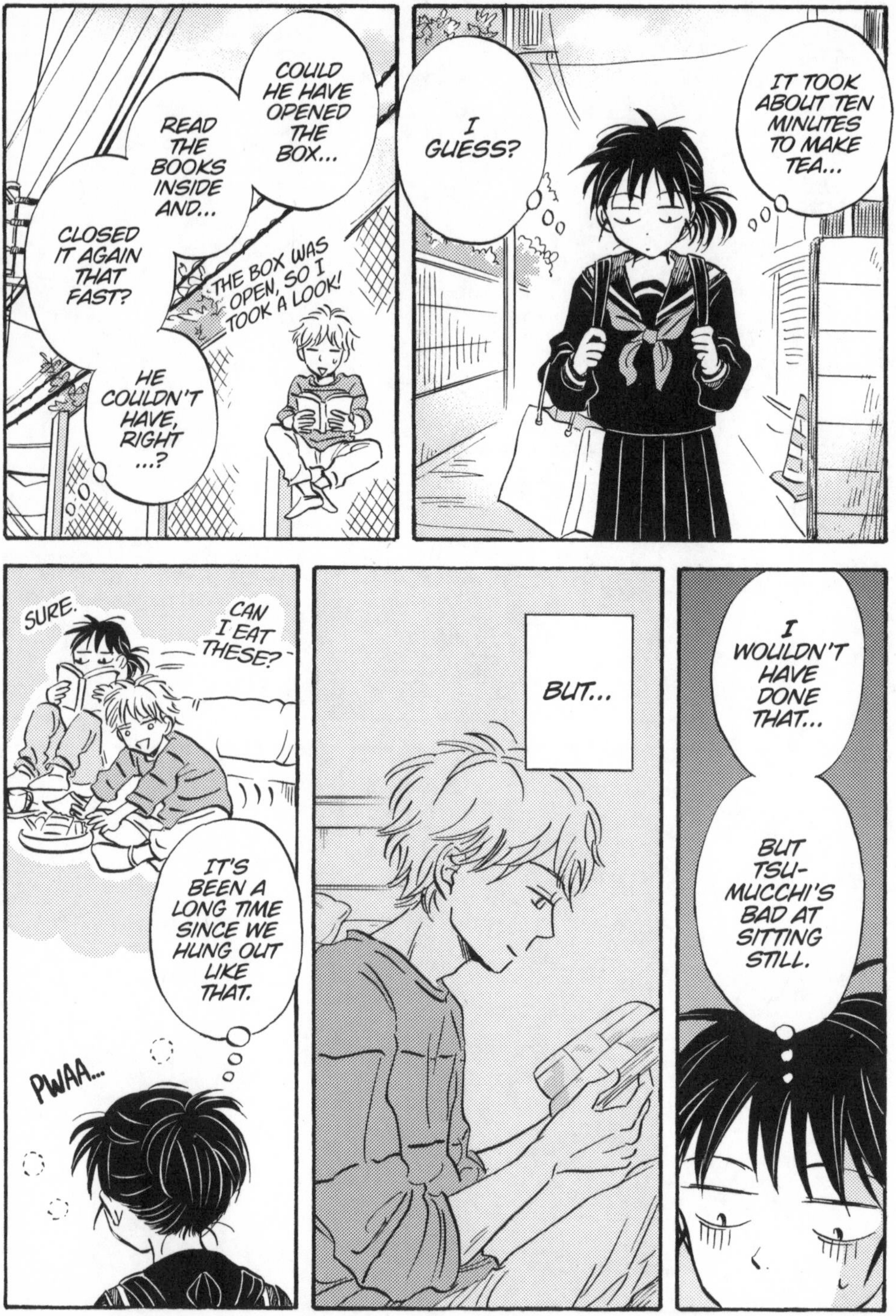
IT TOOK ABOUT TEN MINUTES TO MAKE TEA...
I GUESS?
COULD HE HAVE OPENED THE BOX...
READ THE BOOKS INSIDE AND...
CLOSED IT AGAIN THAT FAST?
THE BOX WAS OPEN, SO I TOOK A LOOK!
HE COULDN'T HAVE, RIGHT ...?
I WOULDN'T HAVE DONE THAT...
BUT TSU-MUCCHI'S BAD AT SITTING STILL.
BUT...
CAN I EAT THESE?
SURE.
IT'S BEEN A LONG TIME SINCE WE HUNG OUT LIKE THAT.
PWAA...

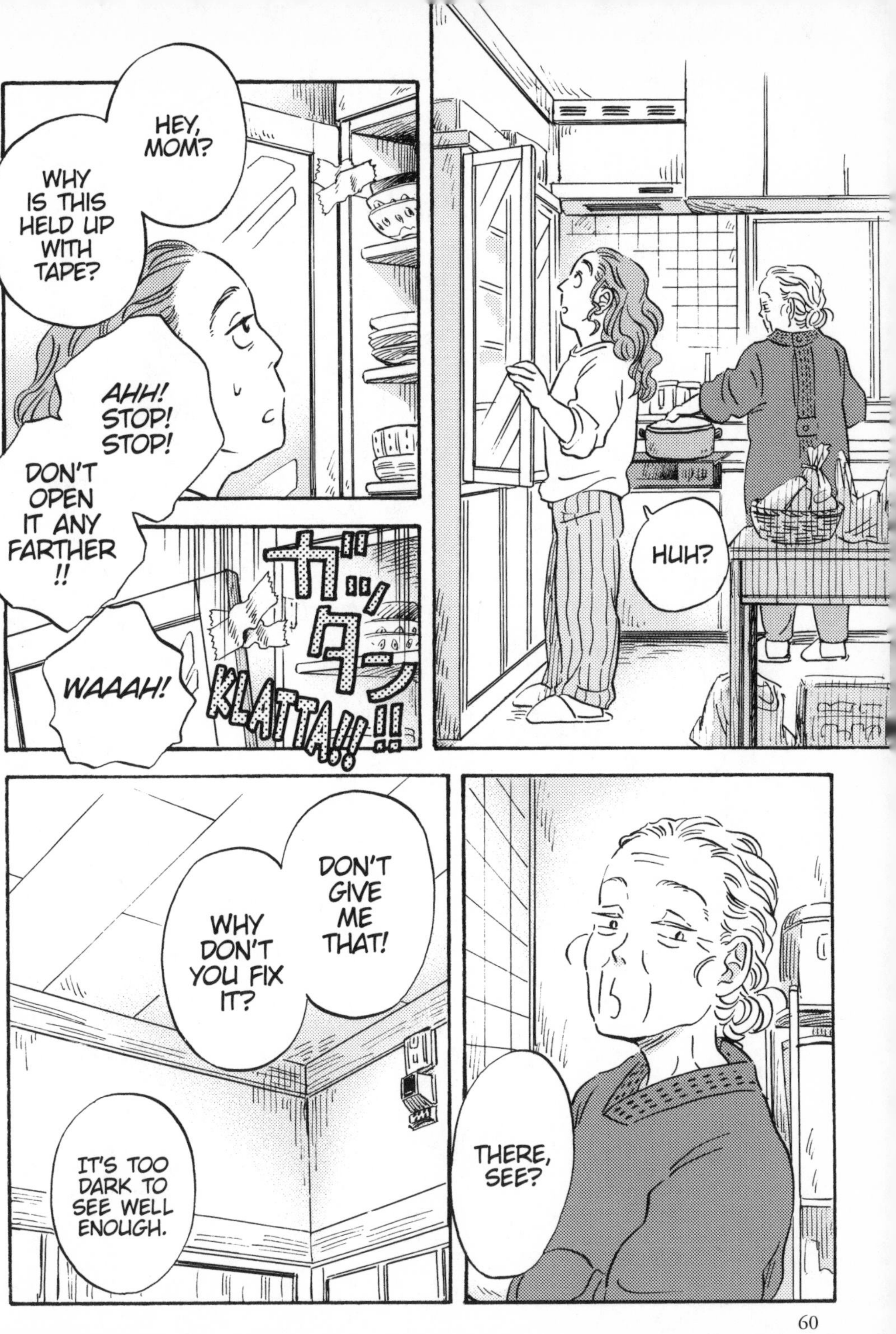
HUH?
HEY, MOM?
WHY IS THIS HELD UP WITH TAPE?
AHH! STOP! STOP! DON'T OPEN IT ANY FARTHER!!
ガダーン
KLATTA!!!!
WAAAH!
THERE, SEE?
DON'T GIVE ME THAT!
WHY DON'T YOU FIX IT?
IT'S TOO DARK TO SEE WELL ENOUGH.

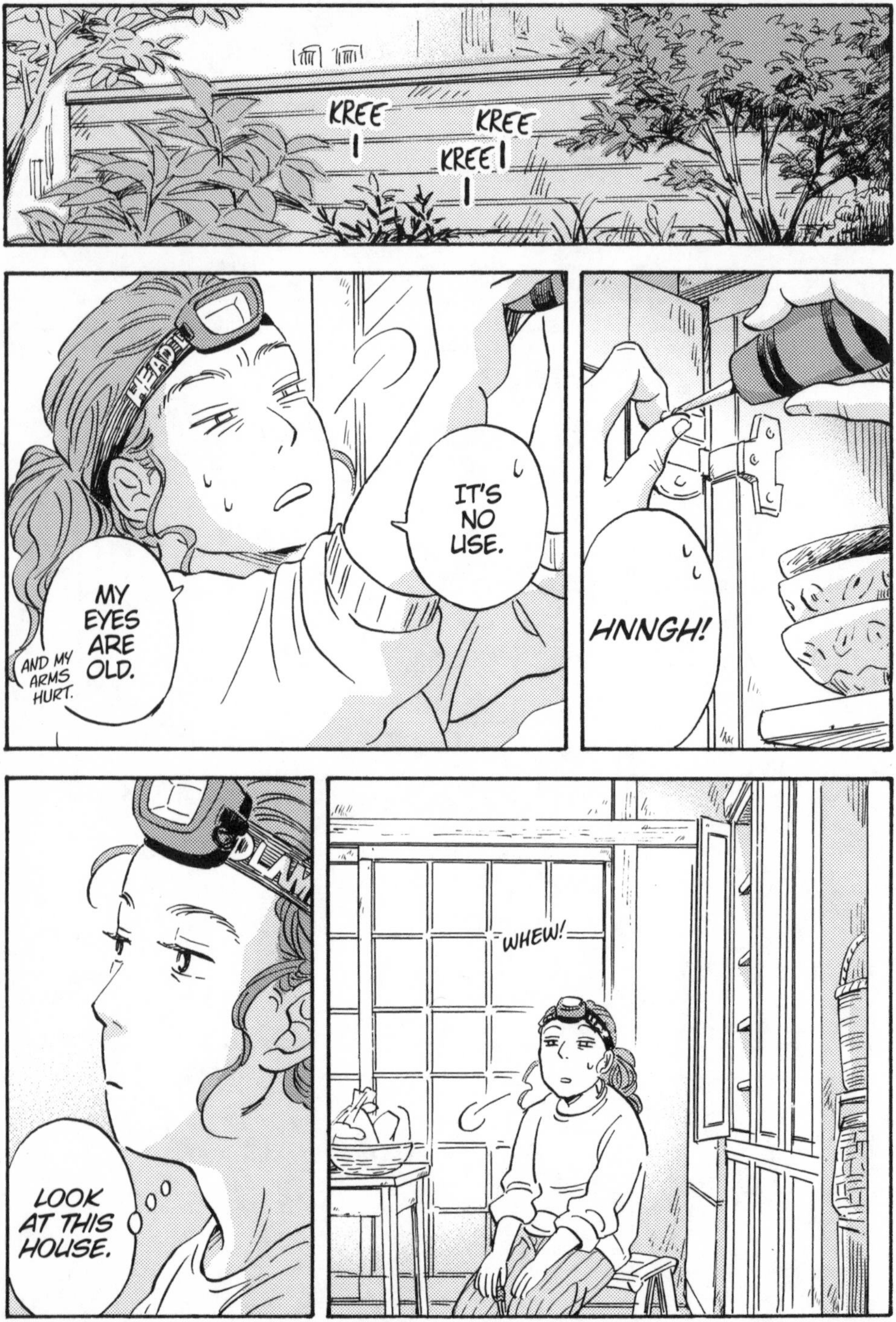
KREE
KREE
KREE
HNNGH!
IT'S NO USE.
MY EYES ARE OLD.
AND MY ARMS HURT.
WHEW!
LOOK AT THIS HOUSE.

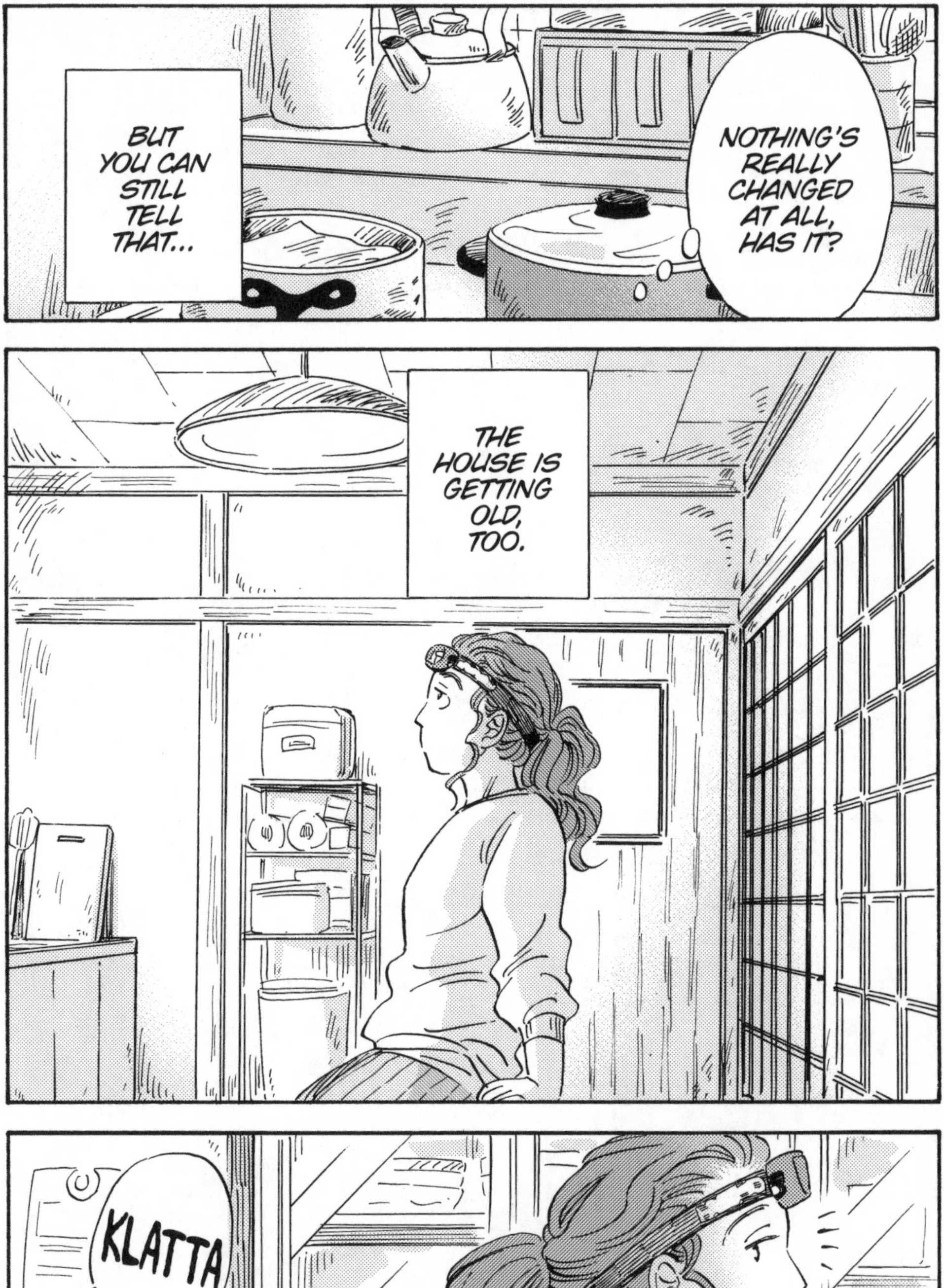
NOTHING'S REALLY CHANGED AT ALL, HAS IT?
BUT YOU CAN STILL TELL THAT...
THE HOUSE IS GETTING OLD, TOO.
KLATTA

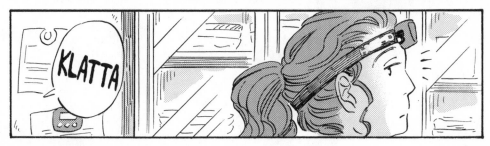

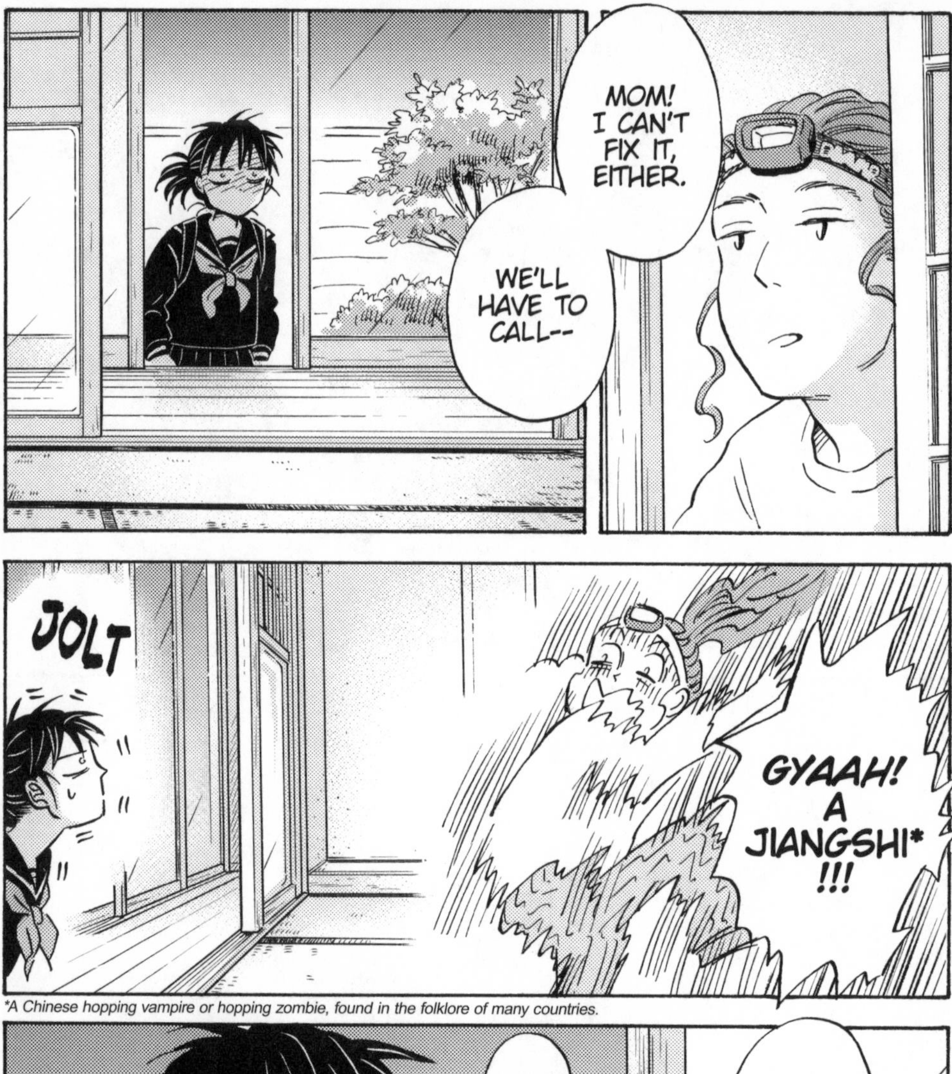
MOM! I CAN'T FIX IT, EITHER.
WE'LL HAVE TO CALL--
GYAAH! A JIANGSHI* !!!
JOLT

*A Chinese hopping vampire or hopping zombie, found in the folklore of many countries.

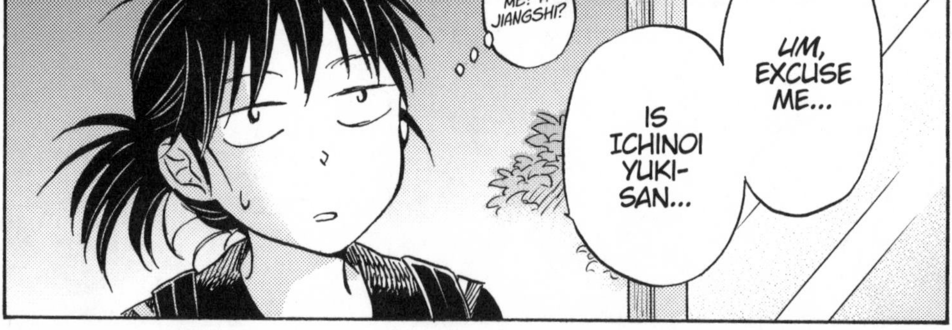
UM, EXCUSE ME...
IS ICHINOI YUKI-SAN...
ME? A JIANGSHI?

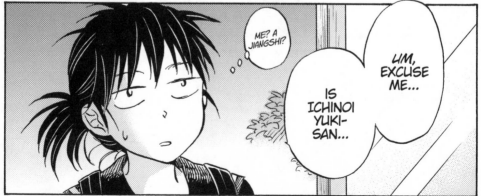

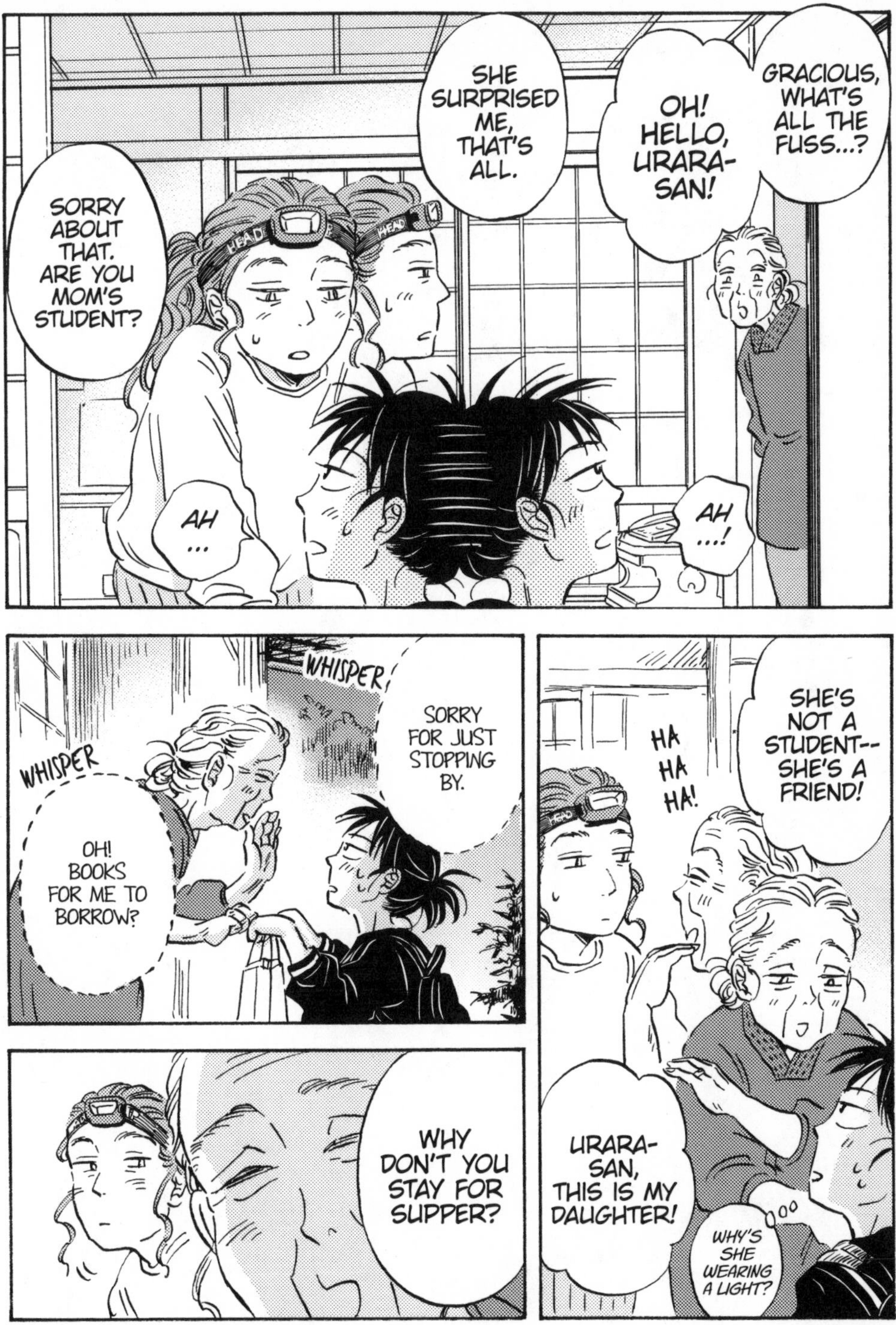
GRACIOUS, WHAT'S ALL THE FUSS...?
OH! HELLO, URARA-SAN!
SHE SURPRISED ME, THAT'S ALL.
SORRY ABOUT THAT. ARE YOU MOM'S STUDENT?
AH ...!
AH ...
SHE'S NOT A STUDENT-- SHE'S A FRIEND!
HA HA HA!
URARA-SAN, THIS IS MY DAUGHTER!
WHY'S SHE WEARING A LIGHT?
WHISPER
SORRY FOR JUST STOPPING BY.
WHISPER
OH! BOOKS FOR ME TO BORROW?
WHY DON'T YOU STAY FOR SUPPER?

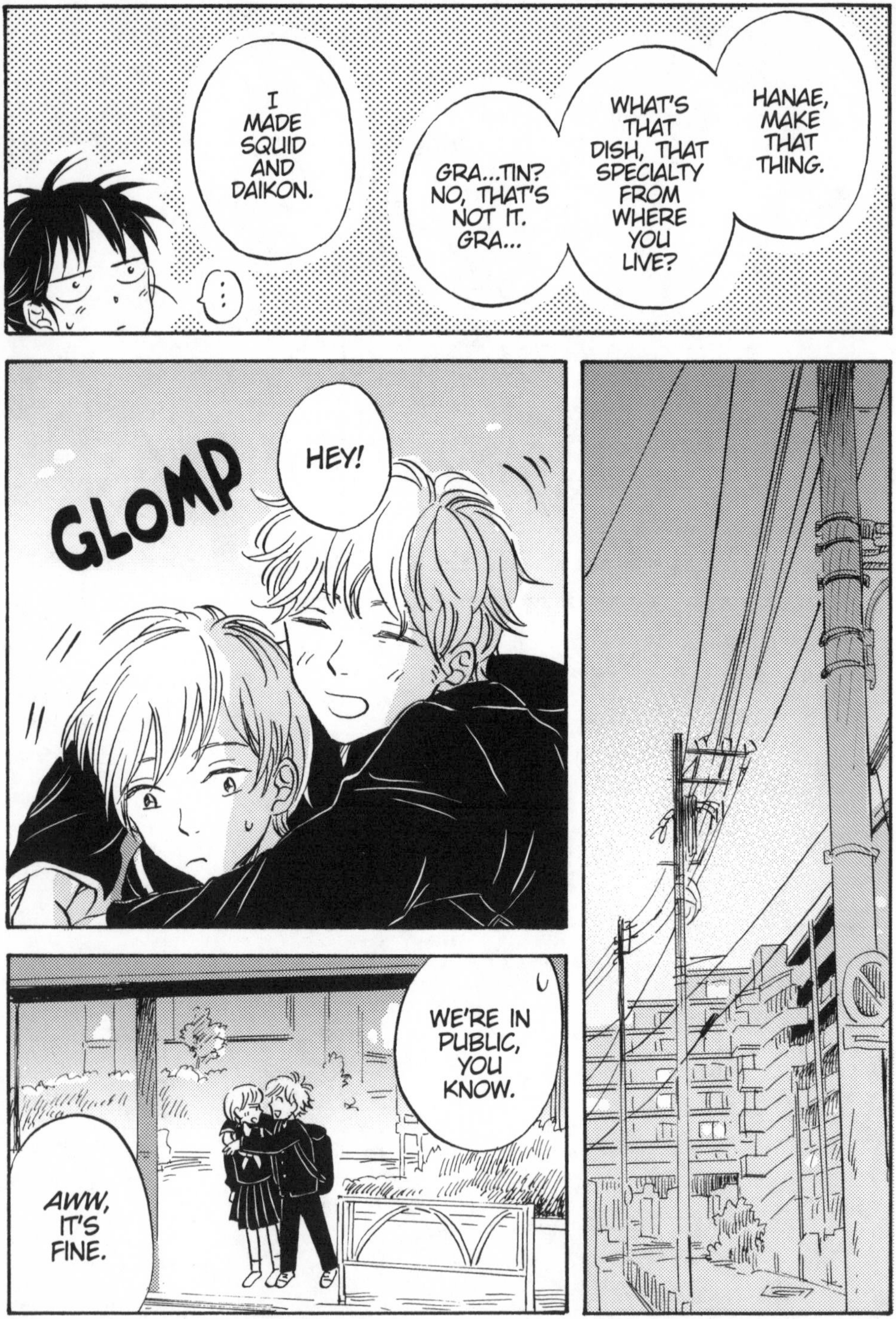
HANAE, MAKE THAT THING.
WHAT'S THAT DISH, THAT SPECIALTY FROM WHERE YOU LIVE?
GRA...TIN? NO, THAT'S NOT IT. GRA...
I MADE SQUID AND DAIKON.
...
HEY!
GLOMP
WE'RE IN PUBLIC, YOU KNOW.
AWW, IT'S FINE.

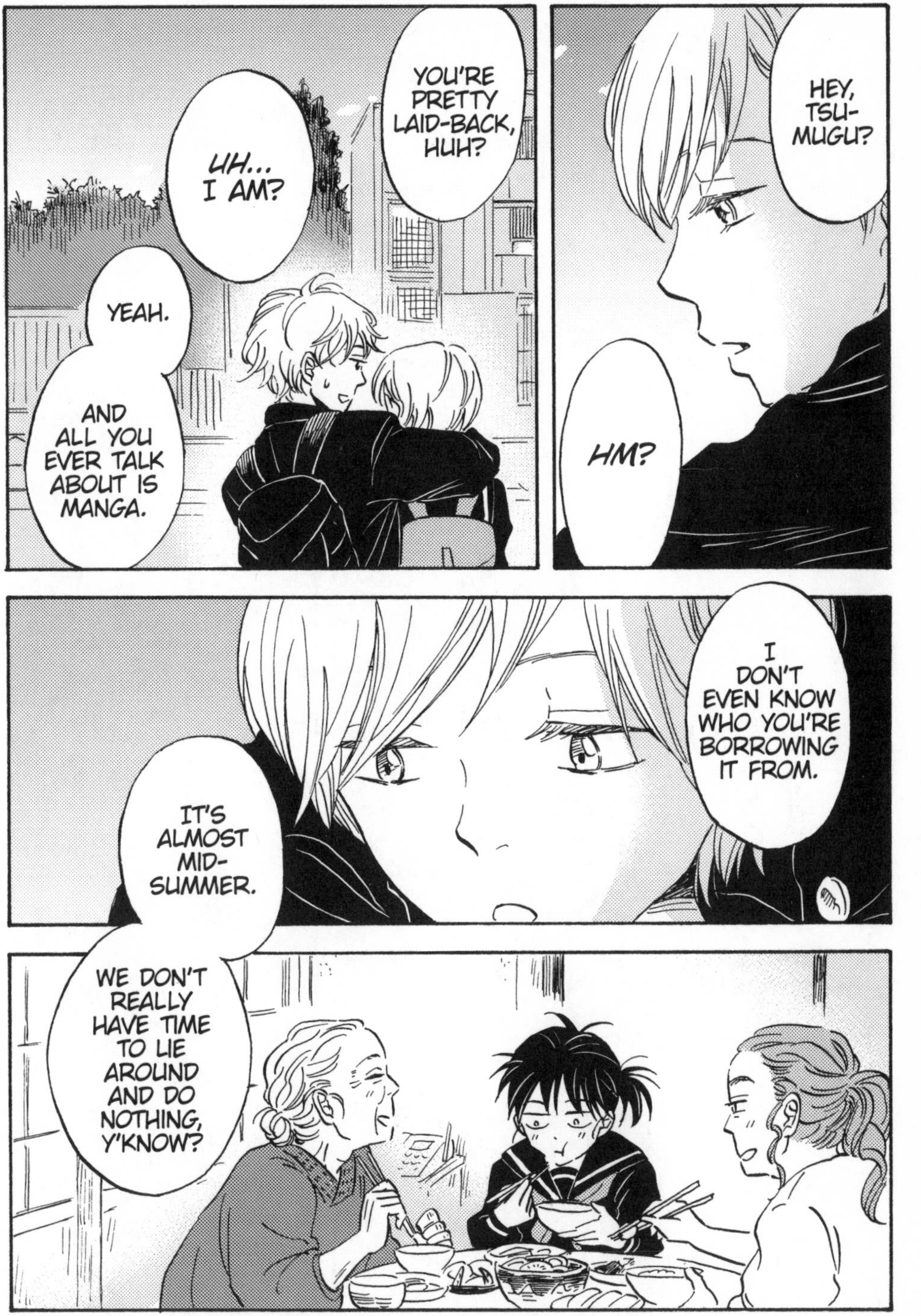
HEY, TSU-MUGU?
HM?
YOU'RE PRETTY LAID-BACK, HUH?
UH... I AM?
YEAH.
AND ALL YOU EVER TALK ABOUT IS MANGA.
I DON'T EVEN KNOW WHO YOU'RE BORROWING IT FROM.
IT'S ALMOST MID-SUMMER.
WE DON'T REALLY HAVE TIME TO LIE AROUND AND DO NOTHING, Y'KNOW?

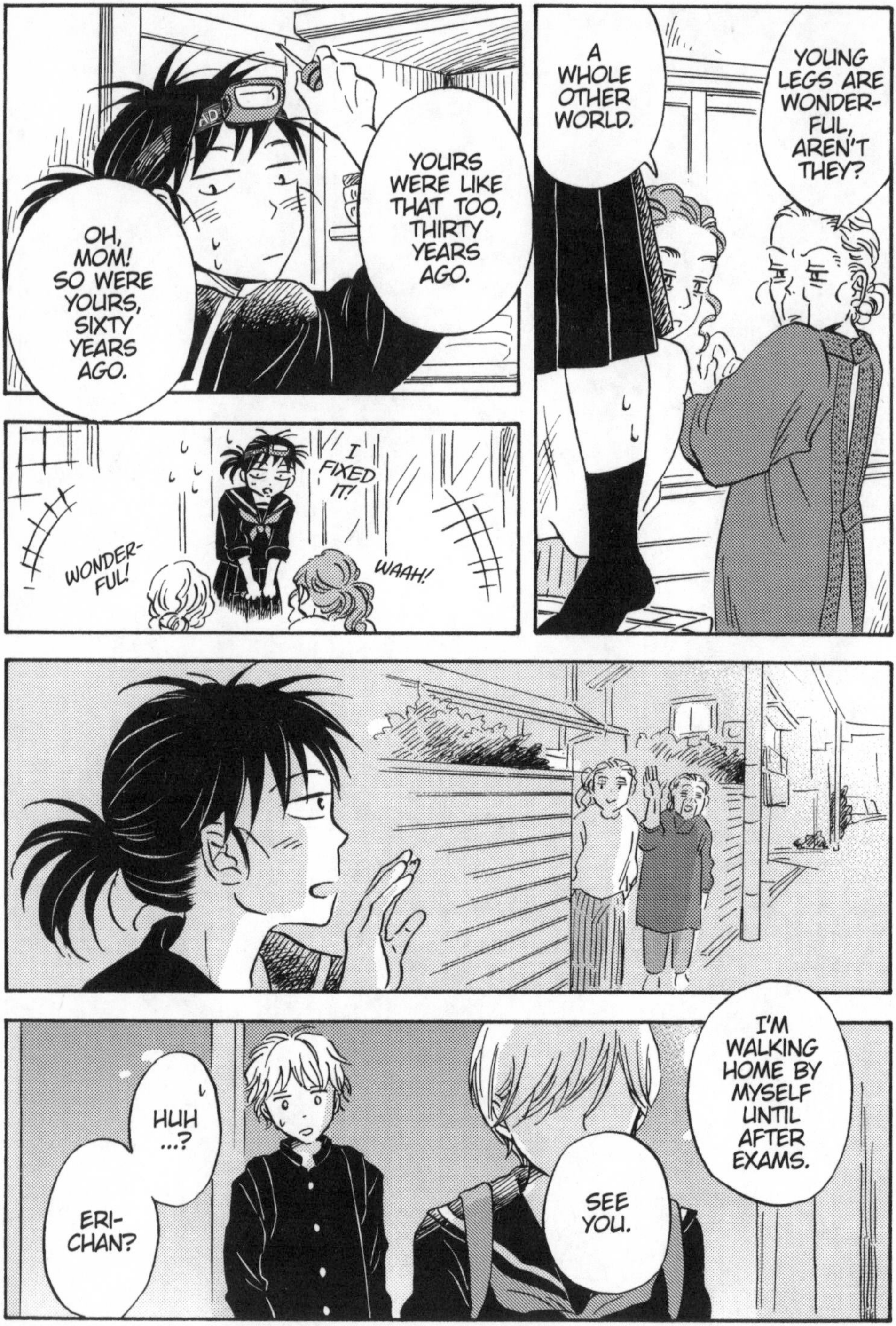
YOUNG LEGS ARE WONDER-FUL, AREN'T THEY?
A WHOLE OTHER WORLD.
YOURS WERE LIKE THAT TOO, THIRTY YEARS AGO.
OH, MOM! SO WERE YOURS, SIXTY YEARS AGO.
I FIXED IT!
WAAH!
WONDER-FUL!
I'M WALKING HOME BY MYSELF UNTIL AFTER EXAMS.
SEE YOU.
HUH ...?
ERI-CHAN?

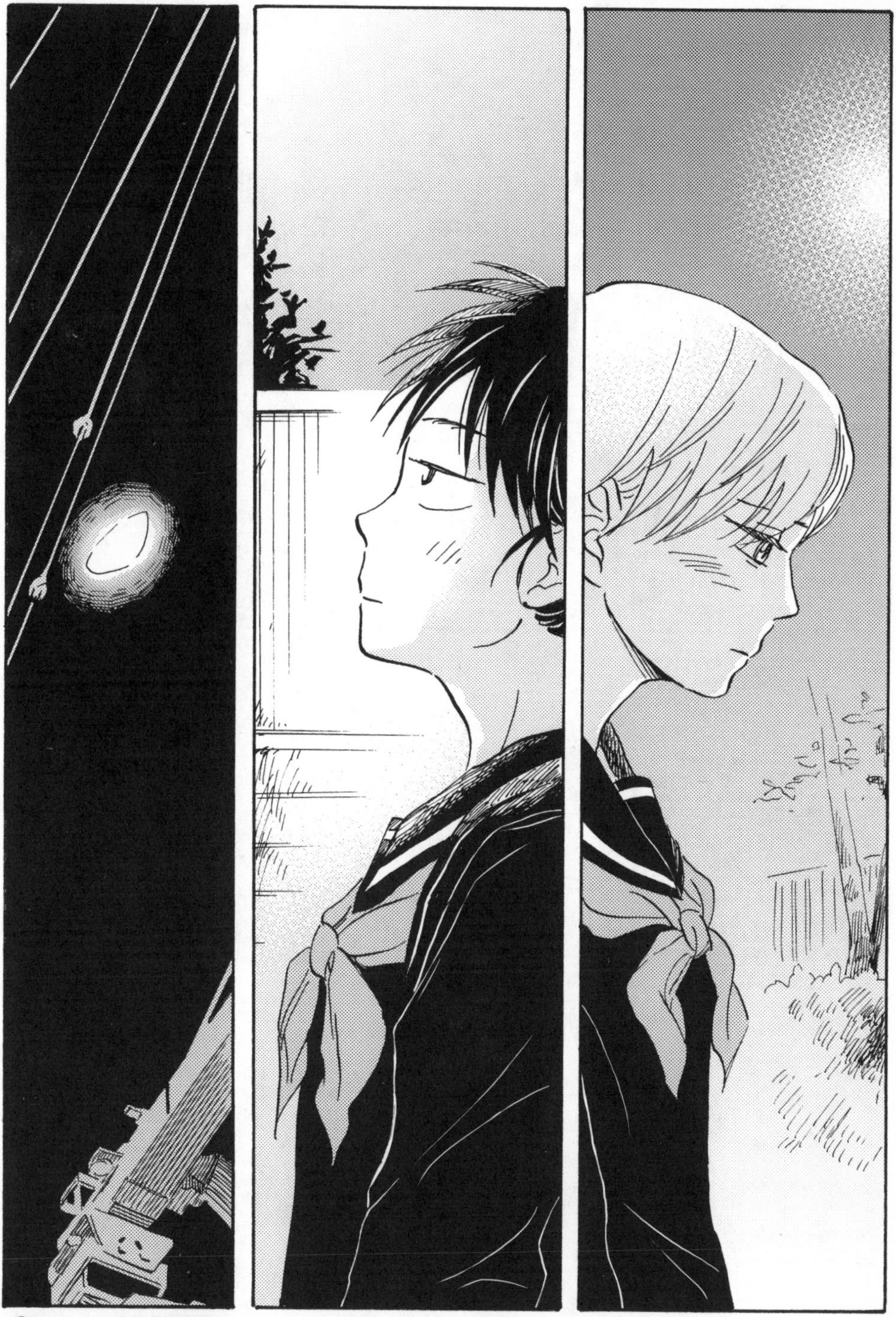

Chapter 15/END

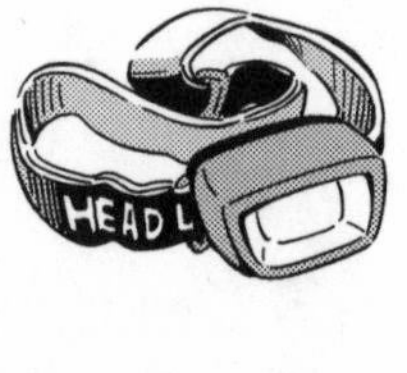
HEAD L

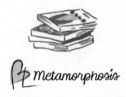
metamorphosis

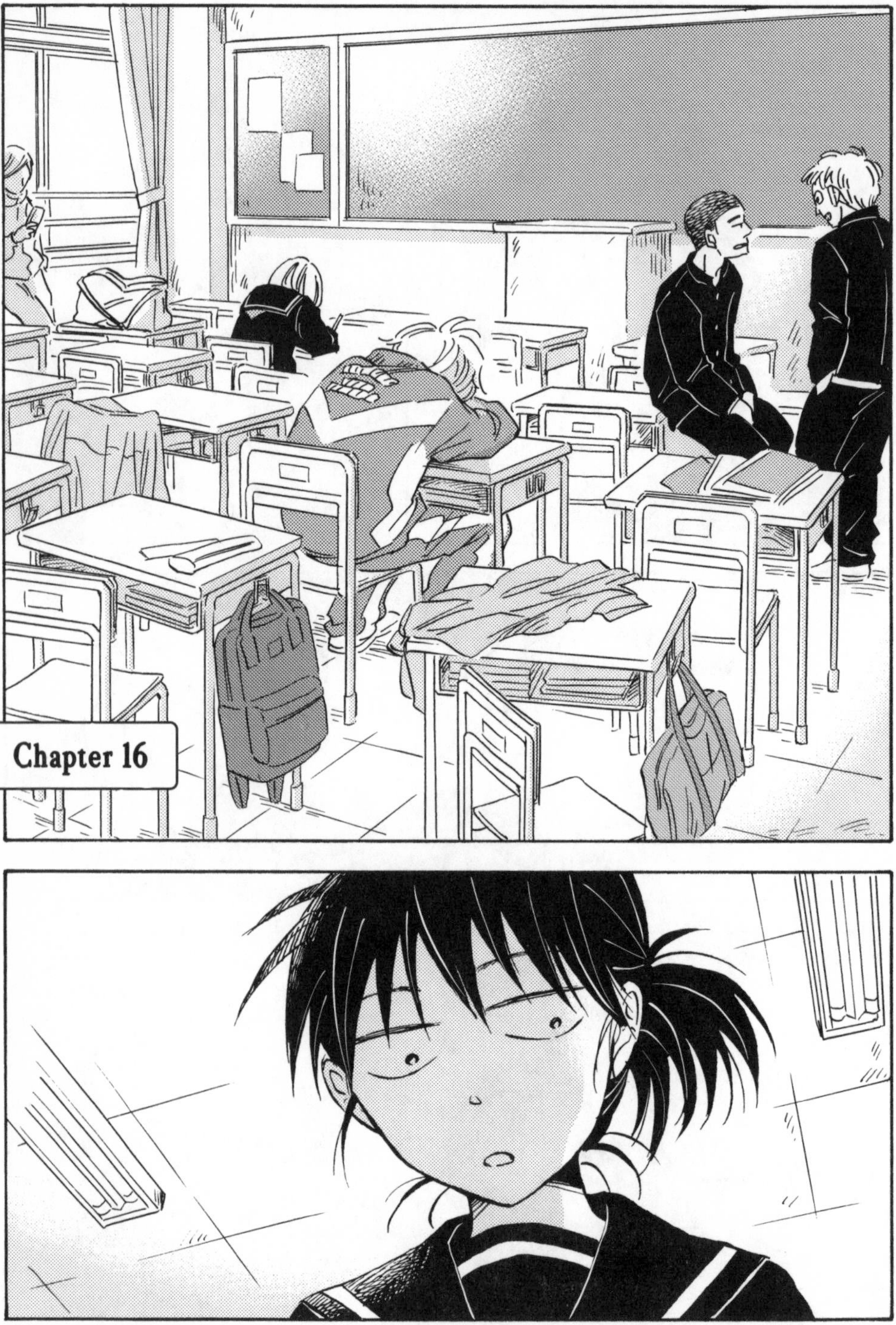
Chapter 16

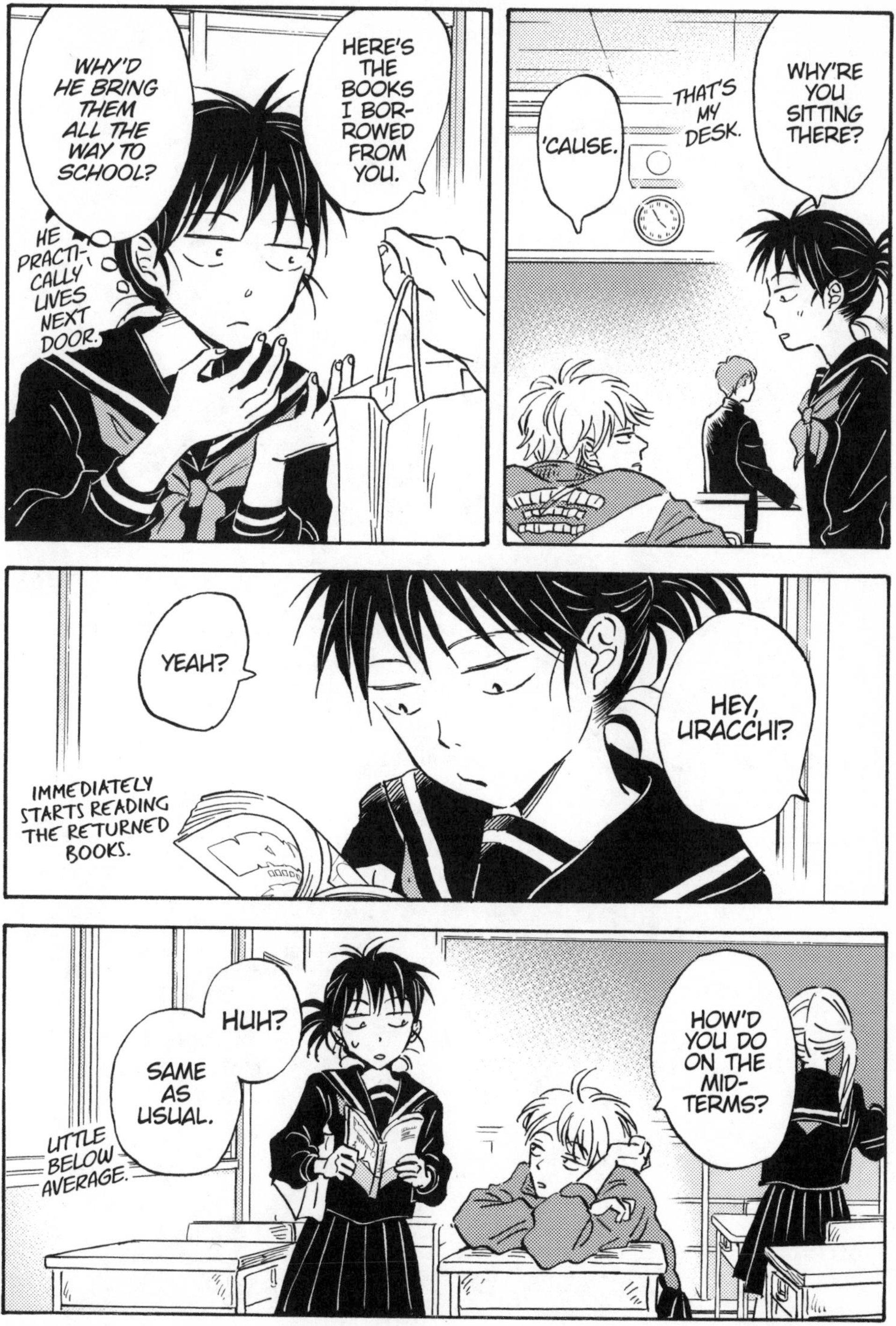
WHY'RE YOU SITTING THERE?
THAT'S MY DESK.
'CAUSE.
HERE'S THE BOOKS I BORROWED FROM YOU.
WHY'D HE BRING THEM ALL THE WAY TO SCHOOL?
HE PRACTICALLY LIVES NEXT DOOR.
HEY, URACCHI?
YEAH?
IMMEDIATELY STARTS READING THE RETURNED BOOKS.
HOW'D YOU DO ON THE MIDTERMS?
HUH?
SAME AS USUAL.
LITTLE BELOW AVERAGE.

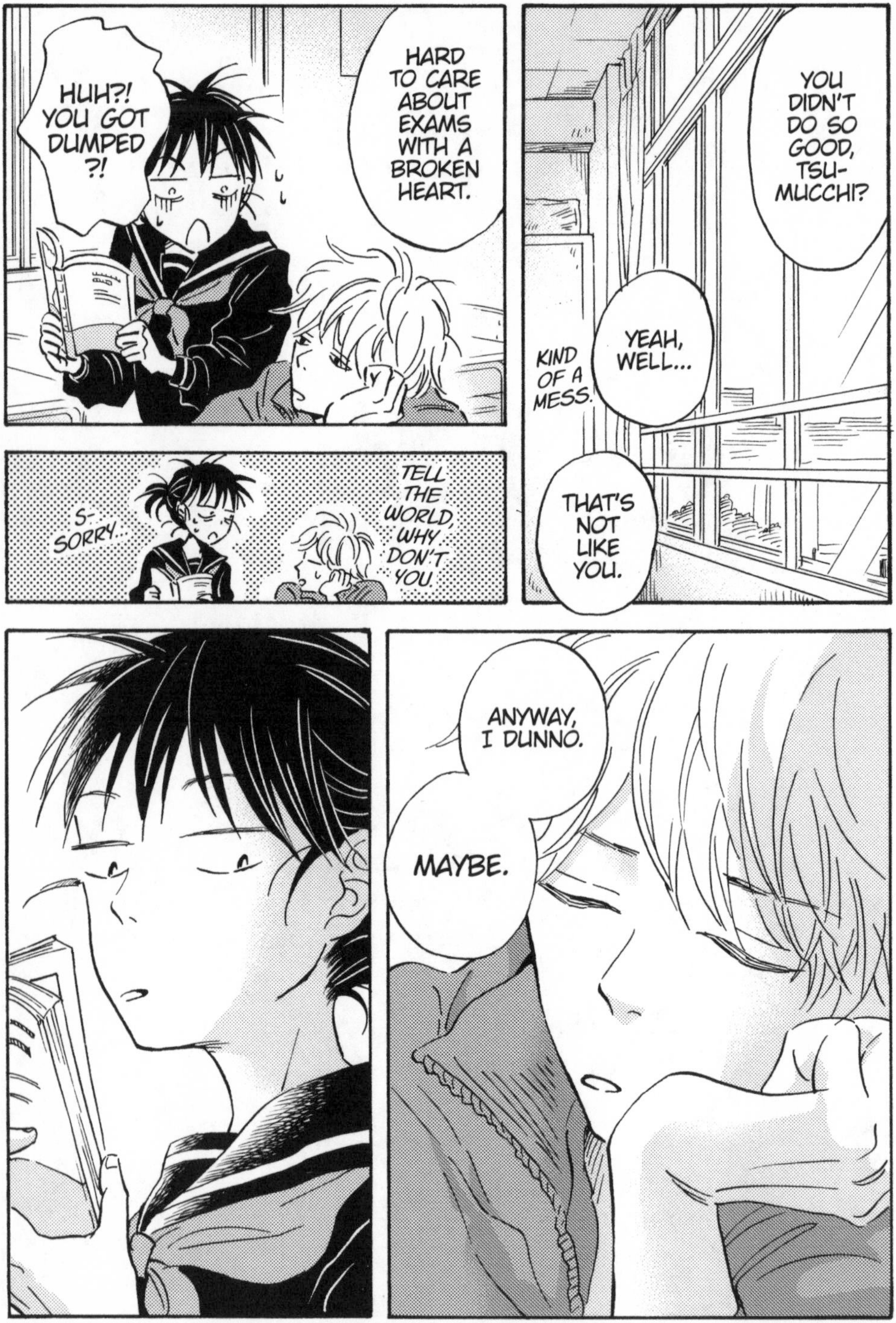
YOU DIDN'T DO SO GOOD, TSU-MUCCHI?
YEAH, WELL...
KIND OF A MESS.
THAT'S NOT LIKE YOU.
HARD TO CARE ABOUT EXAMS WITH A BROKEN HEART.
HUH?! YOU GOT DUMPED?!
TELL THE WORLD, WHY DON'T YOU.
S-SORRY...
ANYWAY, I DUNNO.
MAYBE.

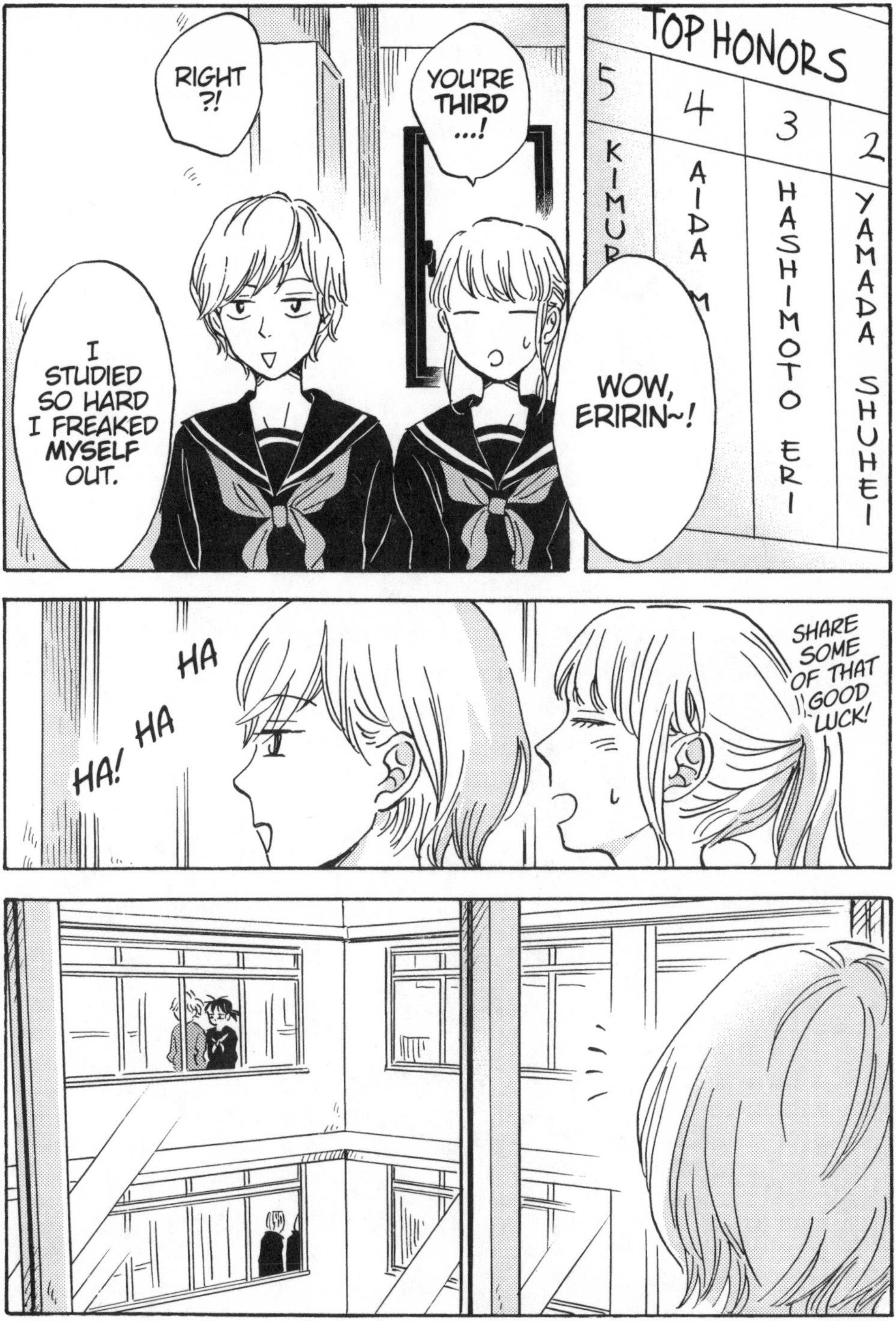
TOP HONORS
2 YAMADA SHUHEI
3 HASHIMOTO ERI
4 AIDA
5 KIMUR
WOW, ERIRIN~!
YOU'RE THIRD ...!
RIGHT ?!
I STUDIED SO HARD I FREAKED MYSELF OUT.
SHARE SOME OF THAT GOOD LUCK!
HA
HA
HA!

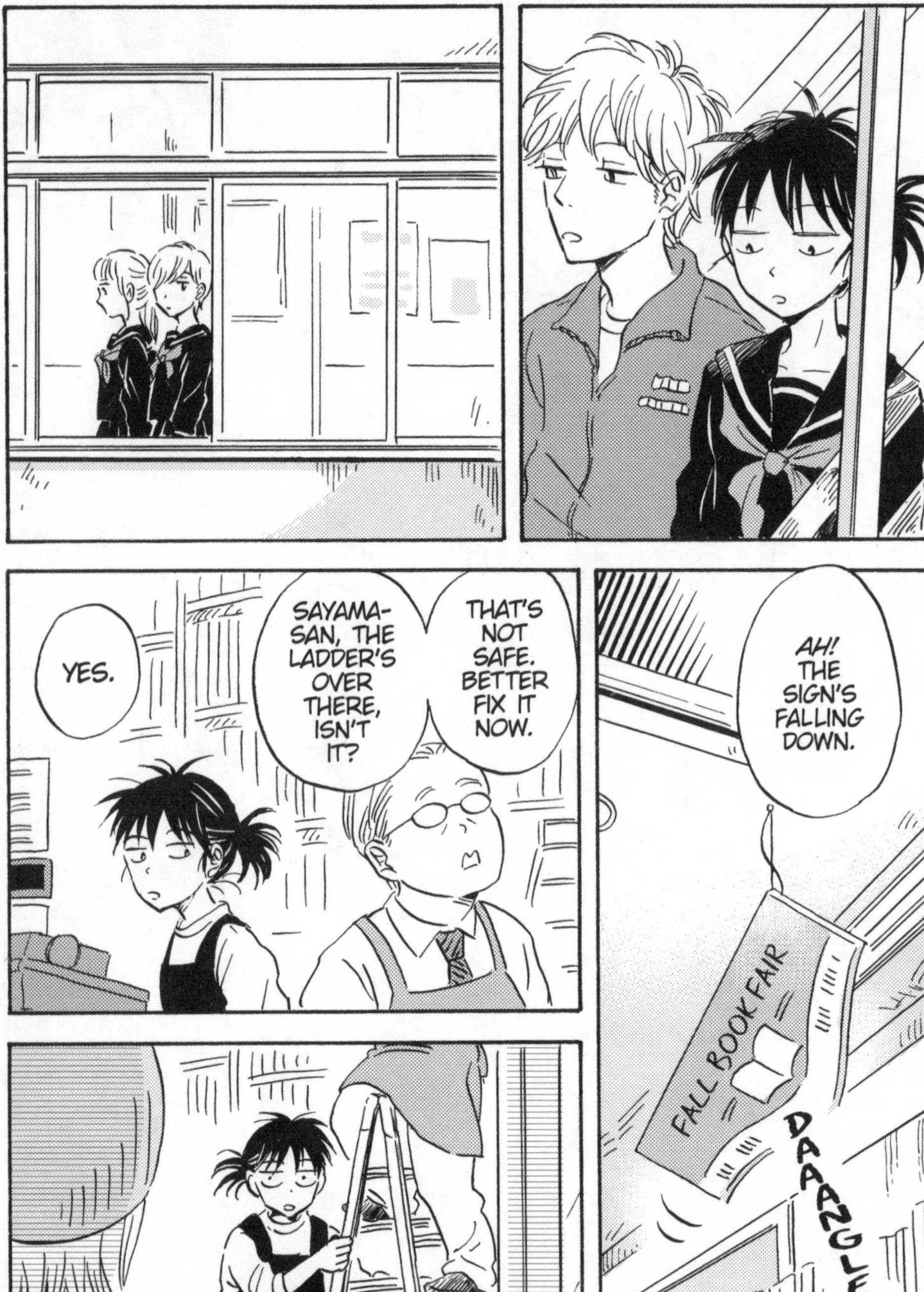
AH! THE SIGN'S FALLING DOWN.
FALL BOOK FAIR
DAAANGLE
THAT'S NOT SAFE. BETTER FIX IT NOW.
SAYAMA-SAN, THE LADDER'S OVER THERE, ISN'T IT?
YES.

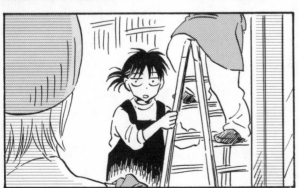

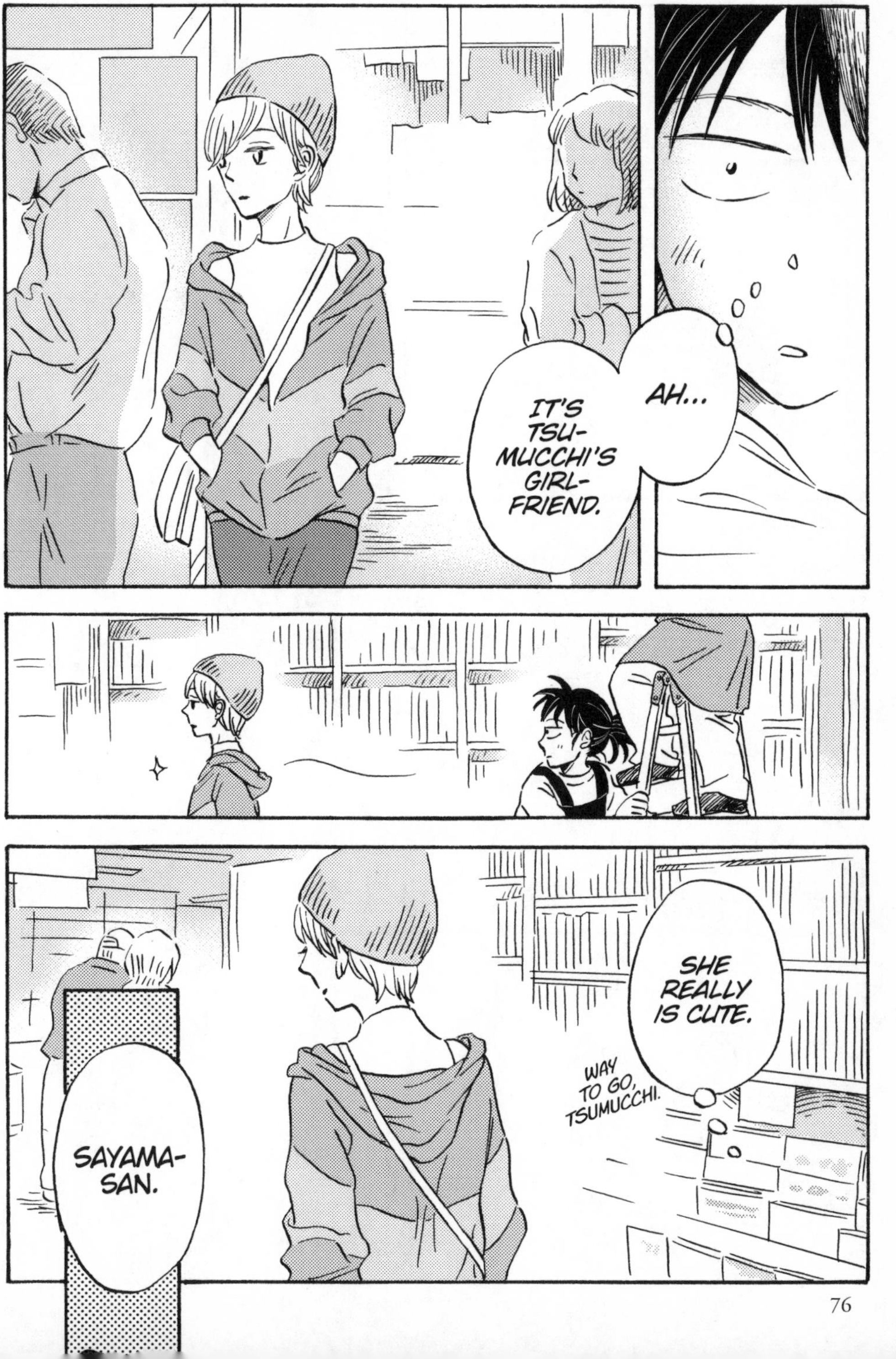
AH...
IT'S TSU-MUCCHI'S GIRL-FRIEND.
SHE REALLY IS CUTE.
WAY TO GO, TSUMUCCHI.
SAYAMA-SAN.

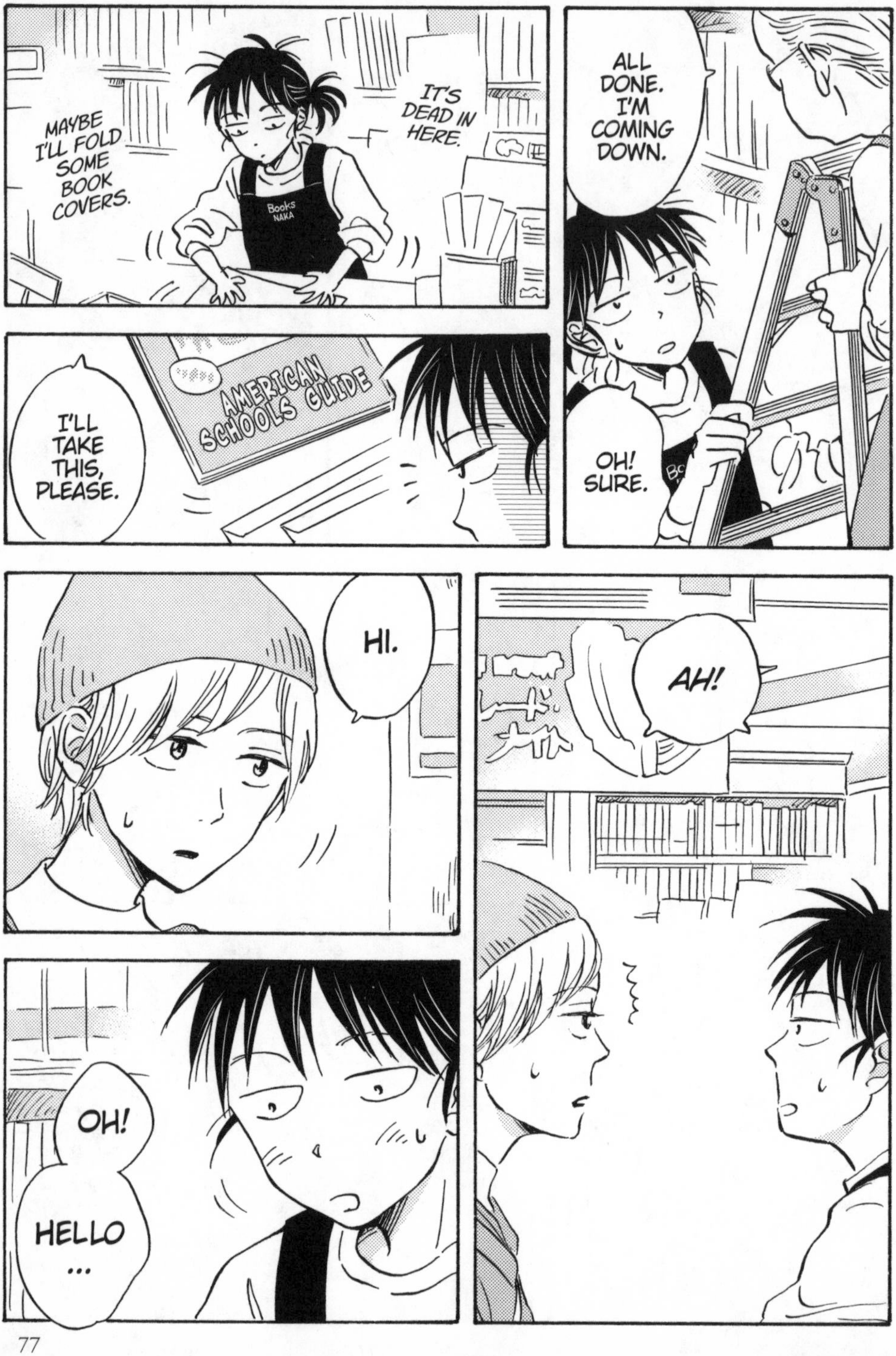
ALL DONE. I'M COMING DOWN.
OH! SURE.
IT'S DEAD IN HERE.
MAYBE I'LL FOLD SOME BOOK COVERS.
Books NAKA
AMERICAN SCHOOLS GUIDE
I'LL TAKE THIS, PLEASE.
AH!
HI.
OH!
HELLO ...

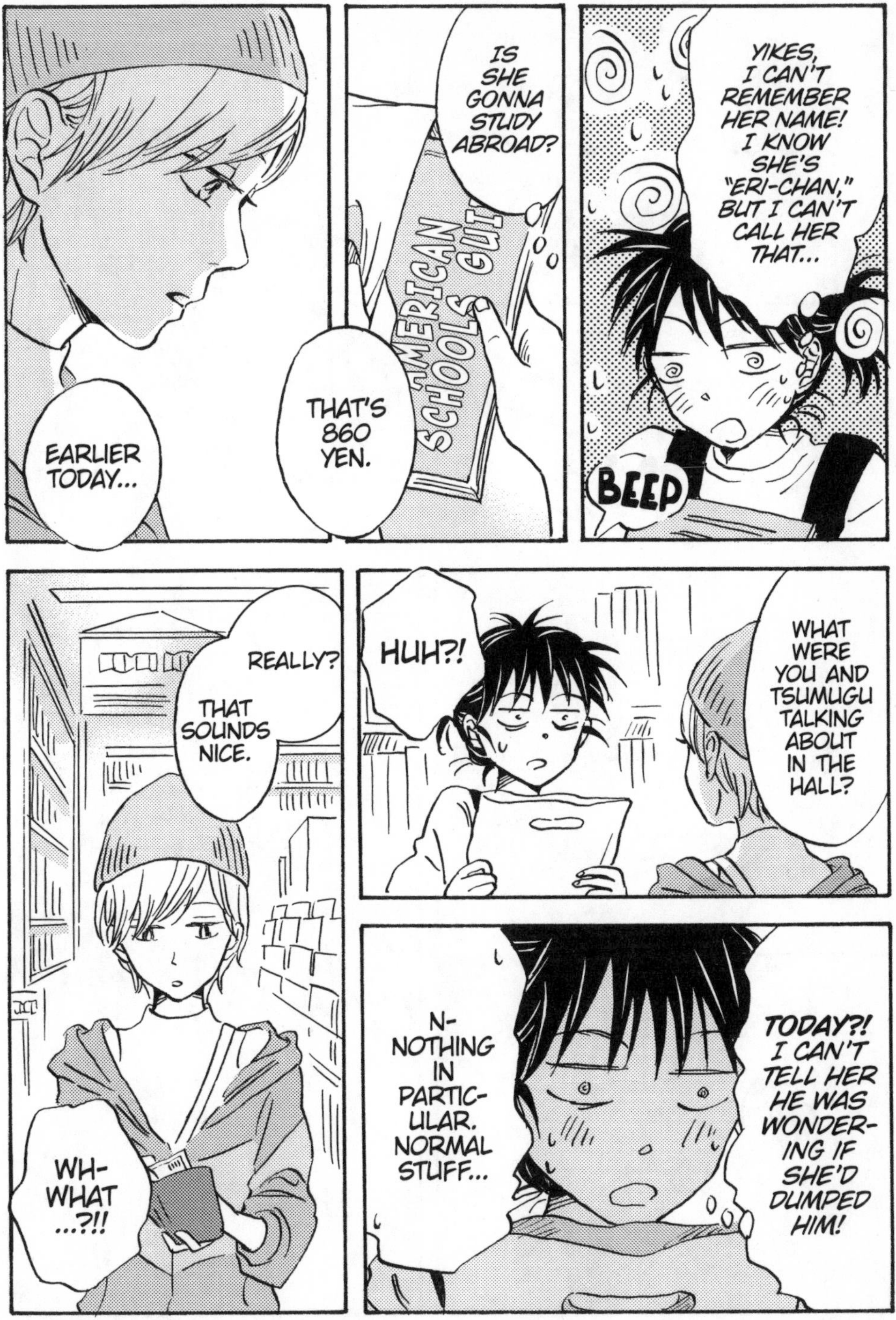
YIKES, I CAN'T REMEMBER HER NAME! I KNOW SHE'S "ERI-CHAN," BUT I CAN'T CALL HER THAT...
BEEP
IS SHE GONNA STUDY ABROAD?
AMERICAN SCHOOLS GUI
THAT'S 860 YEN.
EARLIER TODAY...
WHAT WERE YOU AND TSUMUGU TALKING ABOUT IN THE HALL?
HUH?!
TODAY?! I CAN'T TELL HER HE WAS WONDERING IF SHE'D DUMPED HIM!
N-NOTHING IN PARTICULAR. NORMAL STUFF...
REALLY?
THAT SOUNDS NICE.
WH-WHAT...?!!

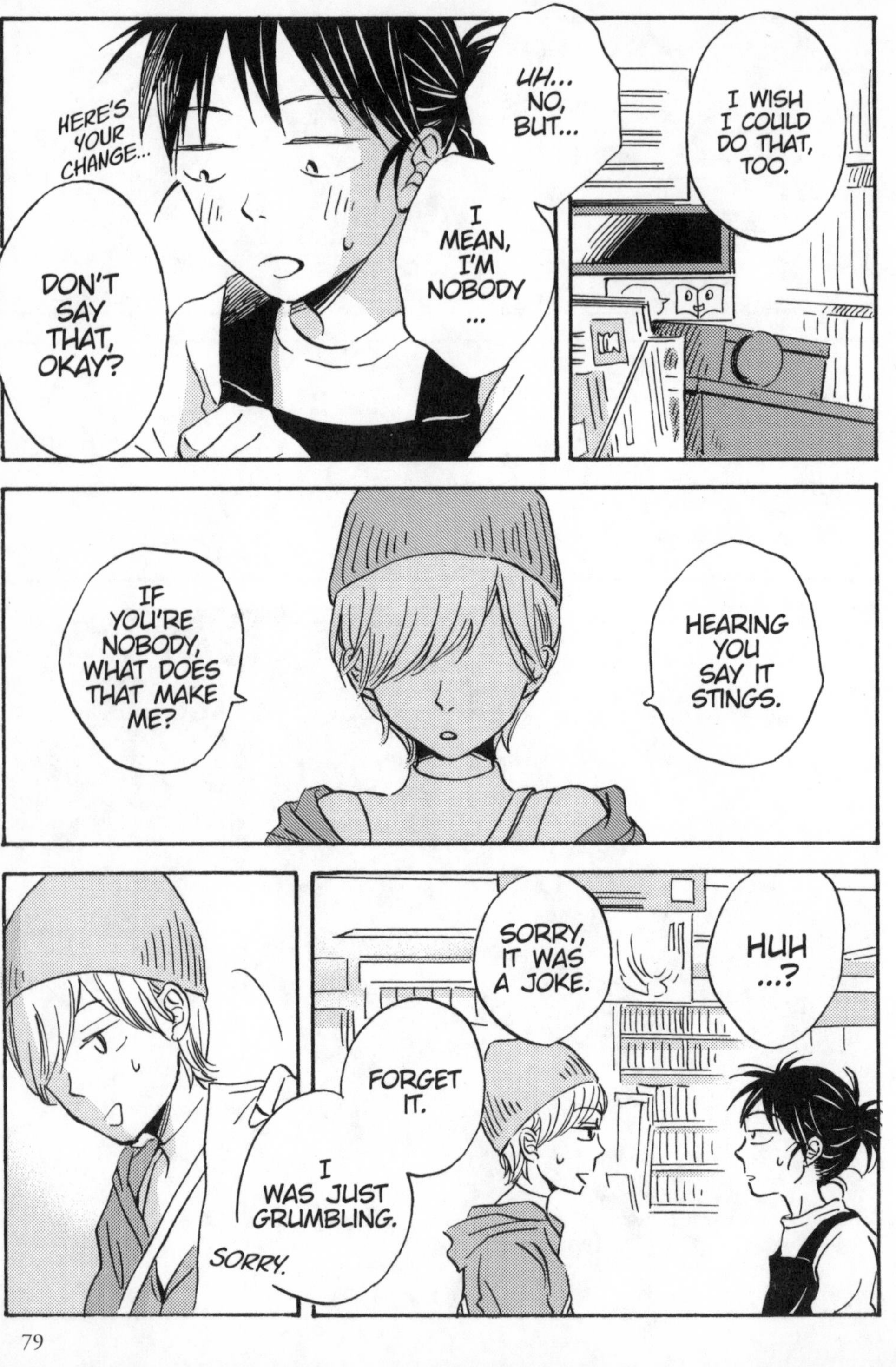
I WISH I COULD DO THAT, TOO.
UH... NO, BUT...
I MEAN, I'M NOBODY...
HERE'S YOUR CHANGE...
DON'T SAY THAT, OKAY?
HEARING YOU SAY IT STINGS.
IF YOU'RE NOBODY, WHAT DOES THAT MAKE ME?
HUH ...?
SORRY, IT WAS A JOKE.
FORGET IT.
I WAS JUST GRUMBLING.
SORRY.

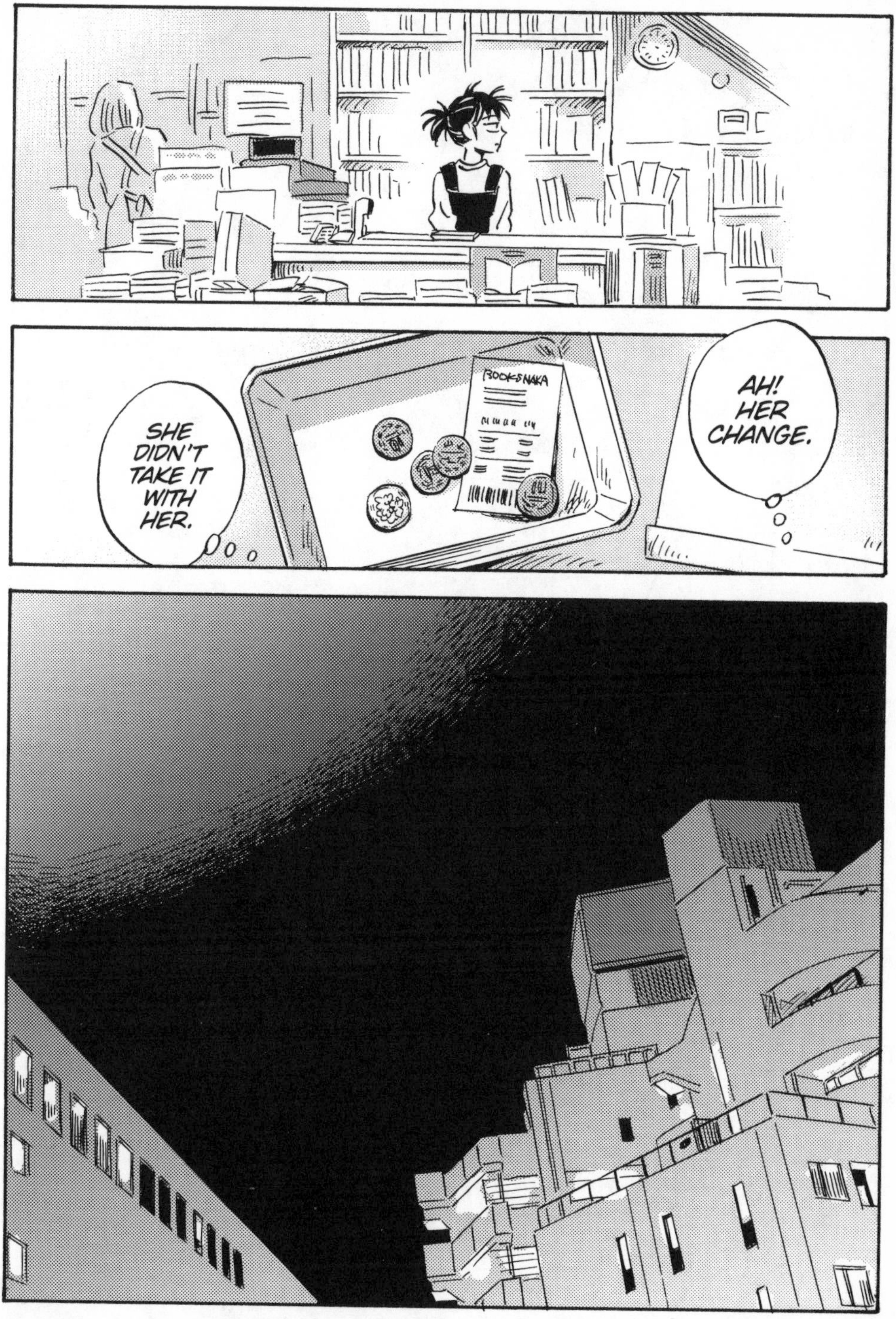
AH! HER CHANGE.
BOOKSNAKA
SHE DIDN'T TAKE IT WITH HER.

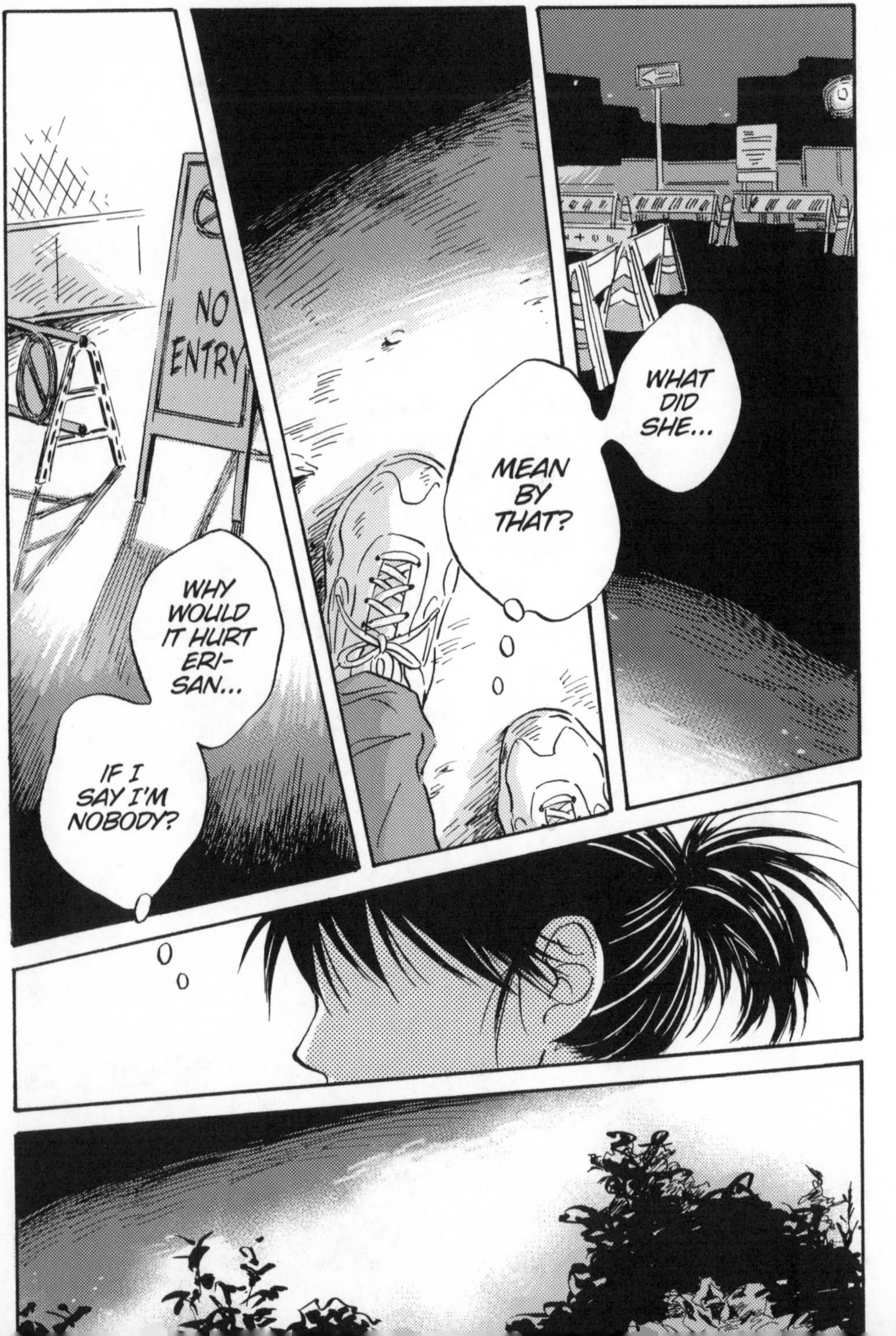
WHAT DID SHE...
MEAN BY THAT?
NO ENTRY
WHY WOULD IT HURT ERI-SAN...
IF I SAY I'M NOBODY?

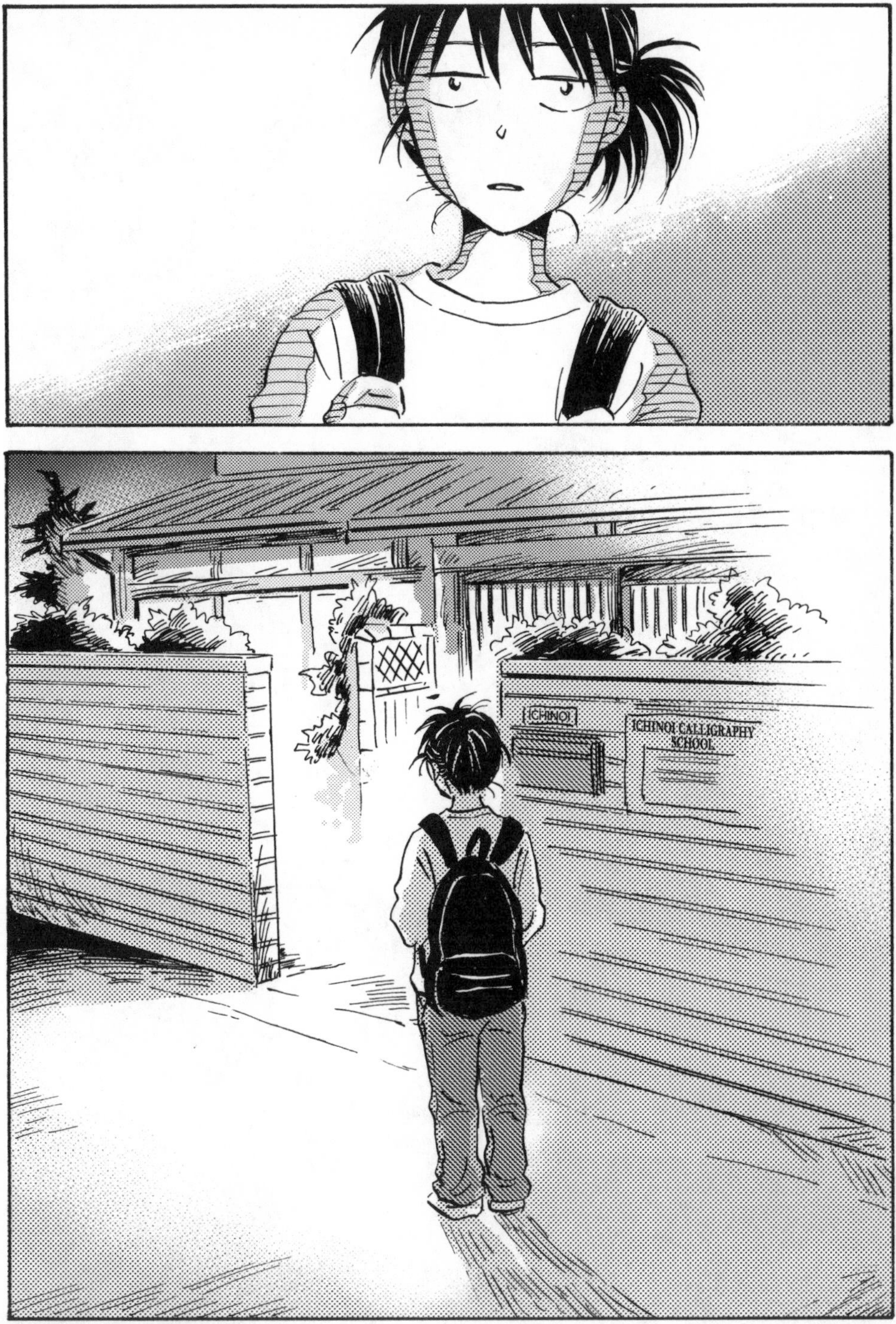
ICHINOI
ICHINOI CALLIGRAPHY SCHOOL

Chapter 16/END

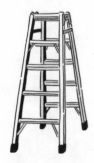

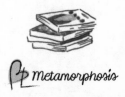
metamorphosis

Chapter 17

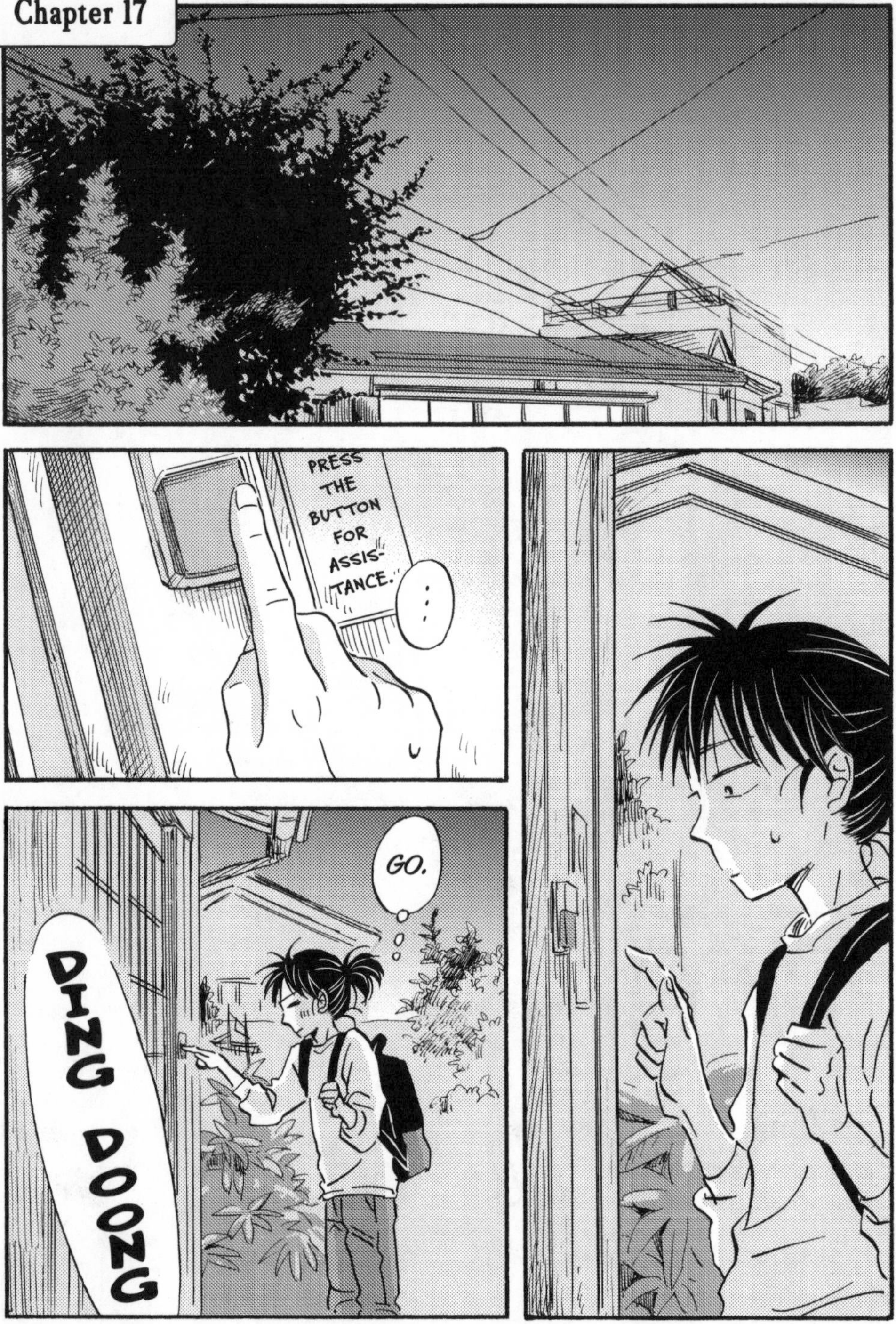
PRESS THE BUTTON FOR ASSISTANCE.
...
GO.
DING DOONG

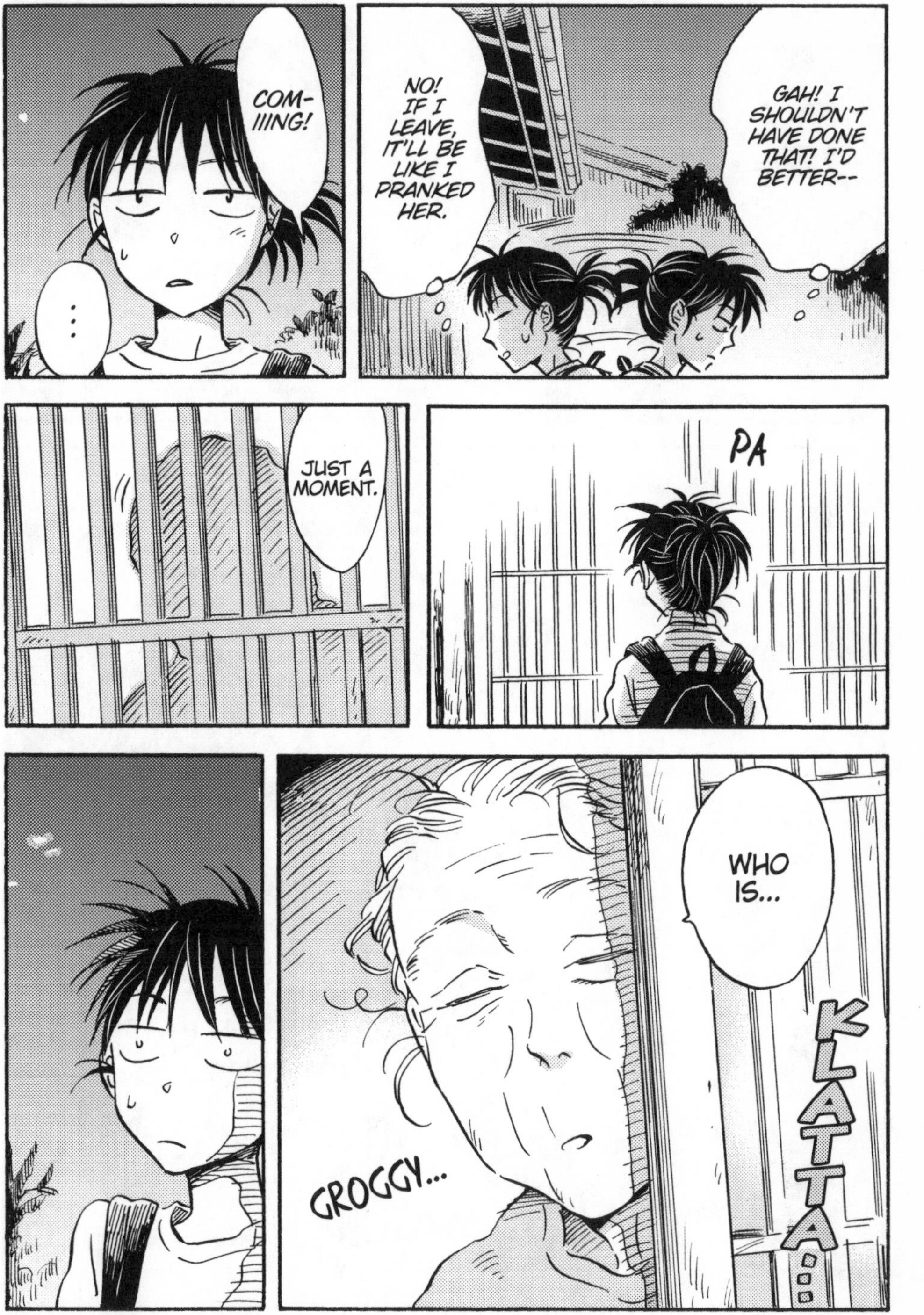
GAH! I SHOULDN'T HAVE DONE THAT! I'D BETTER--
NO! IF I LEAVE, IT'LL BE LIKE I PRANKED HER.
COM-IIING!
...
PA
JUST A MOMENT.
WHO IS...
KLATTA...
GROGGY...

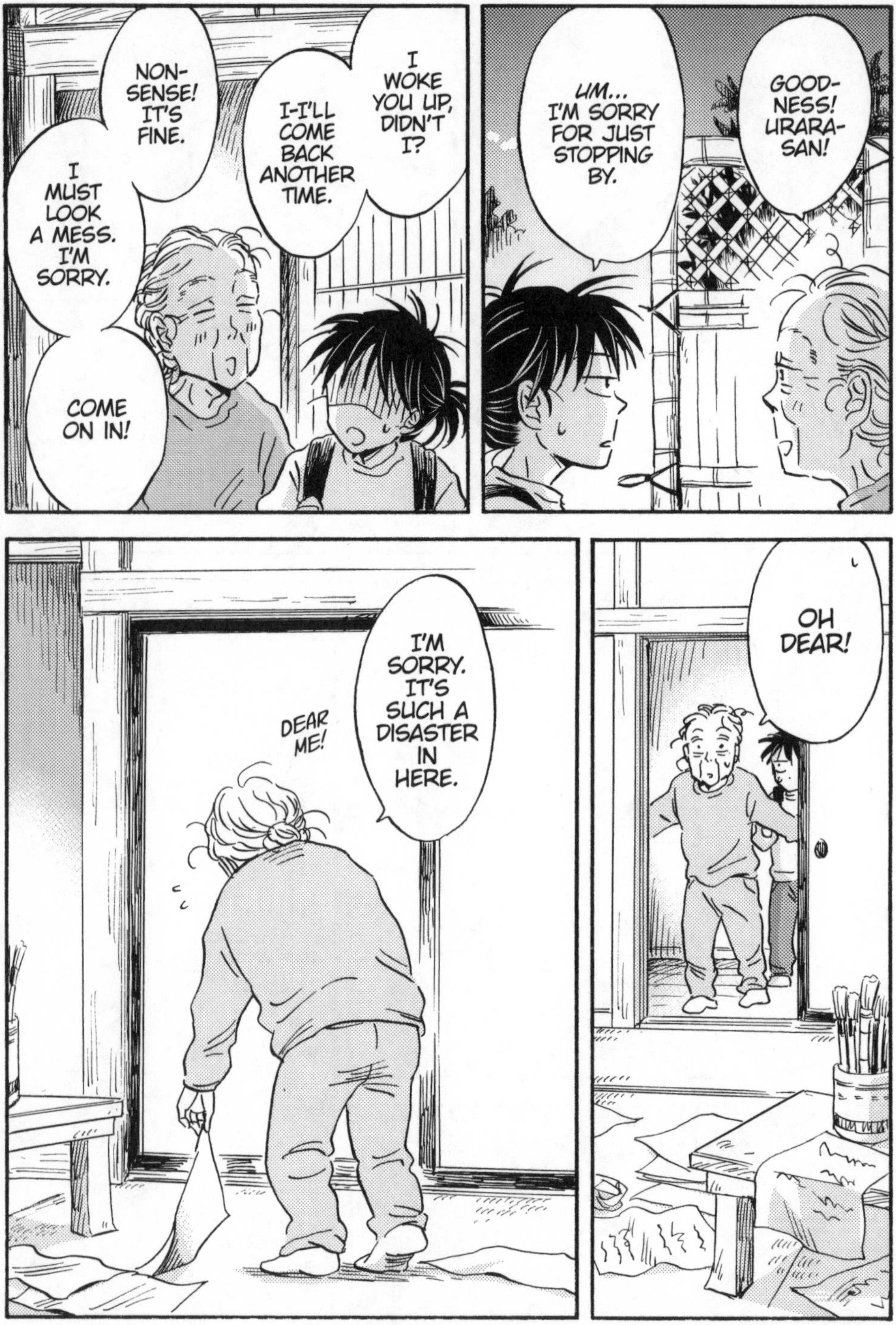
GOOD-NESS! URARA-SAN!
UM... I'M SORRY FOR JUST STOPPING BY.
I WOKE YOU UP, DIDN'T I?
I-I'LL COME BACK ANOTHER TIME.
NON-SENSE! IT'S FINE.
I MUST LOOK A MESS. I'M SORRY.
COME ON IN!
OH DEAR!
I'M SORRY. IT'S SUCH A DISASTER IN HERE.
DEAR ME!

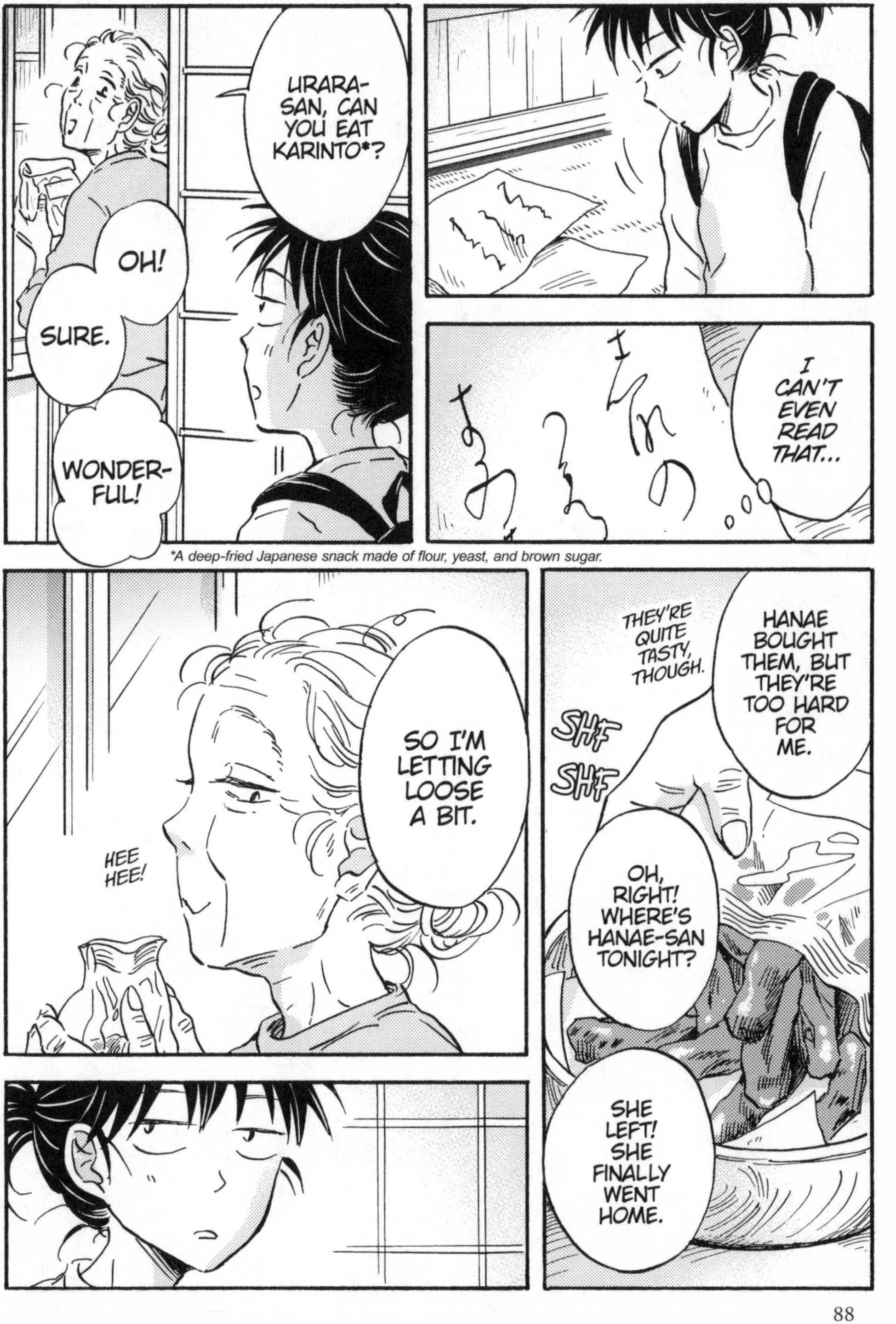
I CAN'T EVEN READ THAT...
URARA-SAN, CAN YOU EAT KARINTO*?
OH!
SURE.
WONDERFUL!
HANAE BOUGHT THEM, BUT THEY'RE TOO HARD FOR ME.
THEY'RE QUITE TASTY, THOUGH.
SHF
SHF
OH, RIGHT! WHERE'S HANAE-SAN TONIGHT?
SHE LEFT! SHE FINALLY WENT HOME.
SO I'M LETTING LOOSE A BIT.
HEE HEE!

*A deep-fried Japanese snack made of flour, yeast, and brown sugar.

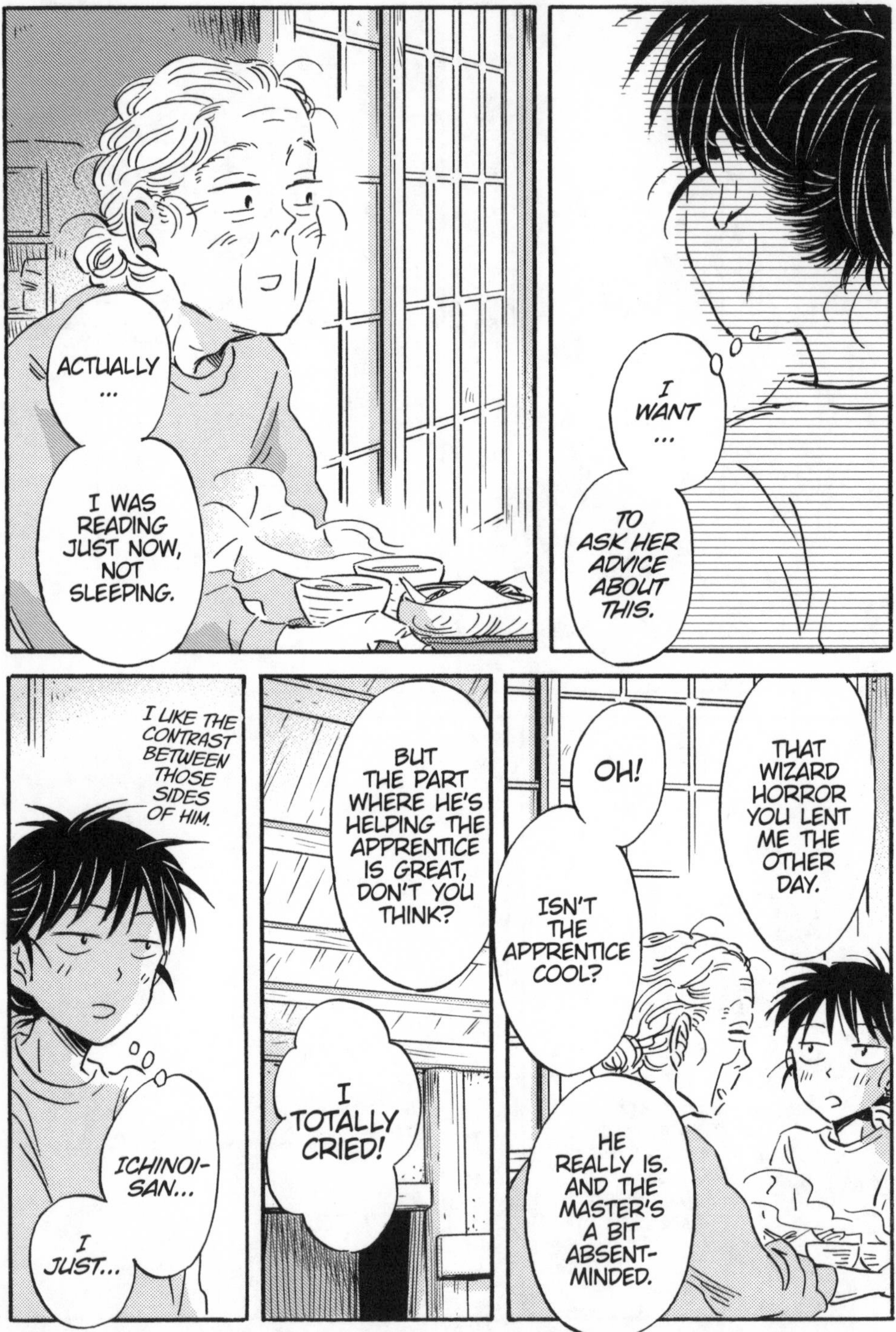
I WANT...
TO ASK HER ADVICE ABOUT THIS.
ACTUALLY...
I WAS READING JUST NOW, NOT SLEEPING.
THAT WIZARD HORROR YOU LENT ME THE OTHER DAY.
OH!
ISN'T THE APPRENTICE COOL?
HE REALLY IS. AND THE MASTER'S A BIT ABSENT-MINDED.
BUT THE PART WHERE HE'S HELPING THE APPRENTICE IS GREAT, DON'T YOU THINK?
I TOTALLY CRIED!
I LIKE THE CONTRAST BETWEEN THOSE SIDES OF HIM.
ICHINOI-SAN...
I JUST...

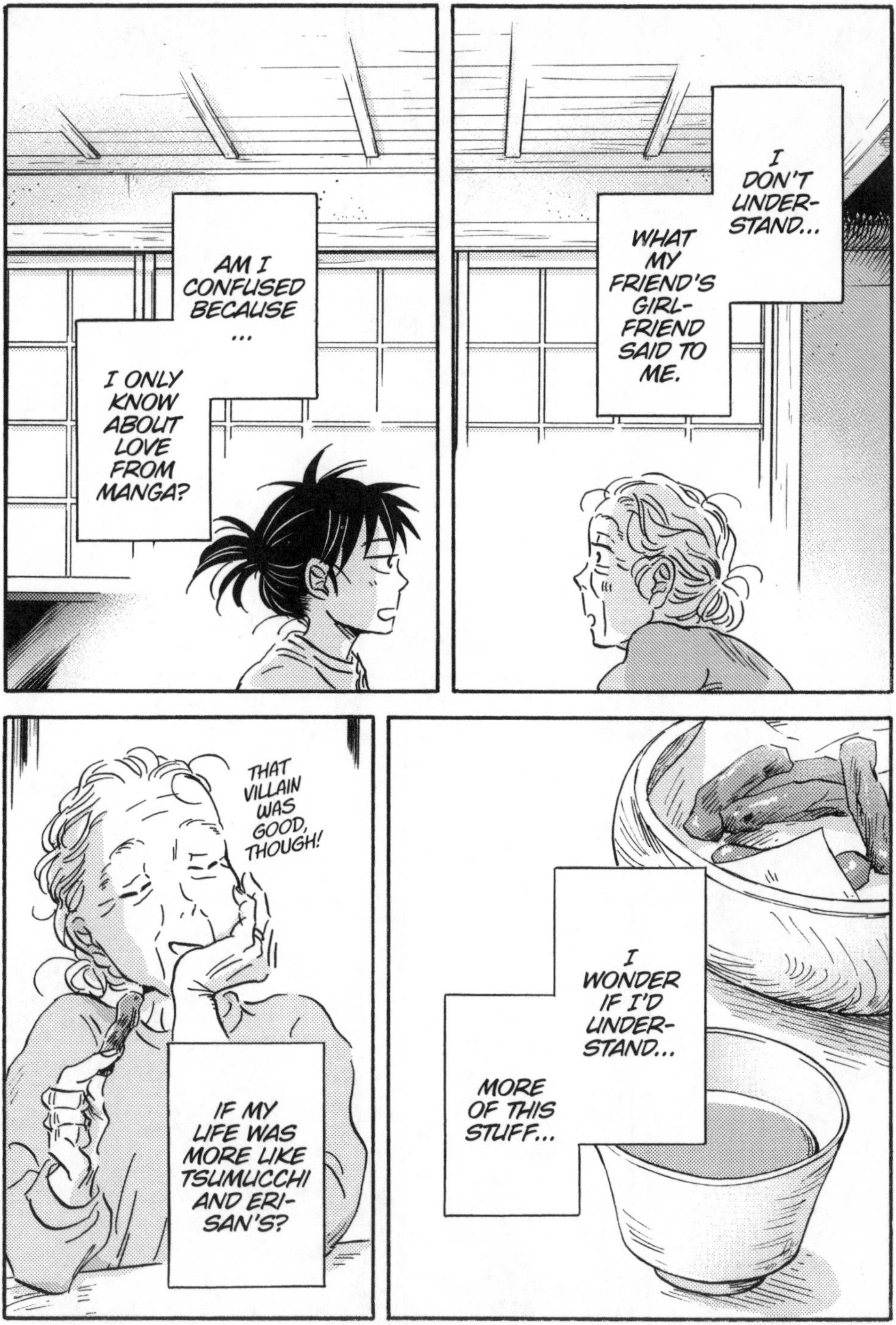
I DON'T UNDER-STAND...
WHAT MY FRIEND'S GIRL-FRIEND SAID TO ME.
AM I CONFUSED BECAUSE ...
I ONLY KNOW ABOUT LOVE FROM MANGA?
I WONDER IF I'D UNDER-STAND...
MORE OF THIS STUFF...
THAT VILLAIN WAS GOOD, THOUGH!
IF MY LIFE WAS MORE LIKE TSUMUCCHI AND ERI-SAN'S?

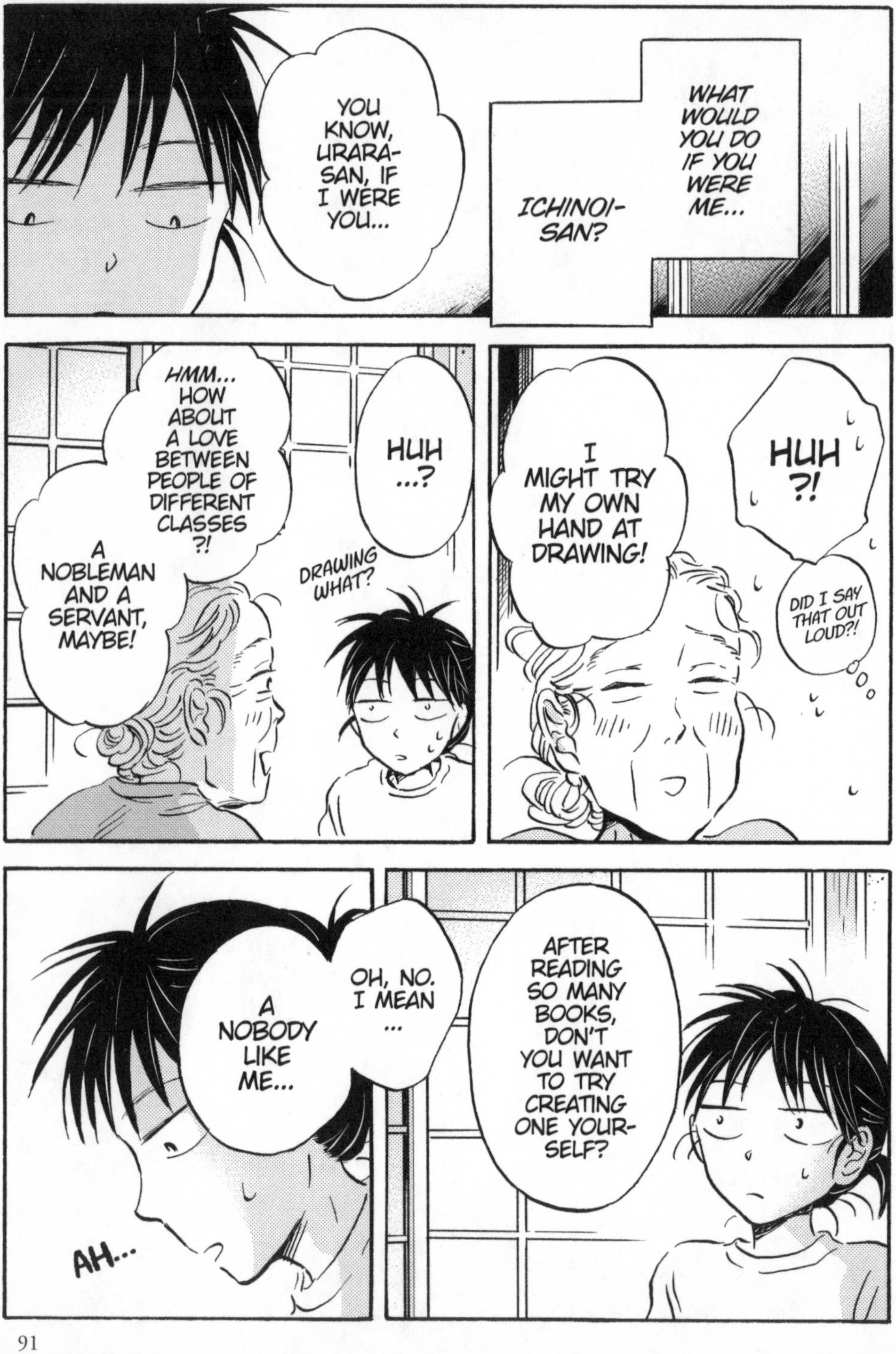
WHAT WOULD YOU DO IF YOU WERE ME...
ICHINOI-SAN?
YOU KNOW, URARA-SAN, IF I WERE YOU...
I MIGHT TRY MY OWN HAND AT DRAWING!
HUH ?!
DID I SAY THAT OUT LOUD?!
HUH ...?
DRAWING WHAT?
HMM... HOW ABOUT A LOVE BETWEEN PEOPLE OF DIFFERENT CLASSES ?!
A NOBLEMAN AND A SERVANT, MAYBE!
AFTER READING SO MANY BOOKS, DON'T YOU WANT TO TRY CREATING ONE YOURSELF?
OH, NO. I MEAN ...
A NOBODY LIKE ME...
AH...

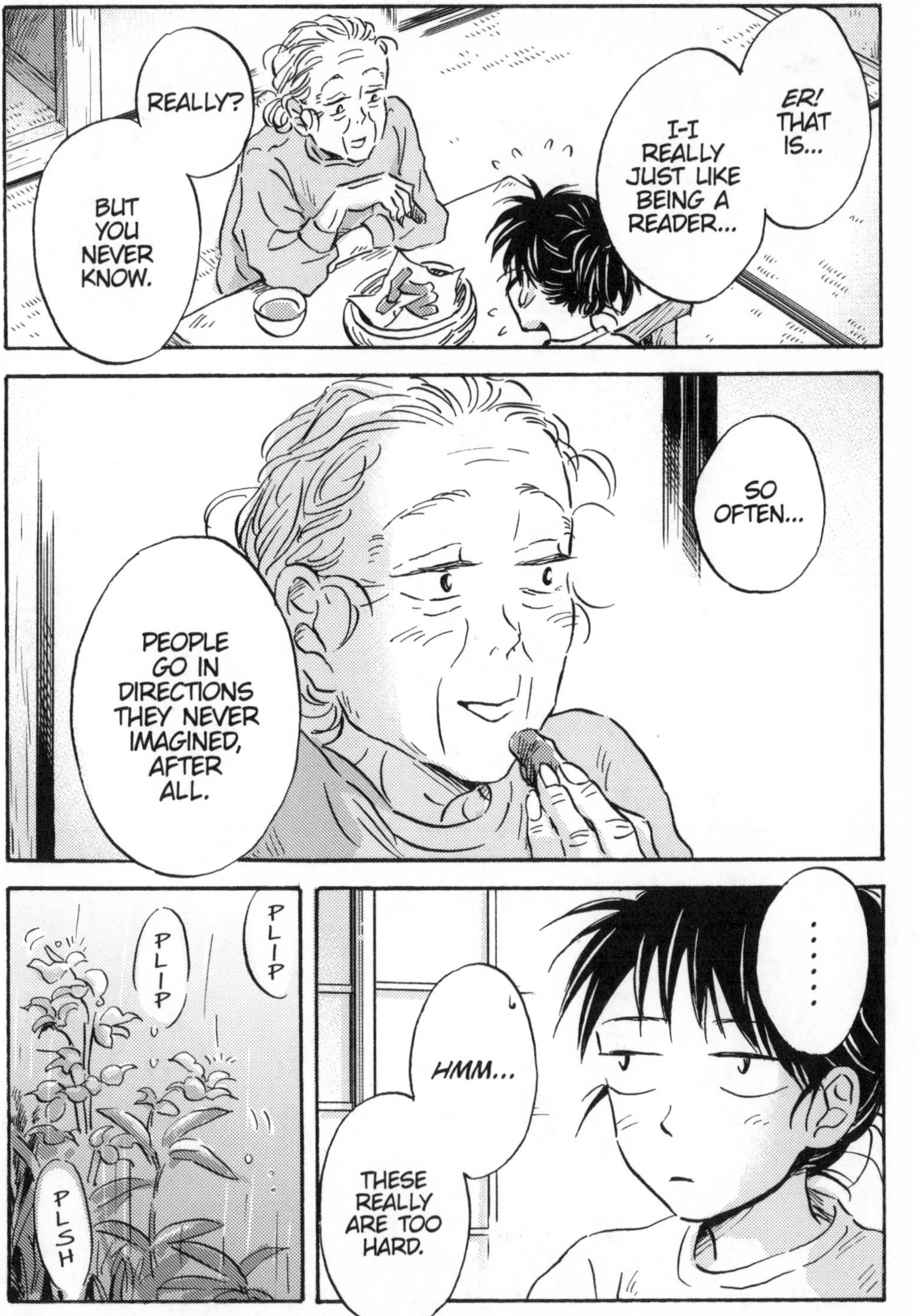
ER! THAT IS...
I-I REALLY JUST LIKE BEING A READER...
REALLY?
BUT YOU NEVER KNOW.
SO OFTEN...
PEOPLE GO IN DIRECTIONS THEY NEVER IMAGINED, AFTER ALL.
......
HMM...
THESE REALLY ARE TOO HARD.
PLIP
PLIP
PLSH

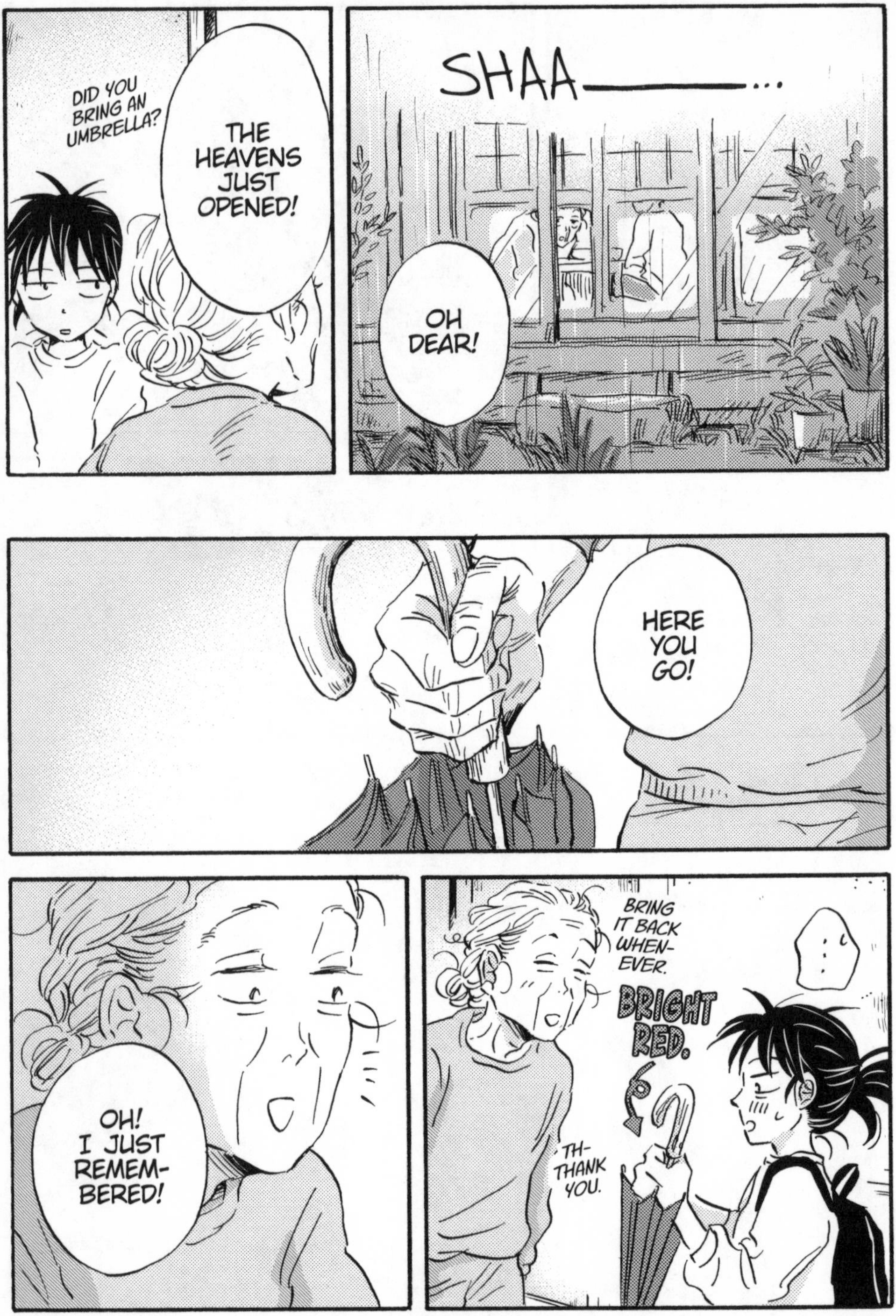
SHAA——...
OH DEAR!
THE HEAVENS JUST OPENED!
DID YOU BRING AN UMBRELLA?
HERE YOU GO!
...
BRING IT BACK WHENEVER.
BRIGHT RED.
TH-THANK YOU.
OH! I JUST REMEMBERED!

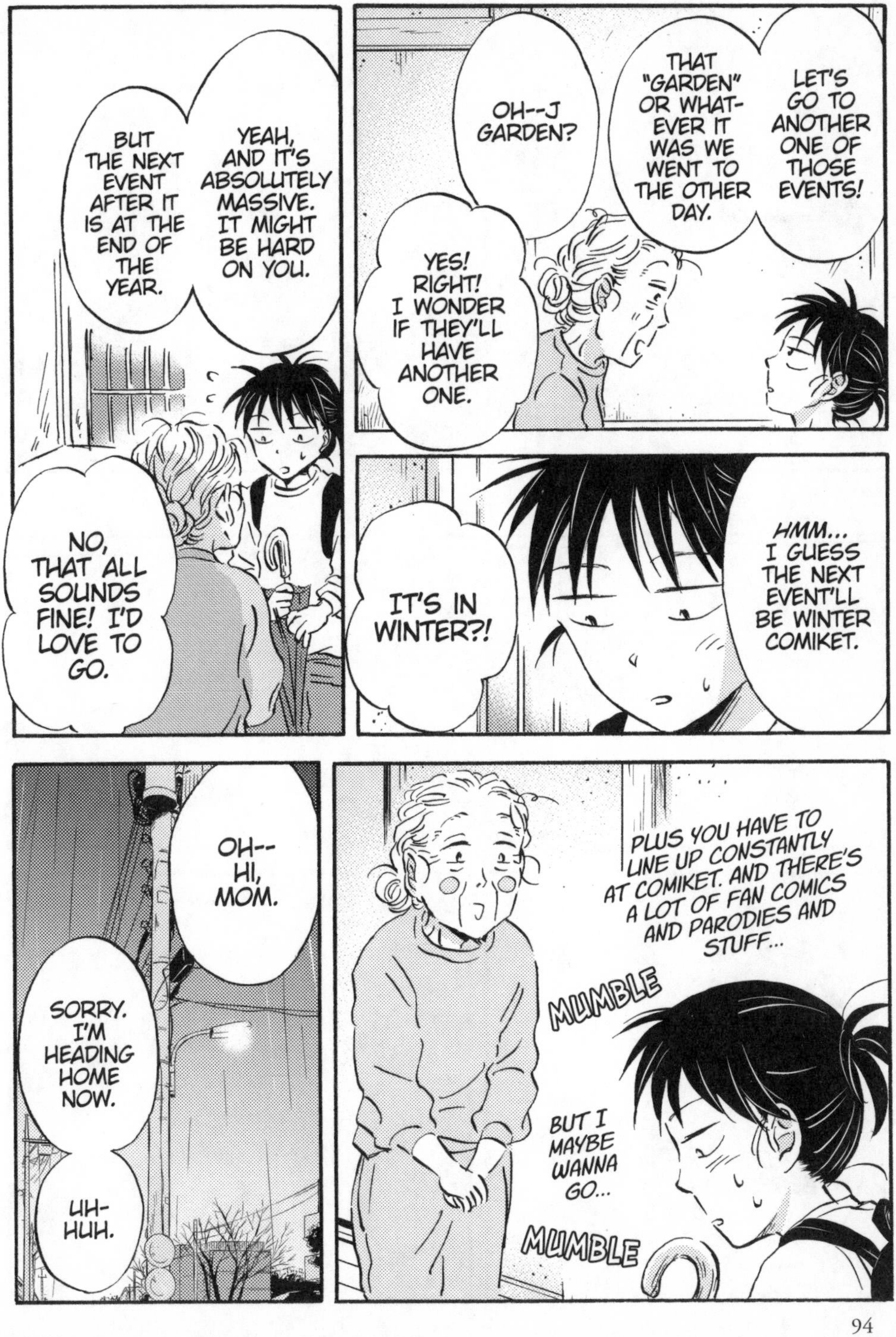
LET'S GO TO ANOTHER ONE OF THOSE EVENTS!
THAT "GARDEN" OR WHATEVER IT WAS WE WENT TO THE OTHER DAY.
OH--J GARDEN?
YES! RIGHT! I WONDER IF THEY'LL HAVE ANOTHER ONE.
HMM... I GUESS THE NEXT EVENT'LL BE WINTER COMIKET.
IT'S IN WINTER?!
YEAH, AND IT'S ABSOLUTELY MASSIVE. IT MIGHT BE HARD ON YOU.
BUT THE NEXT EVENT AFTER IT IS AT THE END OF THE YEAR.
NO, THAT ALL SOUNDS FINE! I'D LOVE TO GO.
PLUS YOU HAVE TO LINE UP CONSTANTLY AT COMIKET. AND THERE'S A LOT OF FAN COMICS AND PARODIES AND STUFF...
MUMBLE
BUT I MAYBE WANNA GO...
MUMBLE
OH-- HI, MOM.
SORRY. I'M HEADING HOME NOW.
UH-HUH.

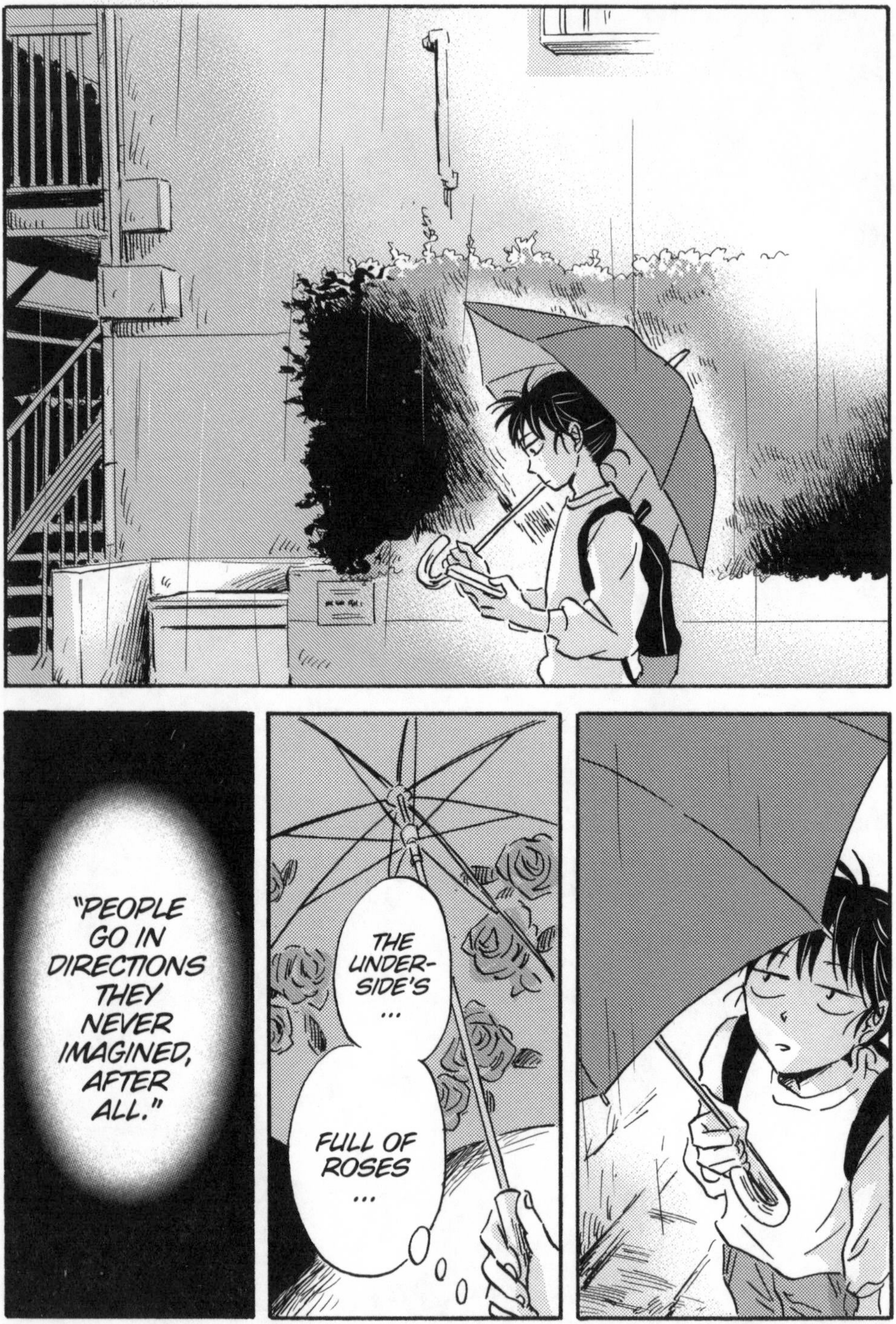
THE UNDER-SIDE'S ...
FULL OF ROSES ...
"PEOPLE GO IN DIRECTIONS THEY NEVER IMAGINED, AFTER ALL."

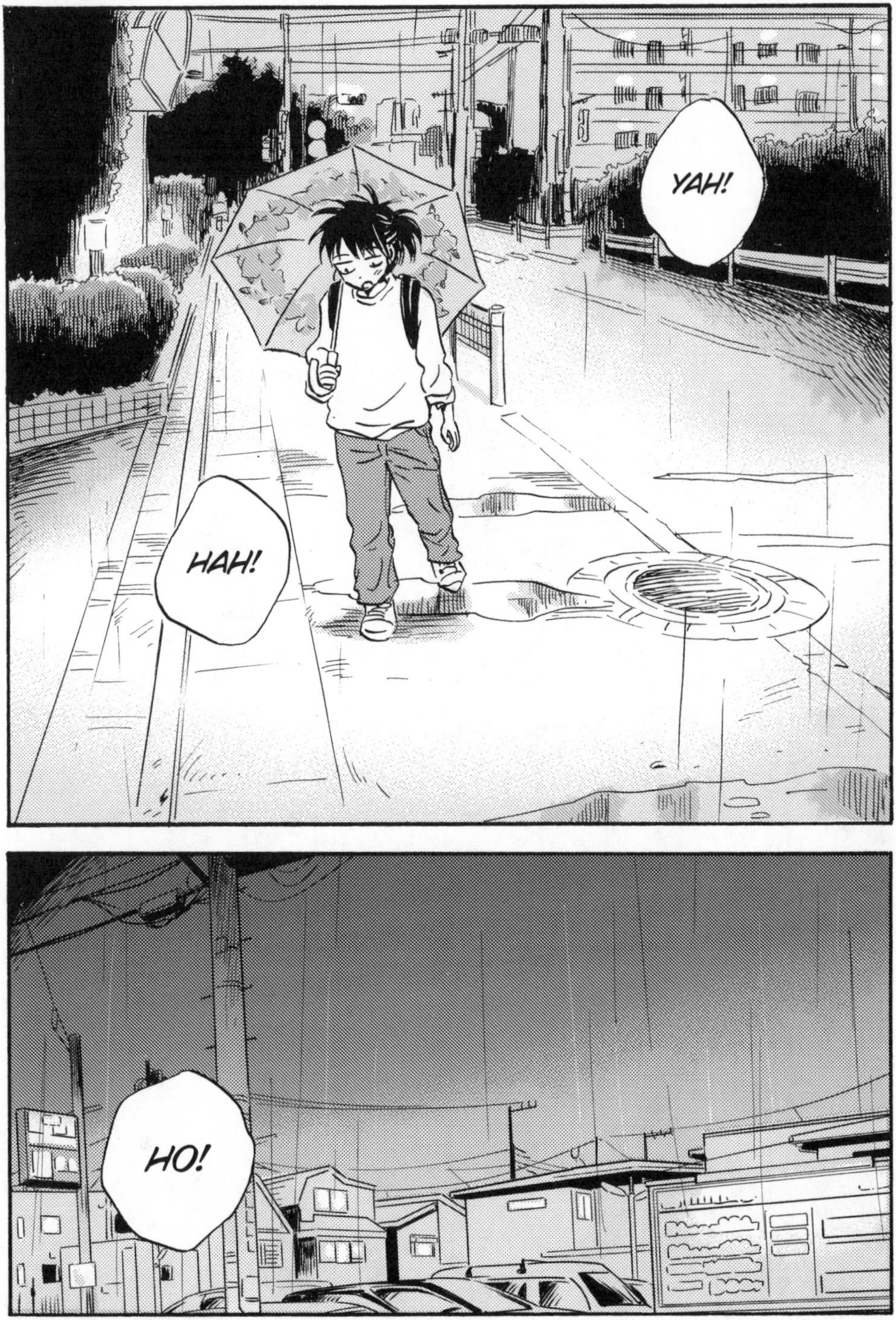
YAH!
HAH!
HO!

Chapter 17/END

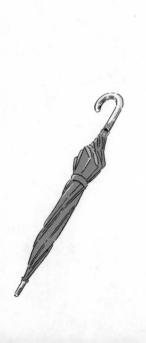

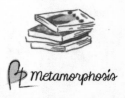
metamorphosis

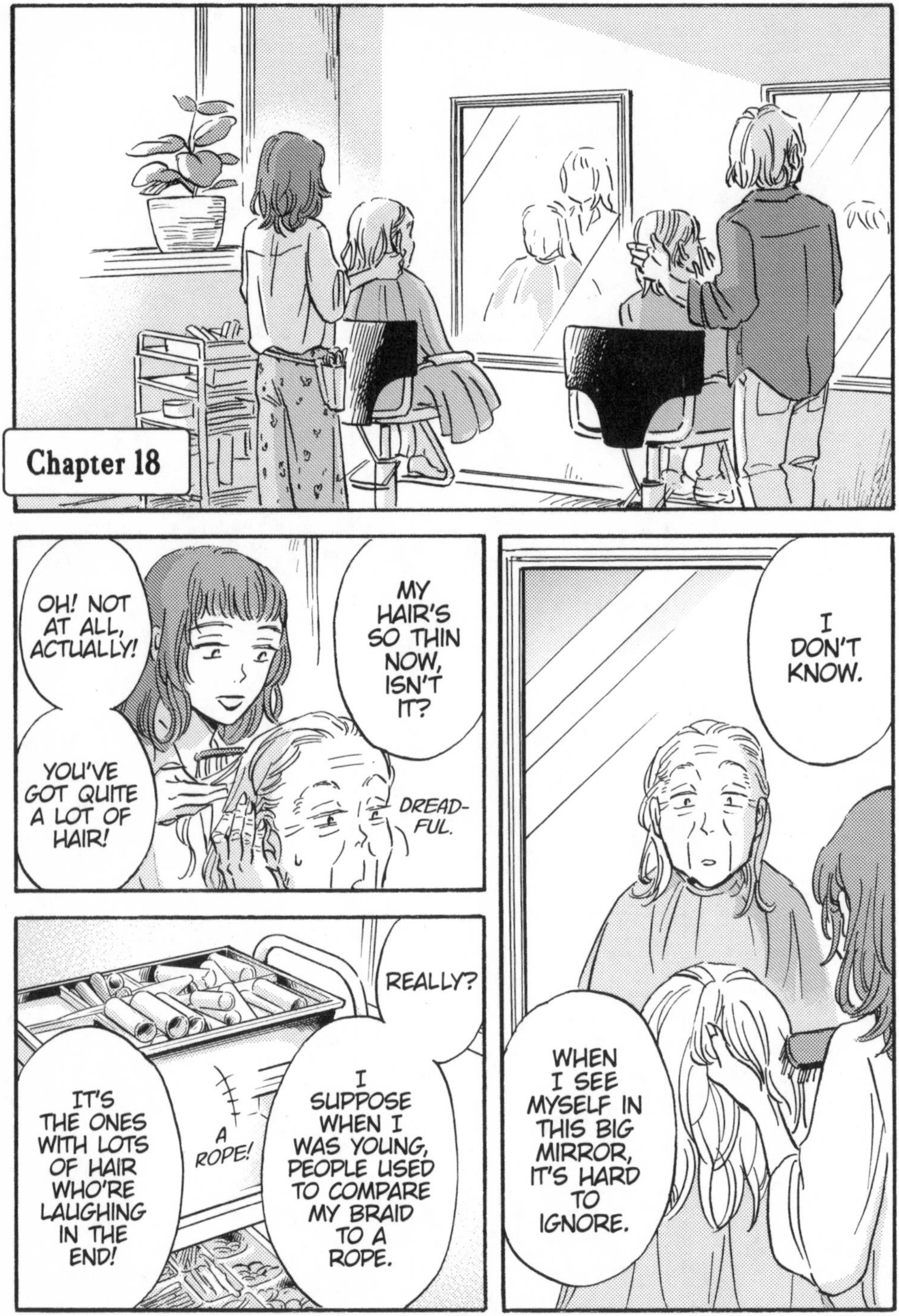
Chapter 18
I DON'T KNOW.
WHEN I SEE MYSELF IN THIS BIG MIRROR, IT'S HARD TO IGNORE.
MY HAIR'S SO THIN NOW, ISN'T IT?
DREADFUL.
OH! NOT AT ALL, ACTUALLY!
YOU'VE GOT QUITE A LOT OF HAIR!
REALLY?
I SUPPOSE WHEN I WAS YOUNG, PEOPLE USED TO COMPARE MY BRAID TO A ROPE.
A ROPE!
IT'S THE ONES WITH LOTS OF HAIR WHO'RE LAUGHING IN THE END!

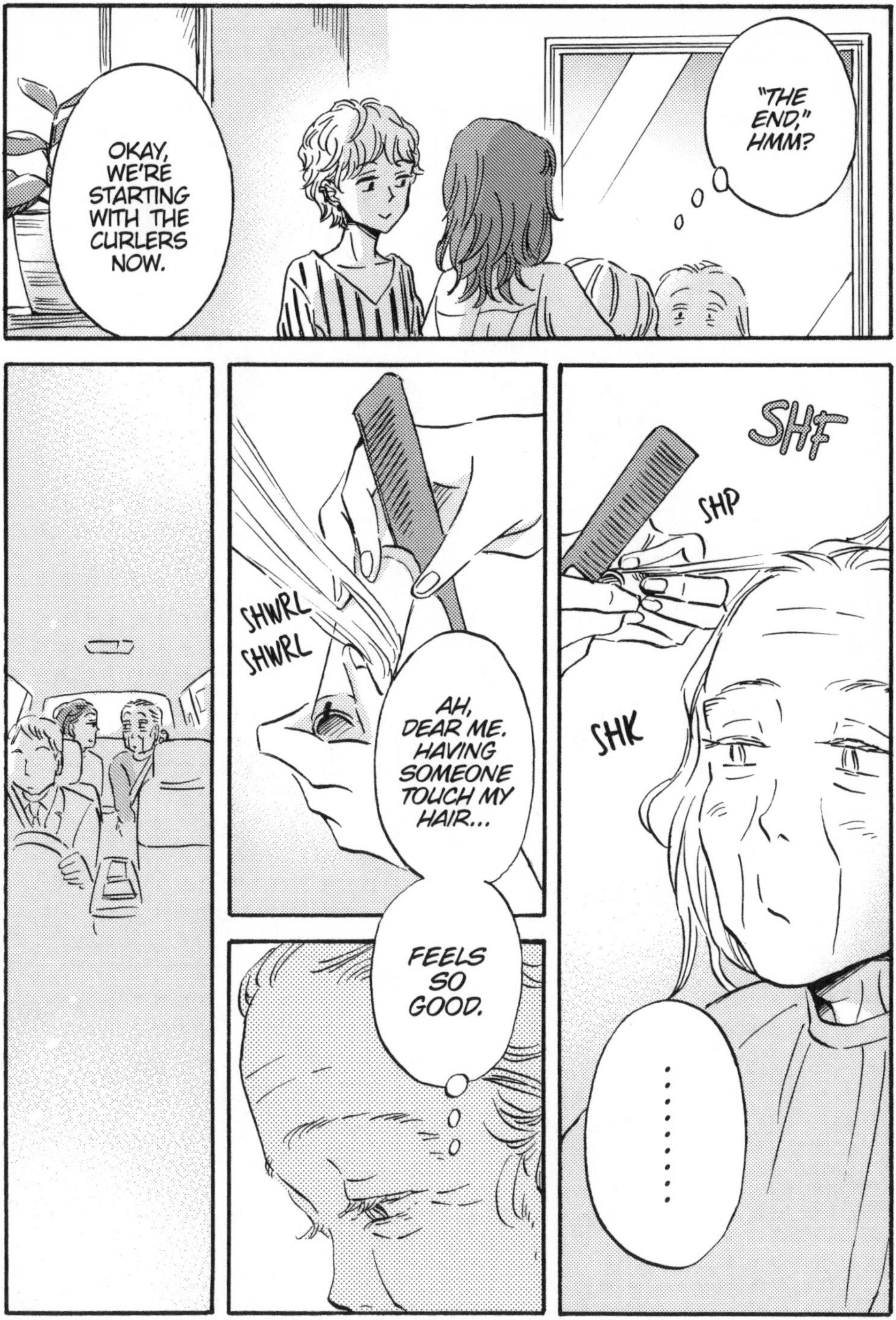
"THE END," HMM?
OKAY, WE'RE STARTING WITH THE CURLERS NOW.
SHF
SHP
SHK
......
SHWRL SHWRL
AH, DEAR ME. HAVING SOMEONE TOUCH MY HAIR...
FEELS SO GOOD.

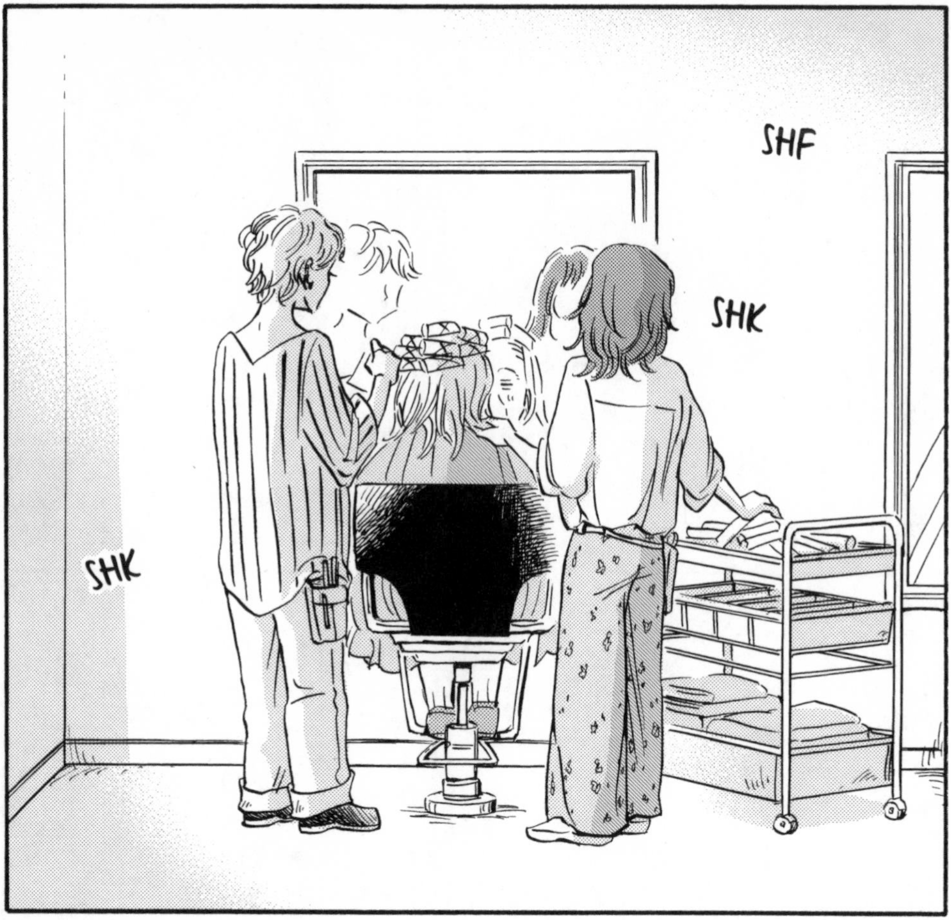
SHF
SHK
SHK

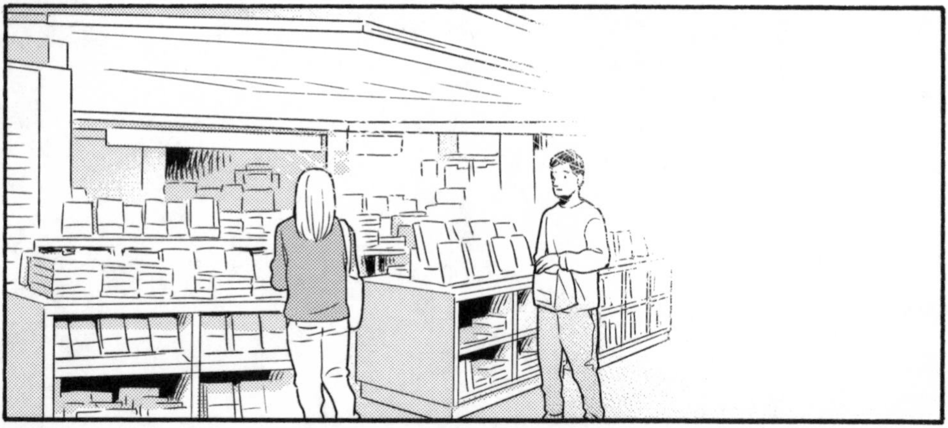

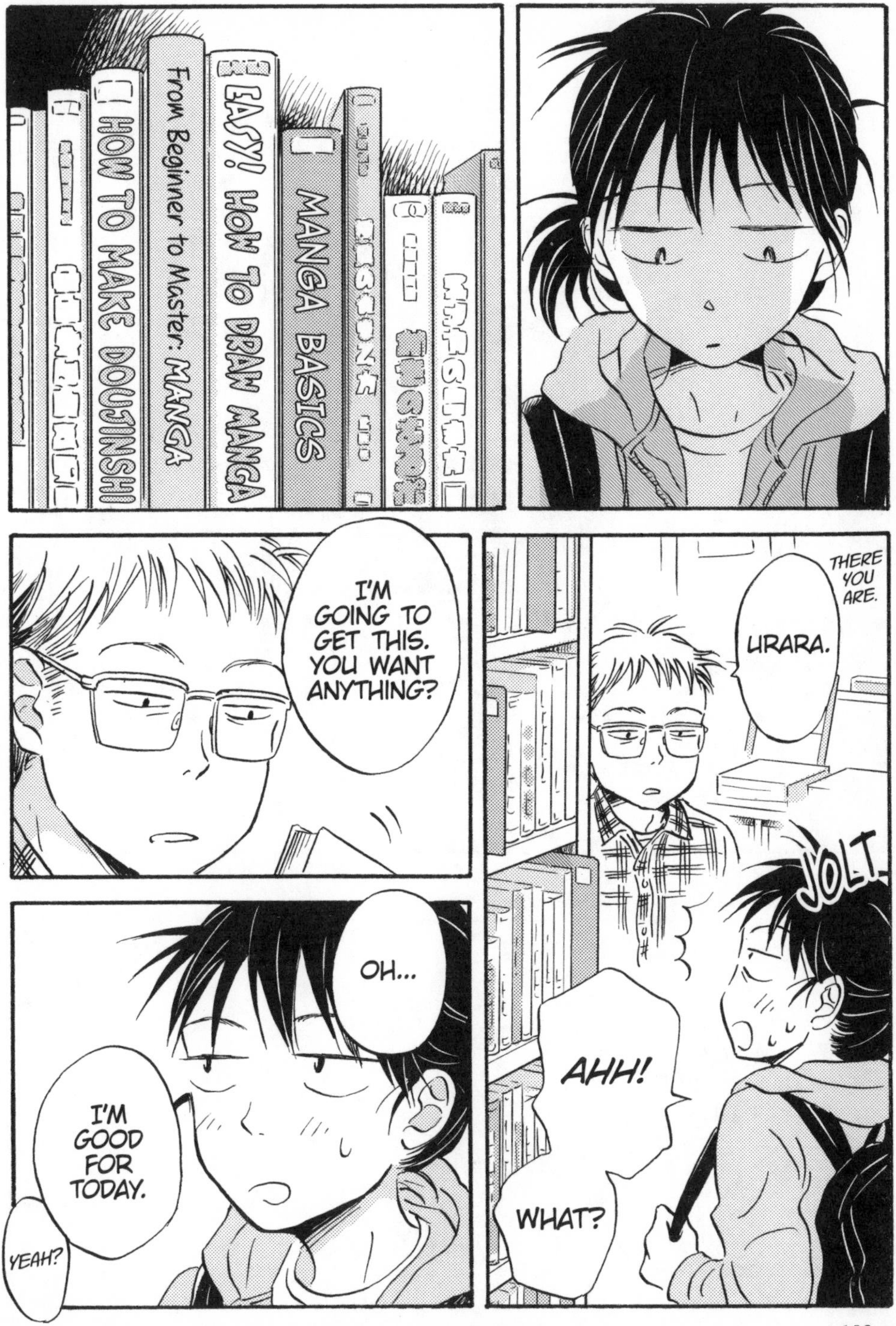
MANGA BASICS
EASY! HOW TO DRAW MANGA
From Beginner to Master: MANGA
HOW TO MAKE DOUJINSHI
THERE YOU ARE.
URARA.
JOLT.
AHH!
WHAT?
I'M GOING TO GET THIS. YOU WANT ANYTHING?
OH...
I'M GOOD FOR TODAY.
YEAH?

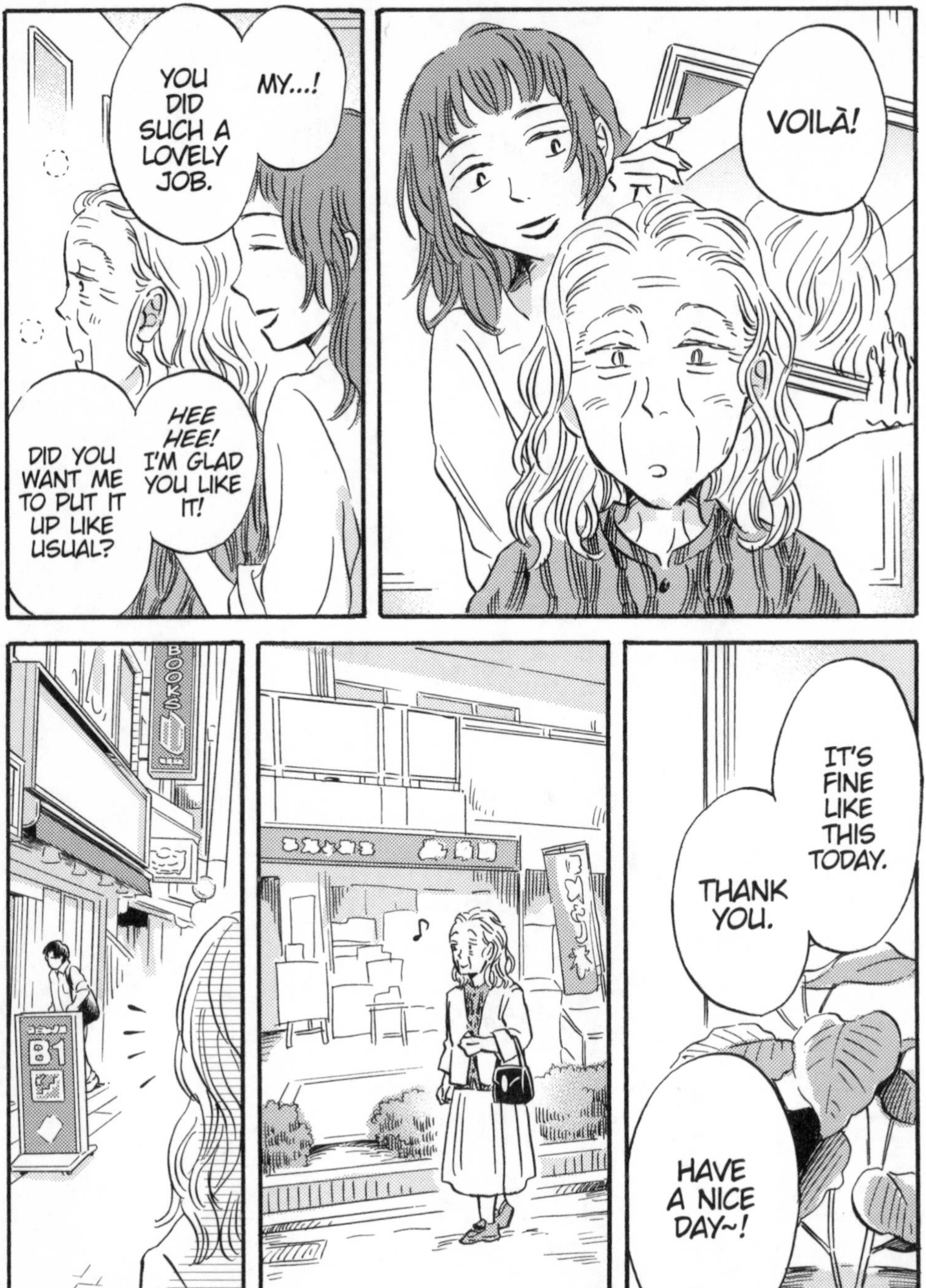
VOILÀ!
MY...!
YOU DID SUCH A LOVELY JOB.
HEE HEE! I'M GLAD YOU LIKE IT!
DID YOU WANT ME TO PUT IT UP LIKE USUAL?
IT'S FINE LIKE THIS TODAY.
THANK YOU.
HAVE A NICE DAY~!
BOOKS
B1

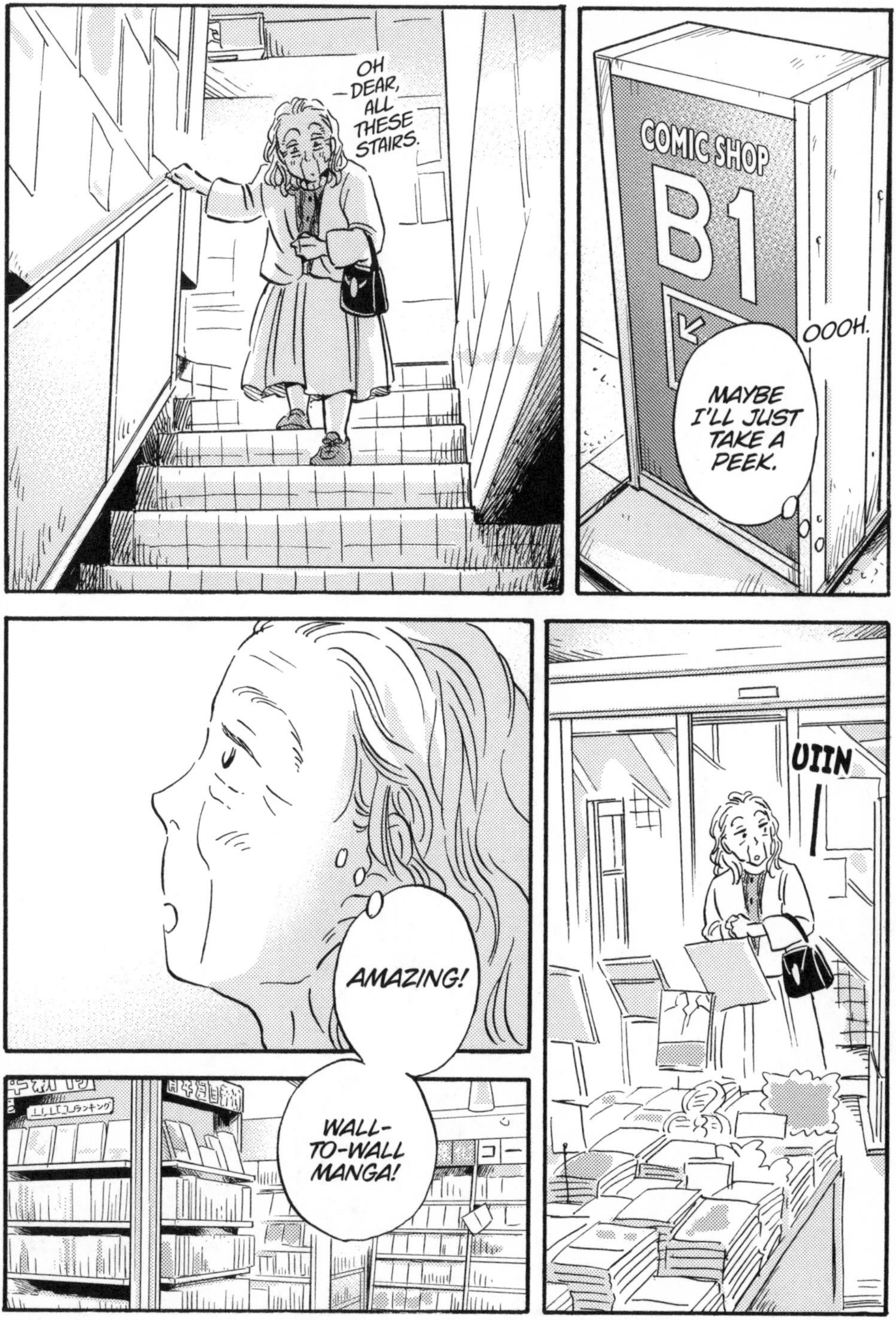
COMIC SHOP
B1
OOOH.
MAYBE I'LL JUST TAKE A PEEK.
OH DEAR, ALL THESE STAIRS.
UIIN
AMAZING!
WALL-TO-WALL MANGA!

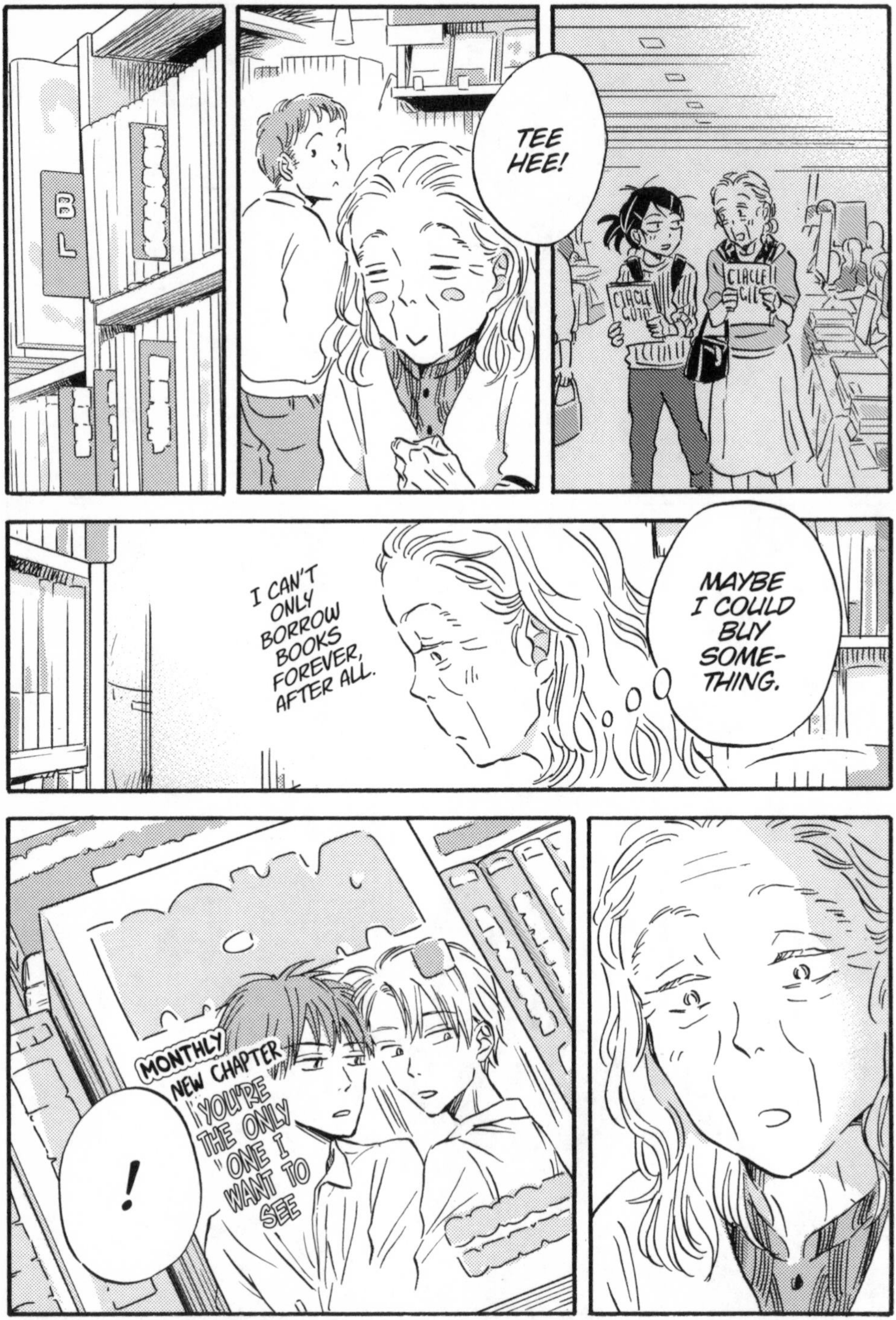
TEE HEE!
BL
MAYBE I COULD BUY SOME-THING.
I CAN'T ONLY BORROW BOOKS FOREVER, AFTER ALL.
MONTHLY
NEW CHAPTER
YOU'RE THE ONLY ONE I WANT TO SEE
!

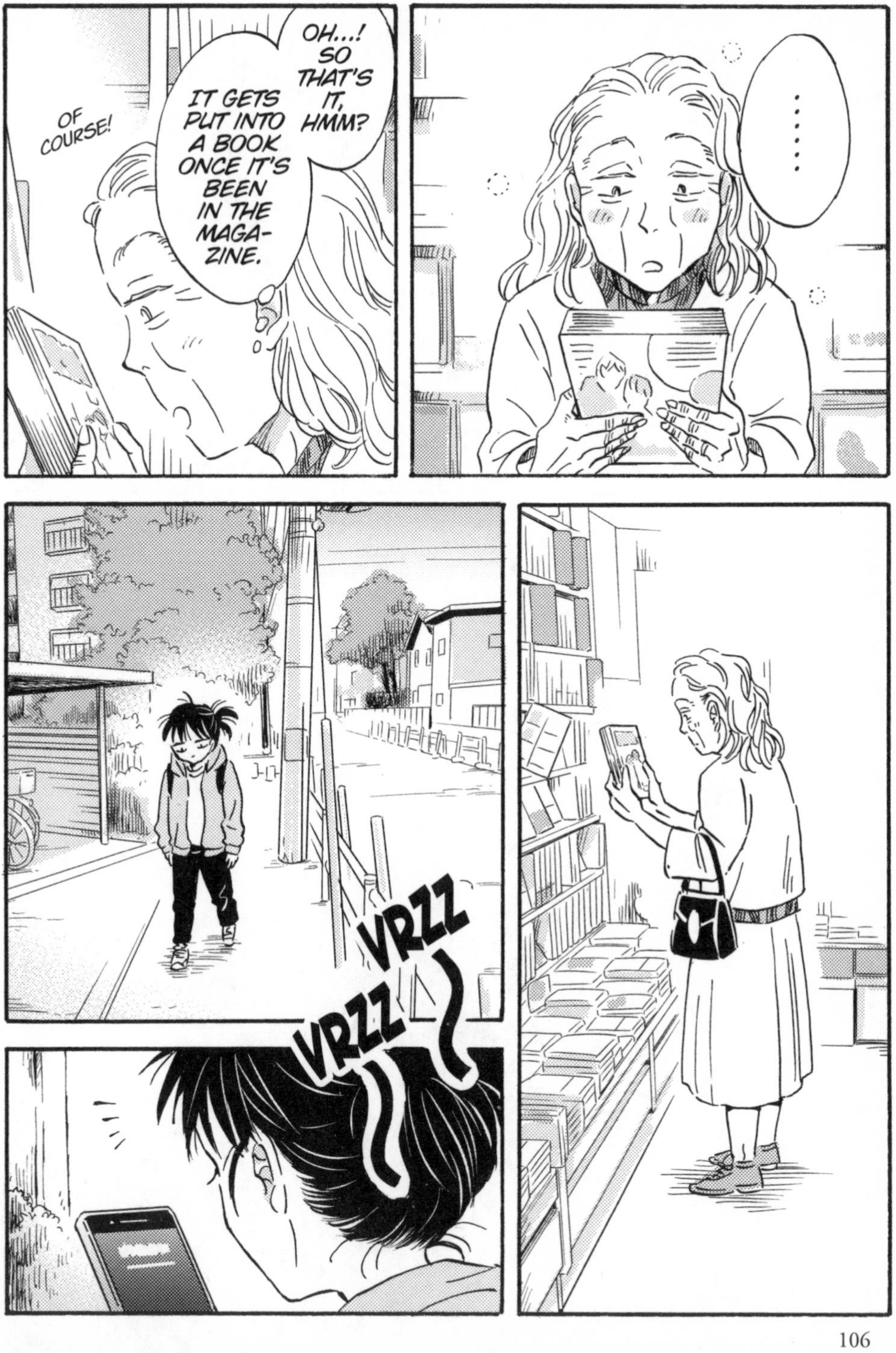
......
OH...! SO THAT'S IT, HMM?
IT GETS PUT INTO A BOOK ONCE IT'S BEEN IN THE MAGA-ZINE.
OF COURSE!
VRZZ
VRZZ

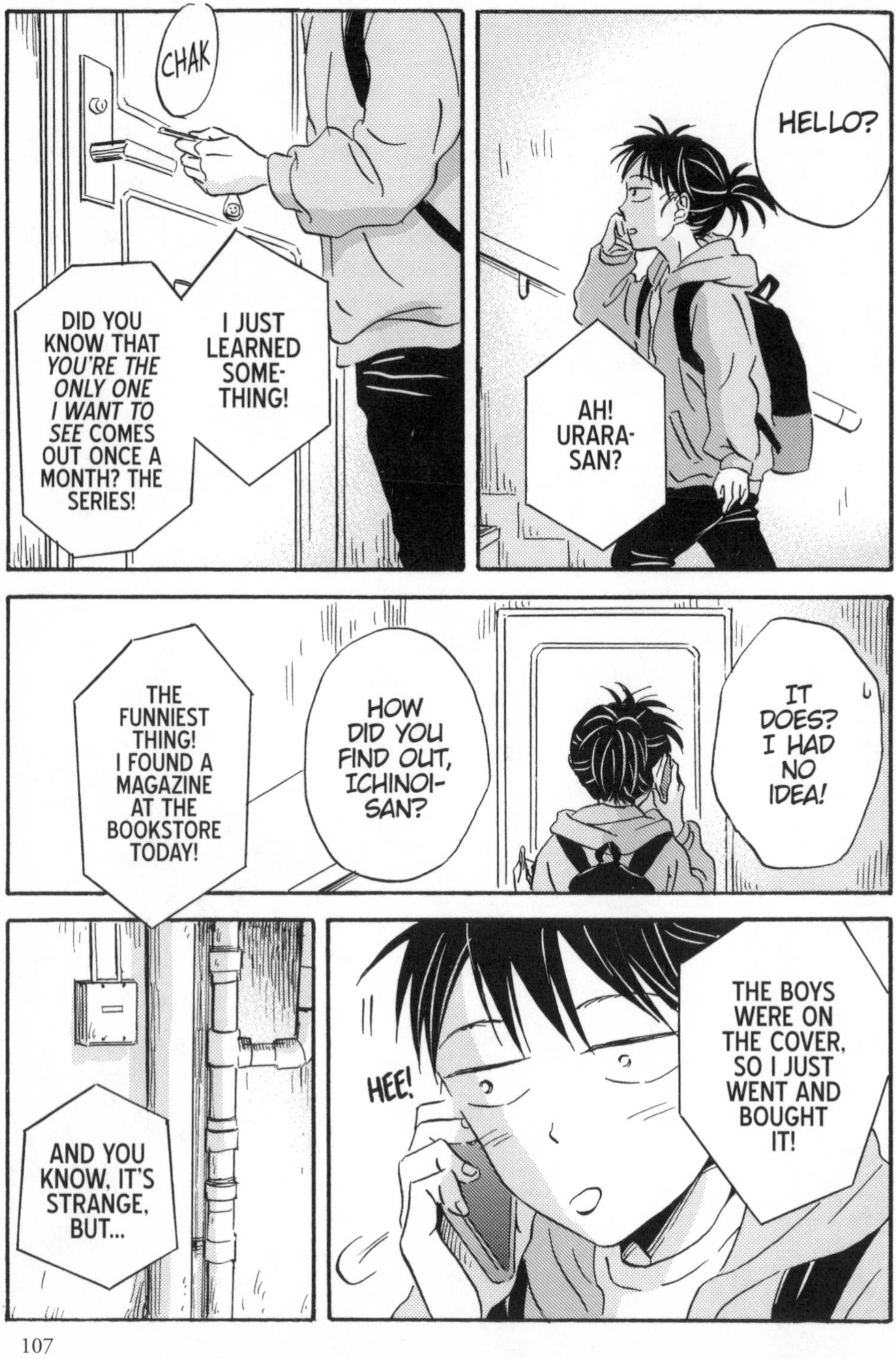
HELLO?
AH! URARA-SAN?
CHAK
I JUST LEARNED SOME-THING!
DID YOU KNOW THAT *YOU'RE THE ONLY ONE I WANT TO SEE* COMES OUT ONCE A MONTH? THE SERIES!
IT DOES? I HAD NO IDEA!
HOW DID YOU FIND OUT, ICHINOI-SAN?
THE FUNNIEST THING! I FOUND A MAGAZINE AT THE BOOKSTORE TODAY!
THE BOYS WERE ON THE COVER, SO I JUST WENT AND BOUGHT IT!
HEE!
AND YOU KNOW, IT'S STRANGE, BUT...

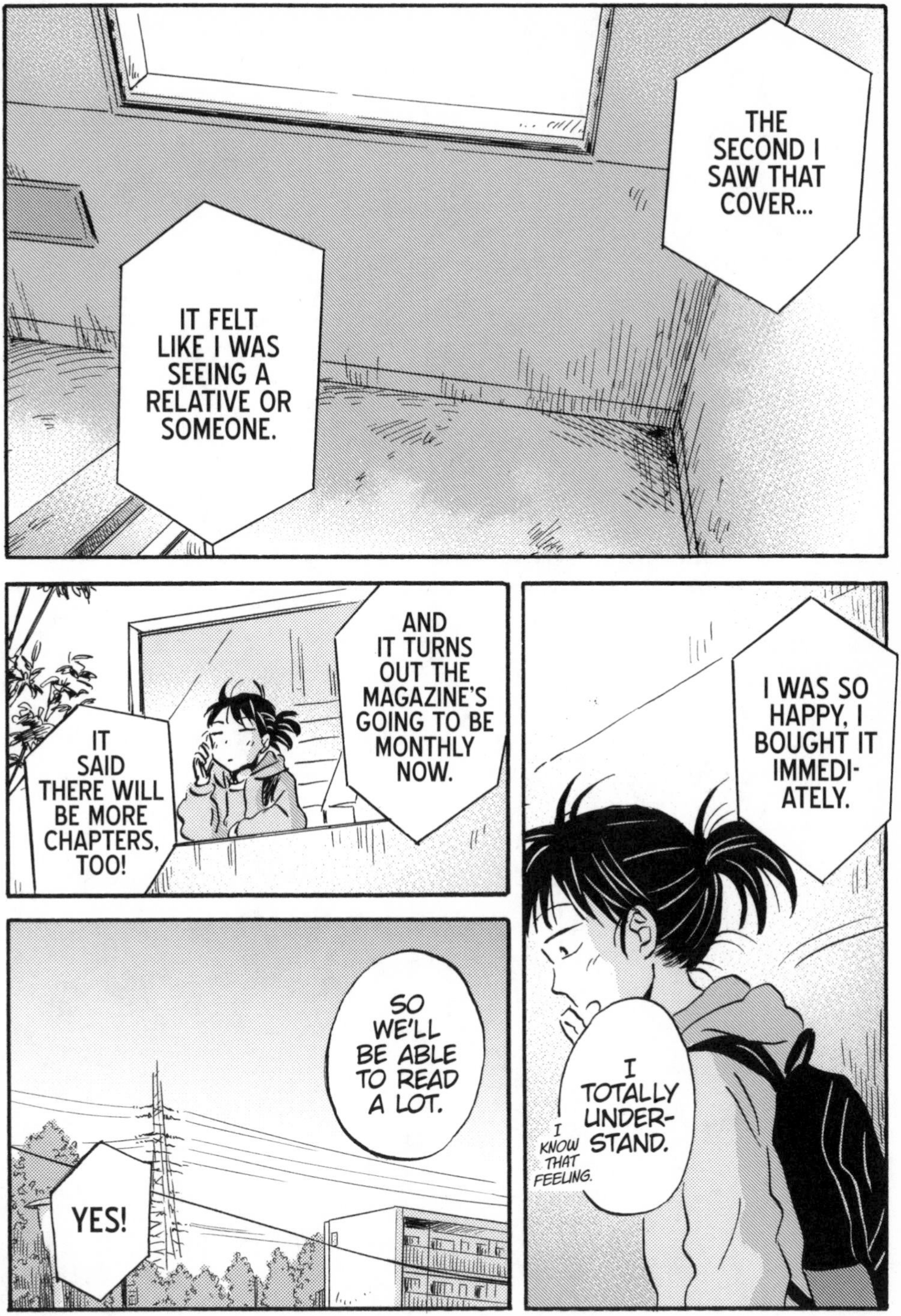
THE SECOND I SAW THAT COVER...
IT FELT LIKE I WAS SEEING A RELATIVE OR SOMEONE.
I WAS SO HAPPY, I BOUGHT IT IMMEDI-ATELY.
I TOTALLY UNDER-STAND.
I KNOW THAT FEELING.
AND IT TURNS OUT THE MAGAZINE'S GOING TO BE MONTHLY NOW.
IT SAID THERE WILL BE MORE CHAPTERS, TOO!
SO WE'LL BE ABLE TO READ A LOT.
YES!

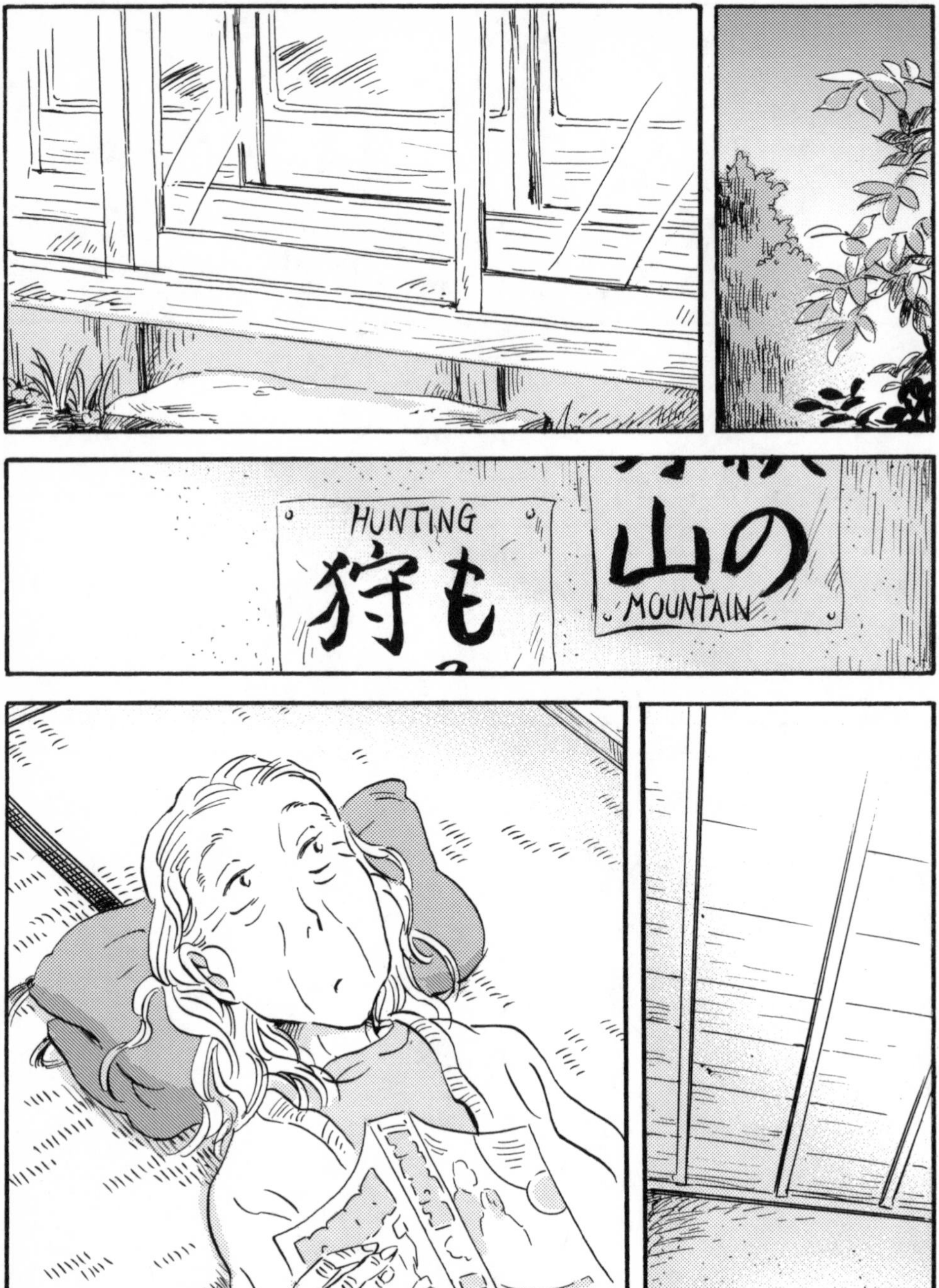
山の
MOUNTAIN
HUNTING
狩も

YAWN
GETTING YOUR HAIR DONE ...
DOES WEAR YOU OUT, HM?
Hey, Mom?
Are you planning to keep living in that house right to the end?

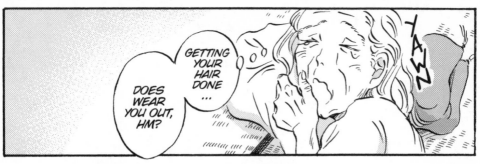

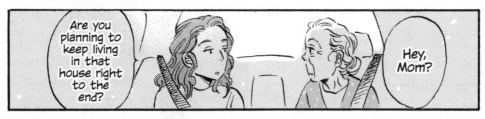

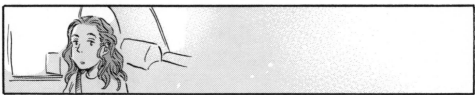

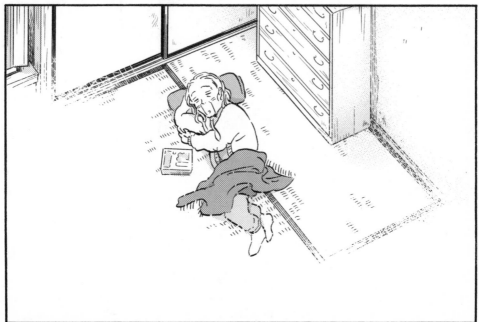

Chapter 18/END

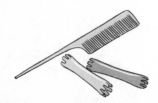

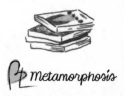

metamorphosis

Chapter 19

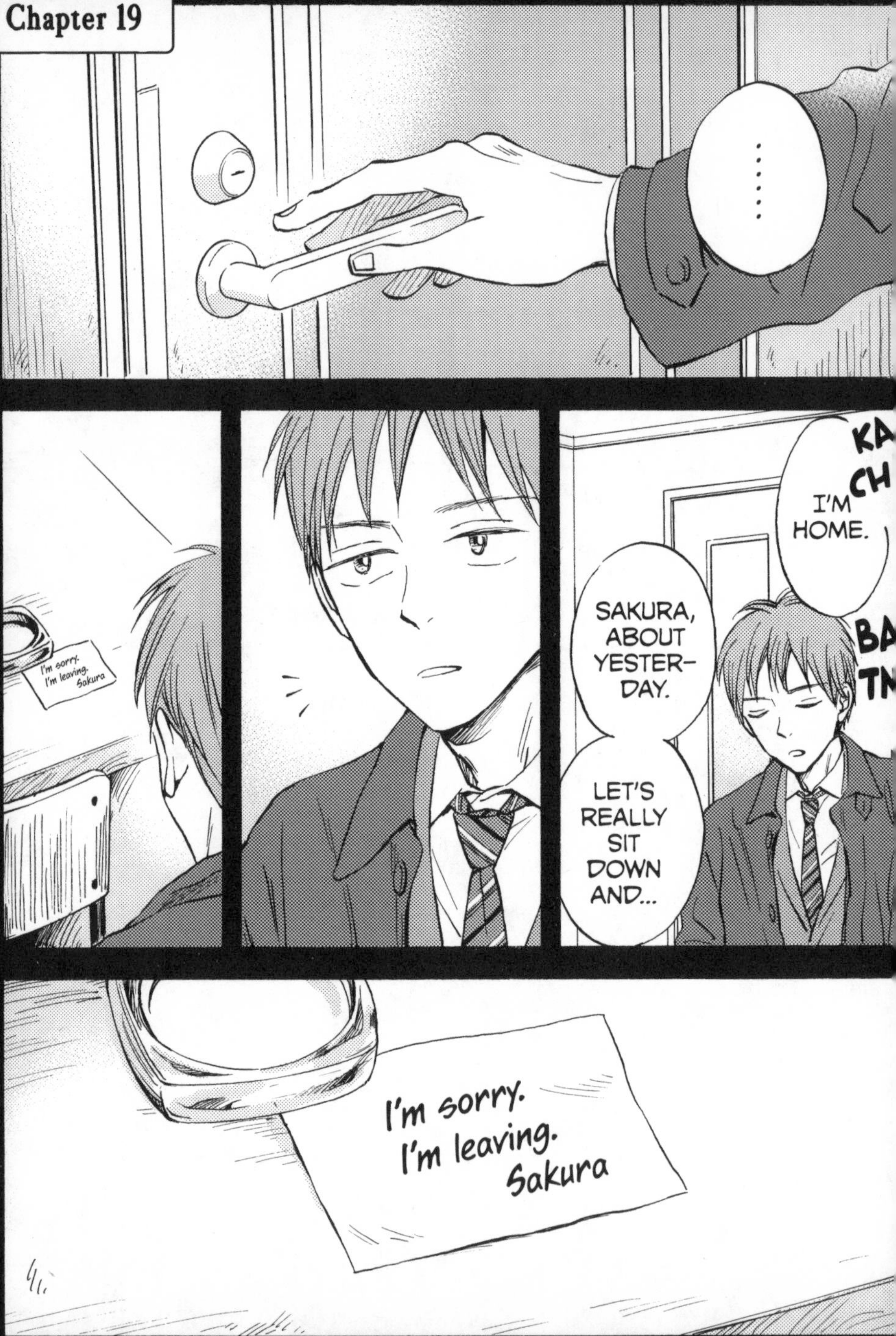
......
KA CH
I'M HOME.
BA TN
SAKURA, ABOUT YESTERDAY.
LET'S REALLY SIT DOWN AND...
I'm sorry. I'm leaving. Sakura
I'm sorry. I'm leaving. Sakura

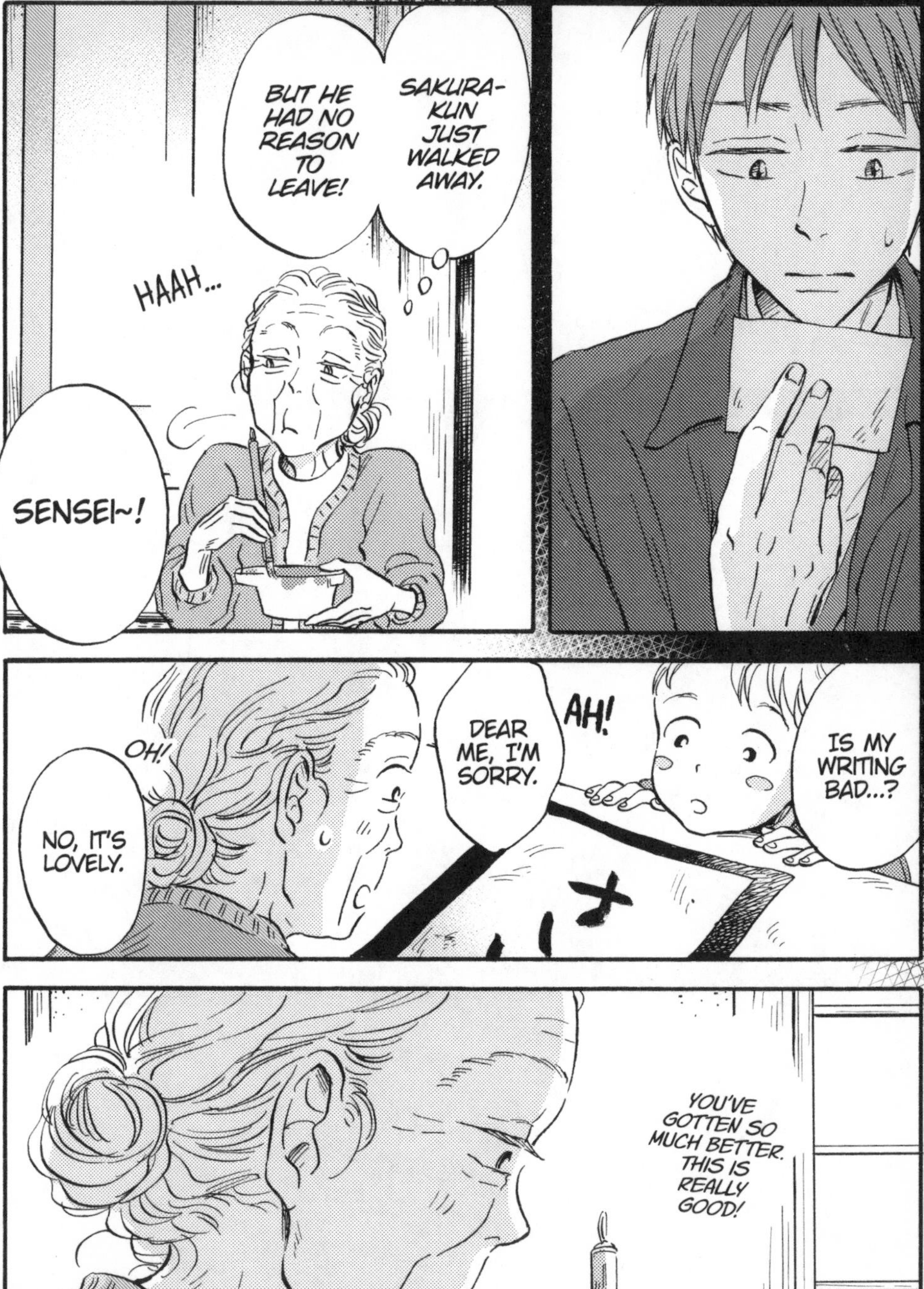
SAKURA-KUN JUST WALKED AWAY.
BUT HE HAD NO REASON TO LEAVE!
HAAH...
SENSEI~!
IS MY WRITING BAD...?
AH!
DEAR ME, I'M SORRY.
OH!
NO, IT'S LOVELY.
YOU'VE GOTTEN SO MUCH BETTER. THIS IS REALLY GOOD!

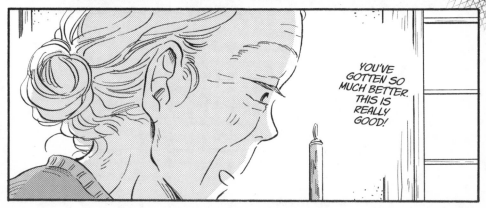

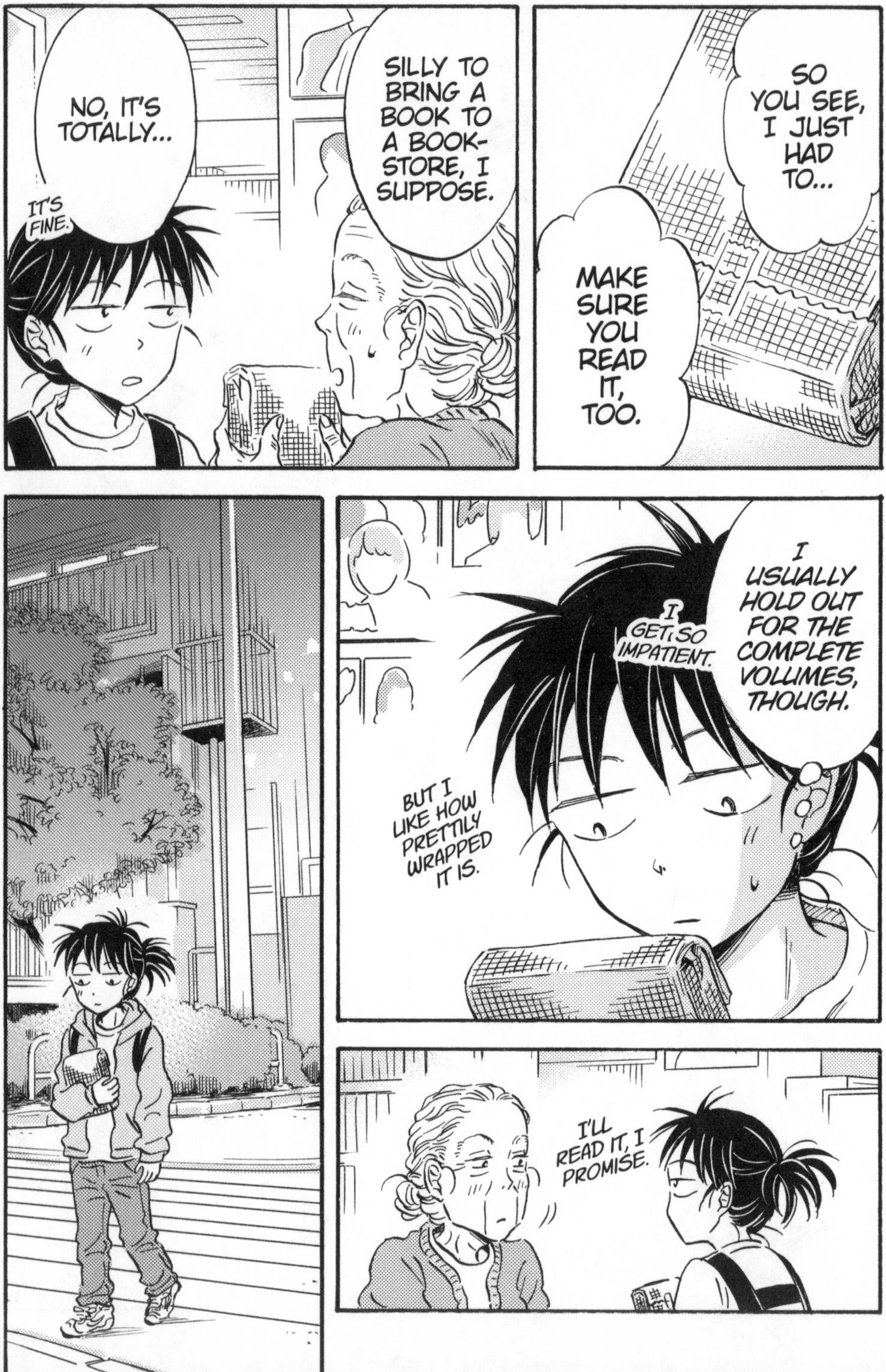
SO YOU SEE, I JUST HAD TO...
MAKE SURE YOU READ IT, TOO.
SILLY TO BRING A BOOK TO A BOOK-STORE, I SUPPOSE.
NO, IT'S TOTALLY...
IT'S FINE.
I USUALLY HOLD OUT FOR THE COMPLETE VOLUMES, THOUGH.
I GET SO IMPATIENT.
BUT I LIKE HOW PRETTILY WRAPPED IT IS.
I'LL READ IT, I PROMISE.

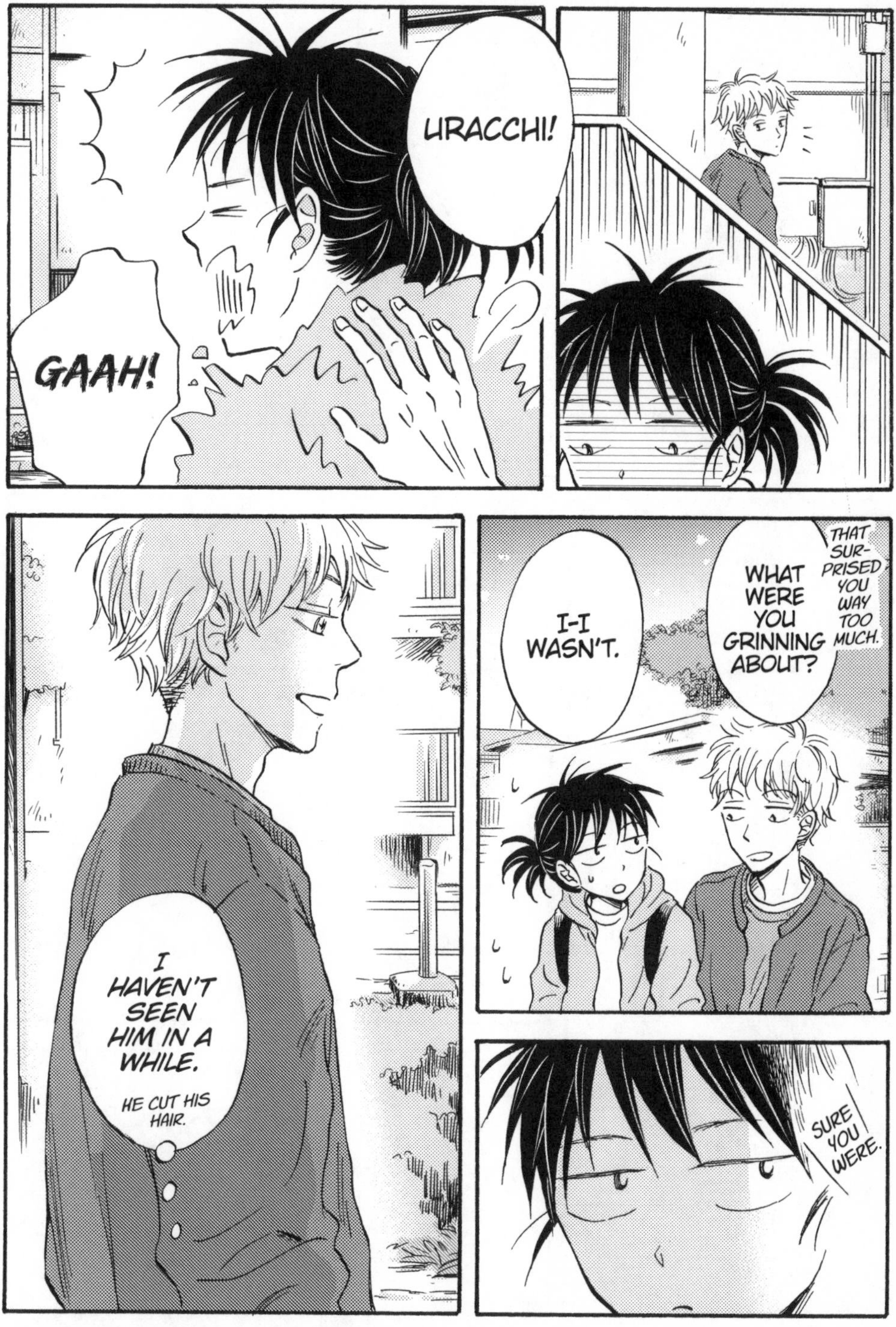
URACCHI!
GAAH!
THAT SUR-PRISED YOU WAY TOO MUCH.
WHAT WERE YOU GRINNING ABOUT?
I-I WASN'T.
SURE YOU WERE.
I HAVEN'T SEEN HIM IN A WHILE.
HE CUT HIS HAIR.

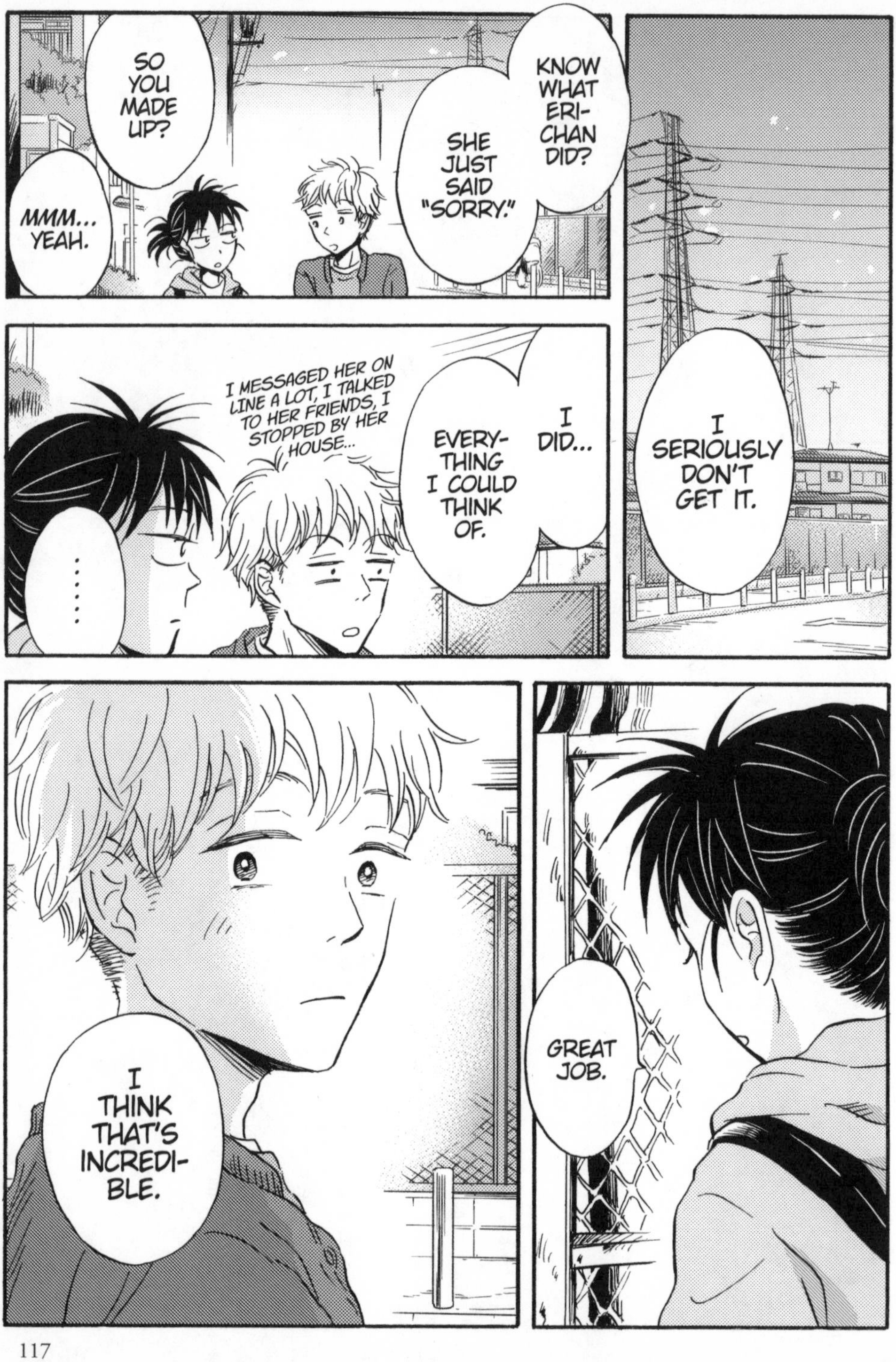
I SERIOUSLY DON'T GET IT.
KNOW WHAT ERI-CHAN DID?
SHE JUST SAID "SORRY."
SO YOU MADE UP?
MMM... YEAH.
I DID...
EVERYTHING I COULD THINK OF.
I MESSAGED HER ON LINE A LOT, I TALKED TO HER FRIENDS, I STOPPED BY HER HOUSE...
......
GREAT JOB.
I THINK THAT'S INCREDIBLE.

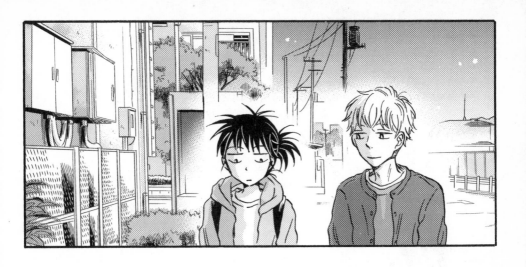

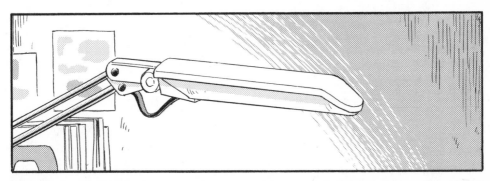

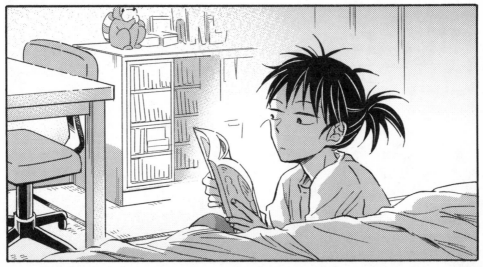

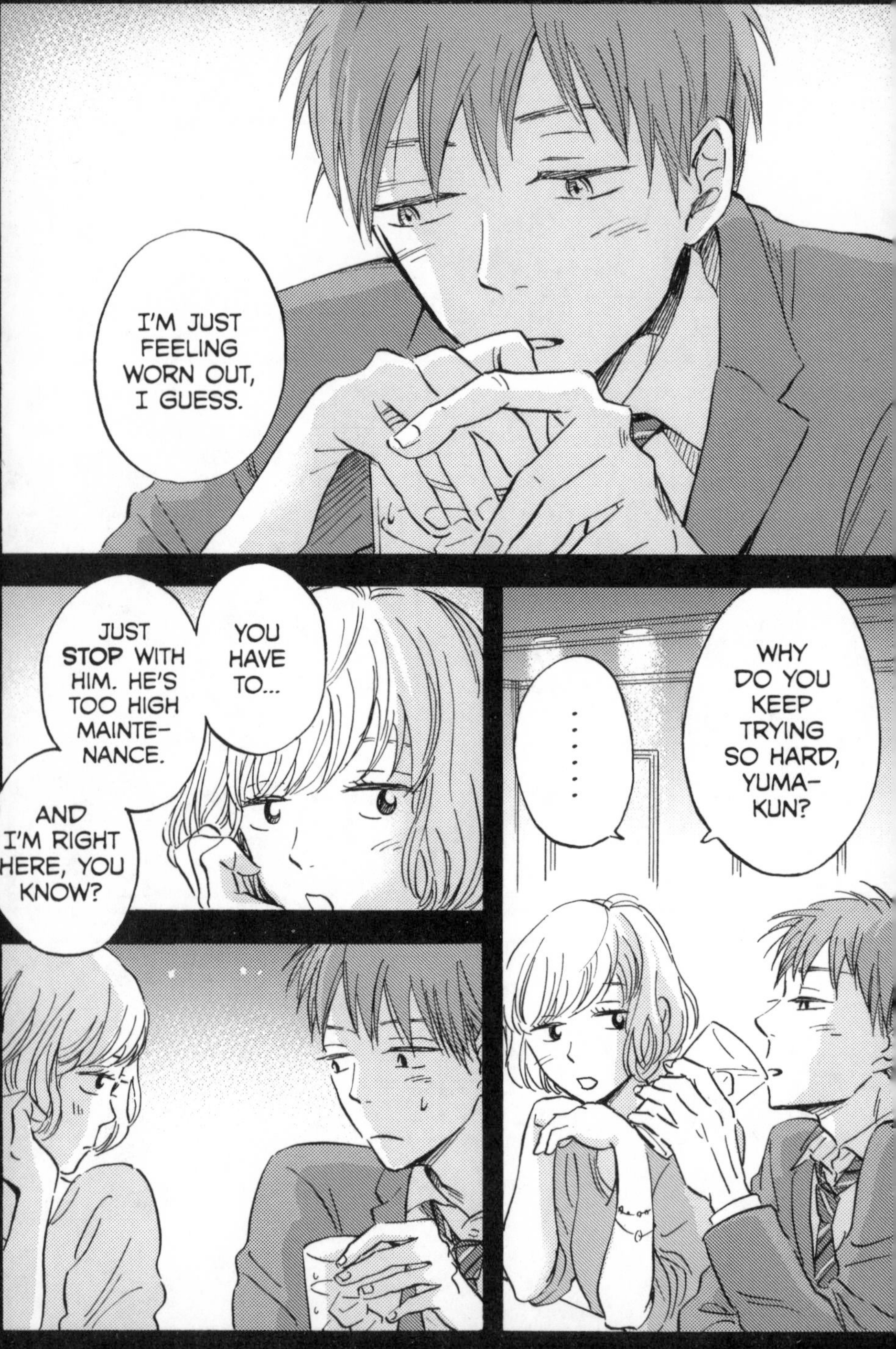
I'M JUST FEELING WORN OUT, I GUESS.
WHY DO YOU KEEP TRYING SO HARD, YUMA-KUN?
......
YOU HAVE TO...
JUST **STOP** WITH HIM. HE'S TOO HIGH MAINTE-NANCE.
AND I'M RIGHT HERE, YOU KNOW?

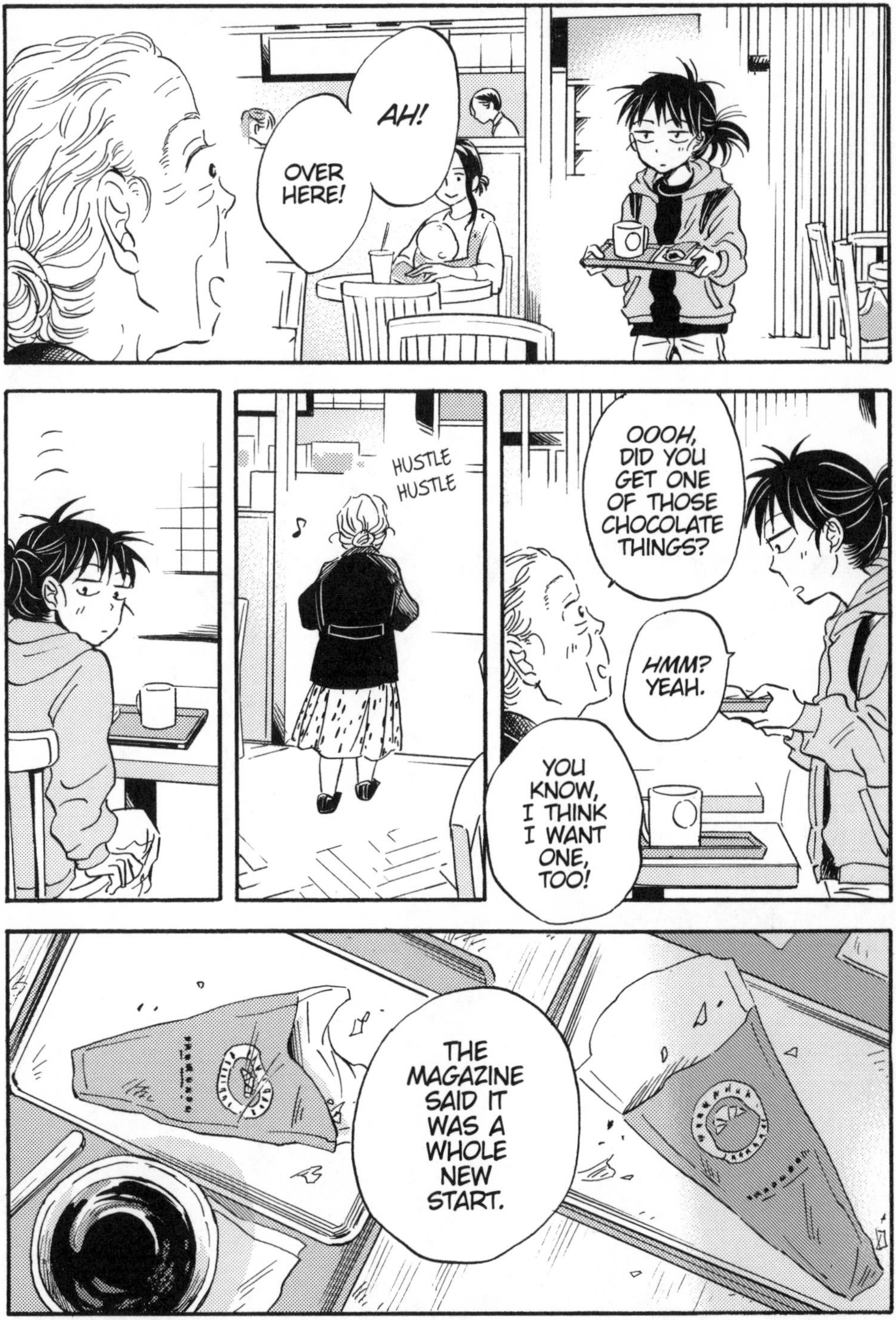
AH!
OVER HERE!
OOOH, DID YOU GET ONE OF THOSE CHOCOLATE THINGS?
HMM? YEAH.
YOU KNOW, I THINK I WANT ONE, TOO!
HUSTLE HUSTLE
THE MAGAZINE SAID IT WAS A WHOLE NEW START.

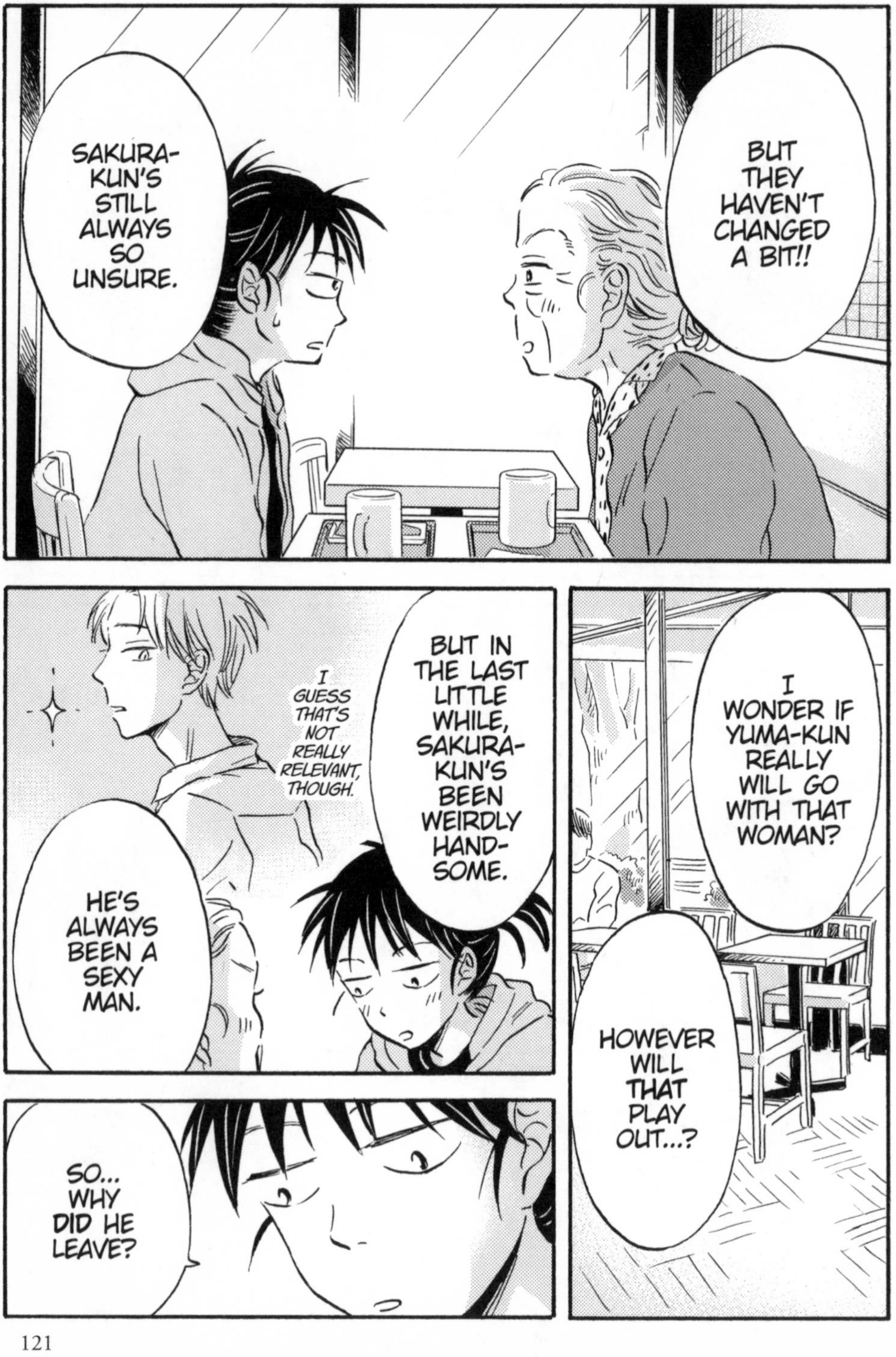
BUT THEY HAVEN'T CHANGED A BIT!!
SAKURA-KUN'S STILL ALWAYS SO UNSURE.
I WONDER IF YUMA-KUN REALLY WILL GO WITH THAT WOMAN?
HOWEVER WILL THAT PLAY OUT...?
BUT IN THE LAST LITTLE WHILE, SAKURA-KUN'S BEEN WEIRDLY HANDSOME.
I GUESS THAT'S NOT REALLY RELEVANT, THOUGH.
HE'S ALWAYS BEEN A SEXY MAN.
SO... WHY DID HE LEAVE?

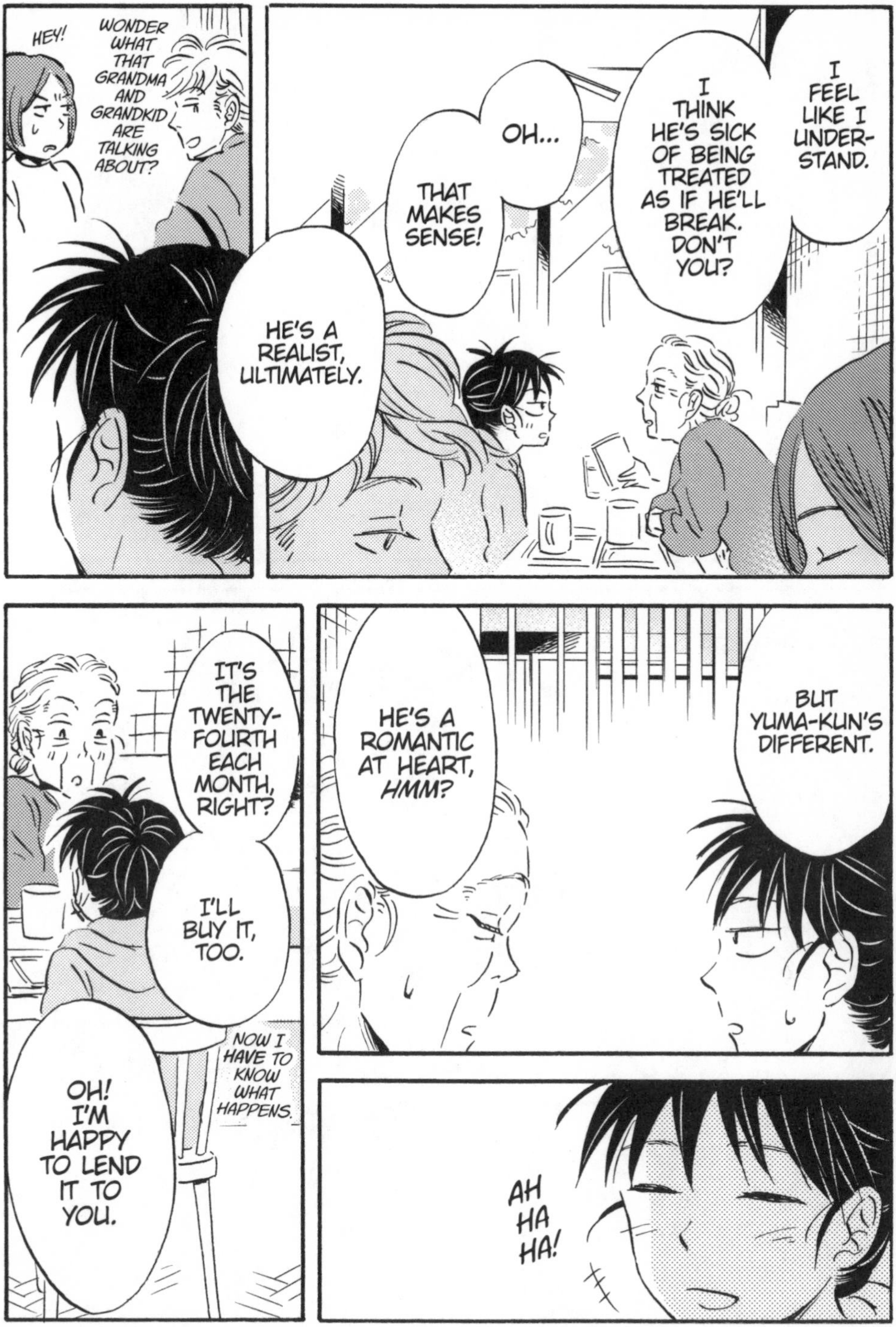
I FEEL LIKE I UNDER-STAND.
I THINK HE'S SICK OF BEING TREATED AS IF HE'LL BREAK. DON'T YOU?
OH... THAT MAKES SENSE!
HE'S A REALIST, ULTIMATELY.
WONDER WHAT THAT GRANDMA AND GRANDKID ARE TALKING ABOUT?
HEY!
BUT YUMA-KUN'S DIFFERENT.
HE'S A ROMANTIC AT HEART, HMM?
AH HA HA!
IT'S THE TWENTY-FOURTH EACH MONTH, RIGHT?
I'LL BUY IT, TOO.
NOW I HAVE TO KNOW WHAT HAPPENS.
OH! I'M HAPPY TO LEND IT TO YOU.

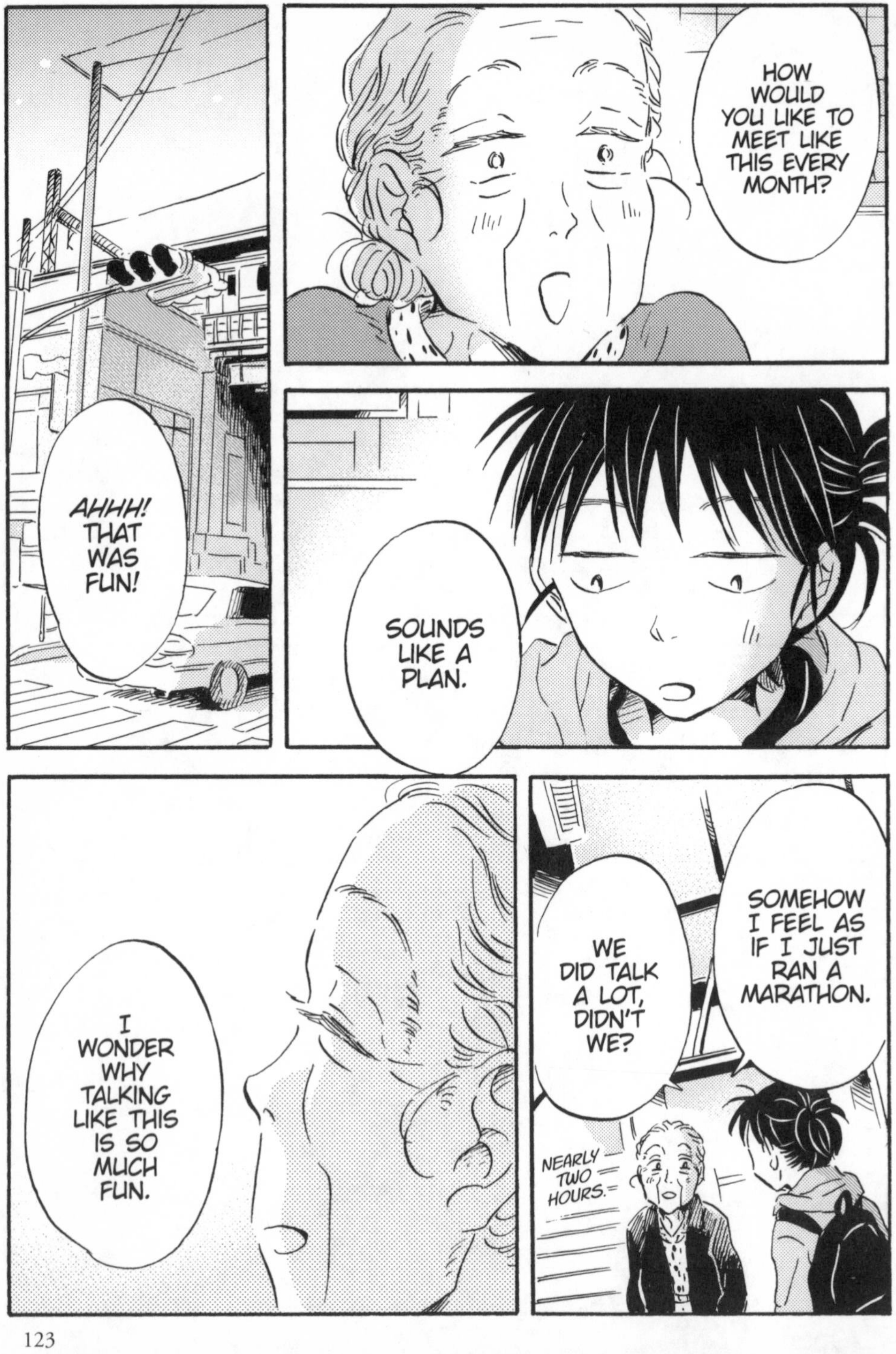
HOW WOULD YOU LIKE TO MEET LIKE THIS EVERY MONTH?
SOUNDS LIKE A PLAN.
AHHH! THAT WAS FUN!
SOMEHOW I FEEL AS IF I JUST RAN A MARATHON.
WE DID TALK A LOT, DIDN'T WE?
NEARLY TWO HOURS.
I WONDER WHY TALKING LIKE THIS IS SO MUCH FUN.

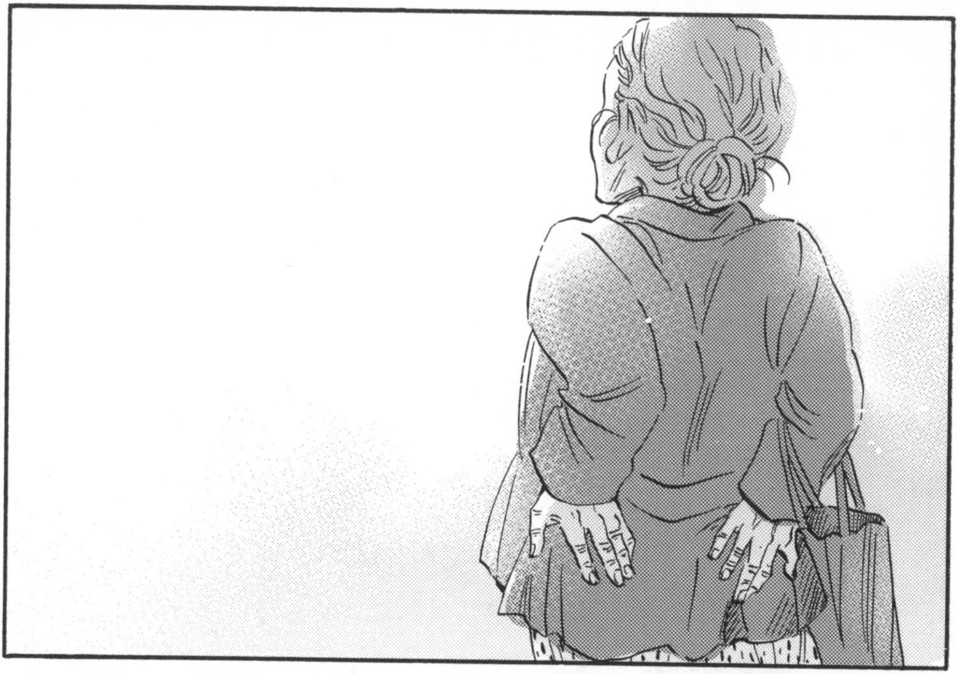

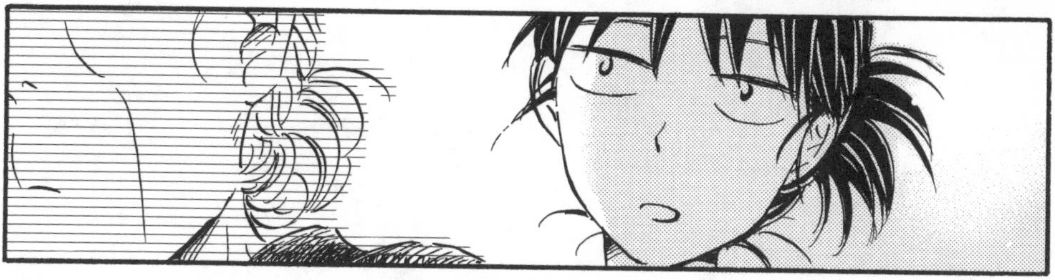

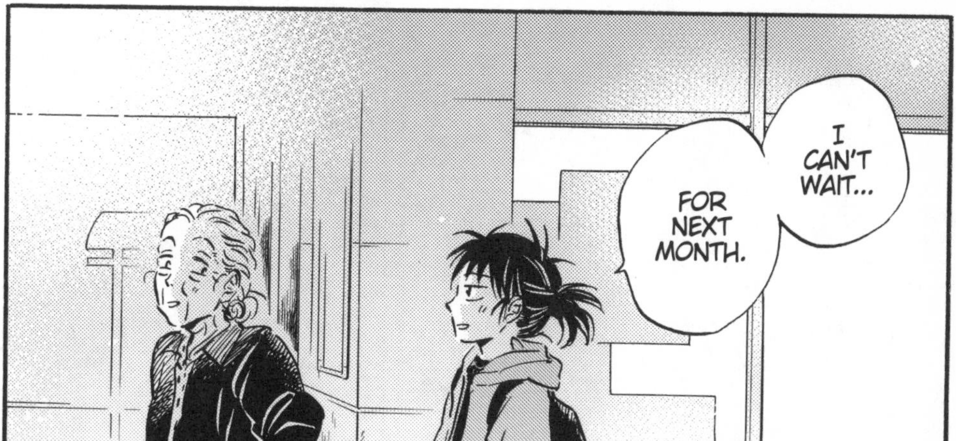
I CAN'T WAIT...
FOR NEXT MONTH.

Chapter 19/END

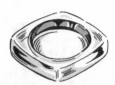

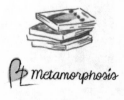
metamorphosis

Chapter 20

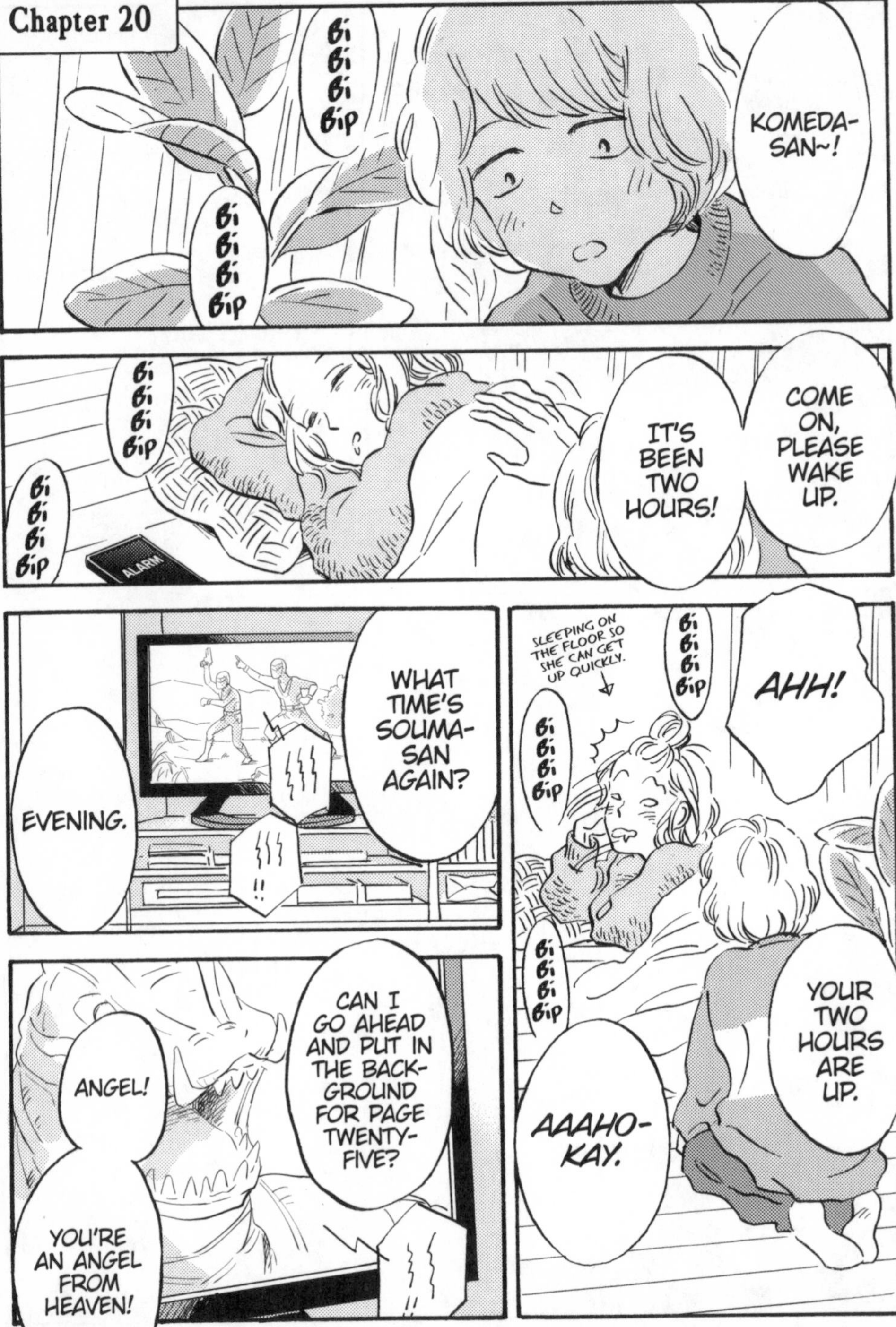
KOMEDA-SAN~!
Bi Bi Bi Bip
Bi Bi Bi Bip
COME ON, PLEASE WAKE UP.
IT'S BEEN TWO HOURS!
Bi Bi Bi Bip
Bi Bi Bi Bip
ALARM
Bi Bi Bi Bip
AHH!
SLEEPING ON THE FLOOR SO SHE CAN GET UP QUICKLY.
Bi Bi Bi Bip
YOUR TWO HOURS ARE UP.
Bi Bi Bi Bip
AAAHO-KAY.
WHAT TIME'S SOUMA-SAN AGAIN?
EVENING.
CAN I GO AHEAD AND PUT IN THE BACK-GROUND FOR PAGE TWENTY-FIVE?
ANGEL!
YOU'RE AN ANGEL FROM HEAVEN!

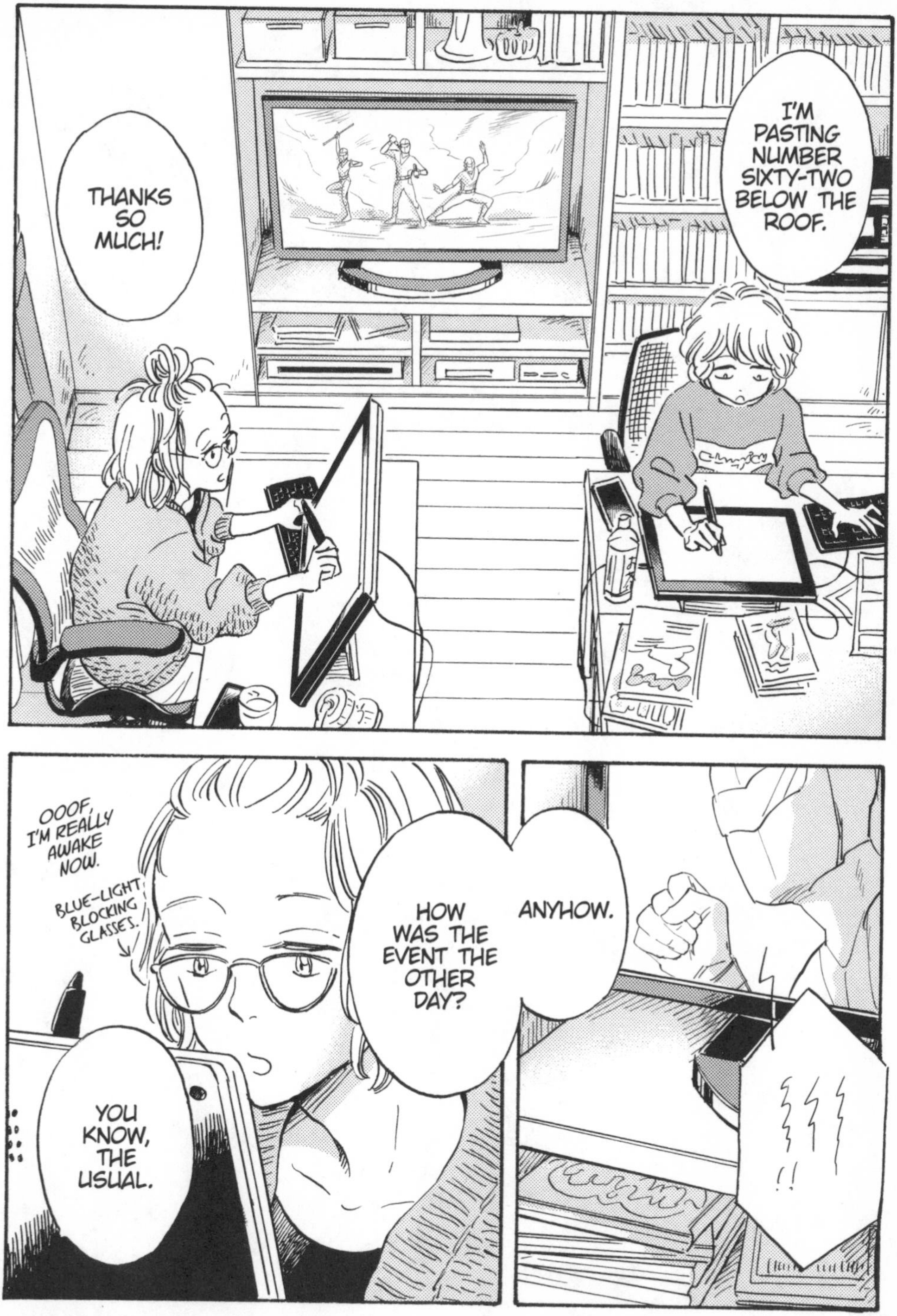
I'M PASTING NUMBER SIXTY-TWO BELOW THE ROOF.
THANKS SO MUCH!
ANYHOW.
HOW WAS THE EVENT THE OTHER DAY?
OOOF, I'M REALLY AWAKE NOW.
BLUE-LIGHT BLOCKING GLASSES.
YOU KNOW, THE USUAL.

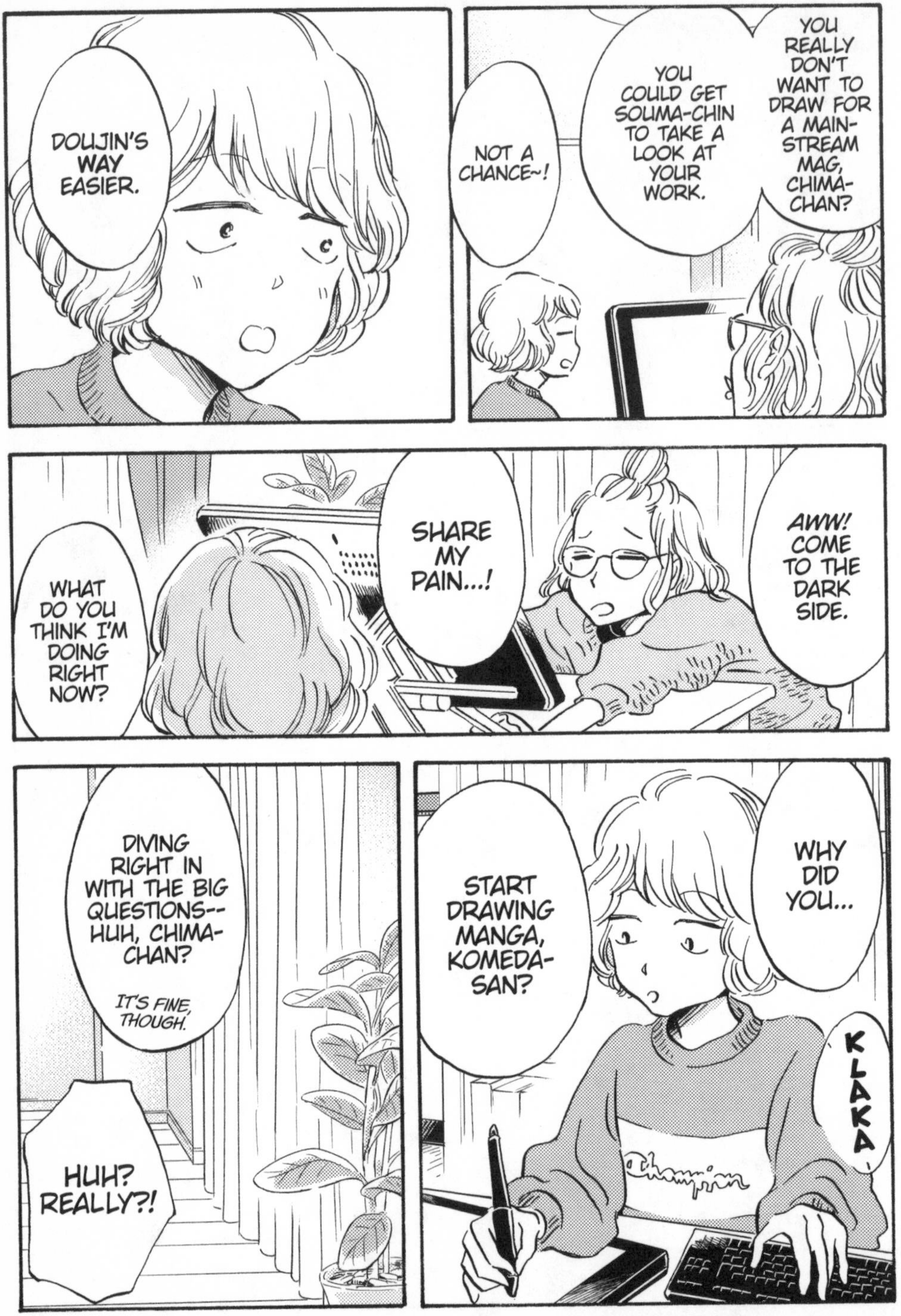
YOU REALLY DON'T WANT TO DRAW FOR A MAIN-STREAM MAG, CHIMA-CHAN?
YOU COULD GET SOUMA-CHIN TO TAKE A LOOK AT YOUR WORK.
NOT A CHANCE~!
DOUJIN'S WAY EASIER.
AWW! COME TO THE DARK SIDE.
SHARE MY PAIN...!
WHAT DO YOU THINK I'M DOING RIGHT NOW?
WHY DID YOU...
START DRAWING MANGA, KOMEDA-SAN?
KLAKA
DIVING RIGHT IN WITH THE BIG QUESTIONS--HUH, CHIMA-CHAN?
IT'S FINE, THOUGH.
HUH? REALLY?!

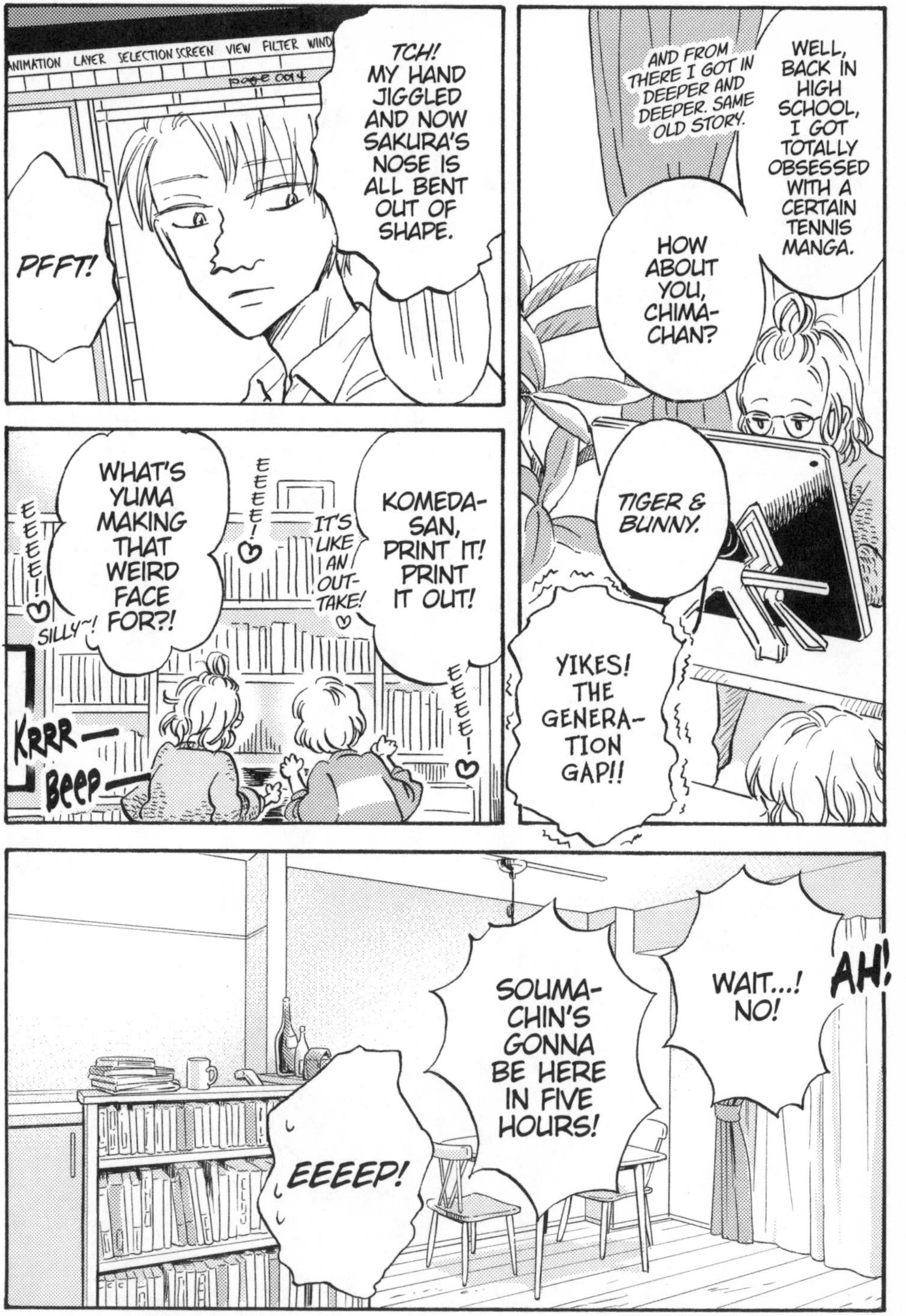
WELL, BACK IN HIGH SCHOOL, I GOT TOTALLY OBSESSED WITH A CERTAIN TENNIS MANGA.
AND FROM THERE I GOT IN DEEPER AND DEEPER. SAME OLD STORY.
HOW ABOUT YOU, CHIMA-CHAN?
TIGER & BUNNY.
YIKES! THE GENERATION GAP!!
ANIMATION LAYER SELECTION SCREEN VIEW FILTER WIND
TCH! MY HAND JIGGLED AND NOW SAKURA'S NOSE IS ALL BENT OUT OF SHAPE.
PFFT!
EEEE!♡
KOMEDA-SAN, PRINT IT! PRINT IT OUT!
EEEE!♡
IT'S LIKE AN OUT-TAKE!♡
WHAT'S YUMA MAKING THAT WEIRD FACE FOR?!
EEEE!♡
SILLY~!
KRRR—
Beep—
AH!
WAIT...! NO!
SOUMA-CHIN'S GONNA BE HERE IN FIVE HOURS!
EEEEP!

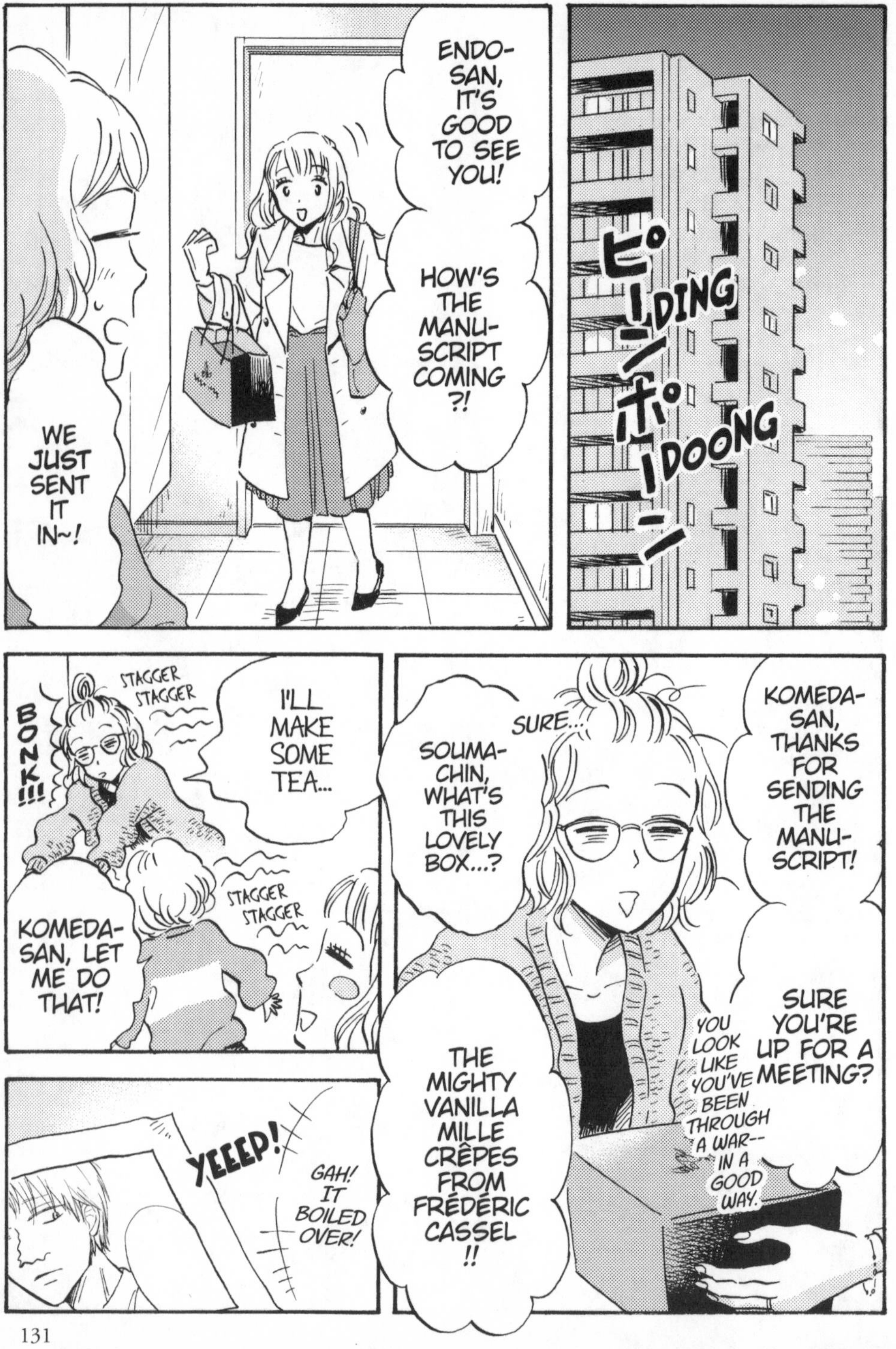
ピーンポーン
DING
DOONG
ENDO-SAN, IT'S GOOD TO SEE YOU!
HOW'S THE MANUSCRIPT COMING?!
WE JUST SENT IT IN~!
KOMEDA-SAN, THANKS FOR SENDING THE MANUSCRIPT!
SURE...
SOUMA-CHIN, WHAT'S THIS LOVELY BOX...?
SURE YOU'RE UP FOR A MEETING?
YOU LOOK LIKE YOU'VE BEEN THROUGH A WAR--IN A GOOD WAY.
THE MIGHTY VANILLA MILLE CRÊPES FROM FRÉDÉRIC CASSEL!!
I'LL MAKE SOME TEA...
STAGGER STAGGER
BONK!!!
KOMEDA-SAN, LET ME DO THAT!
STAGGER STAGGER
YEEEP!
GAH! IT BOILED OVER!

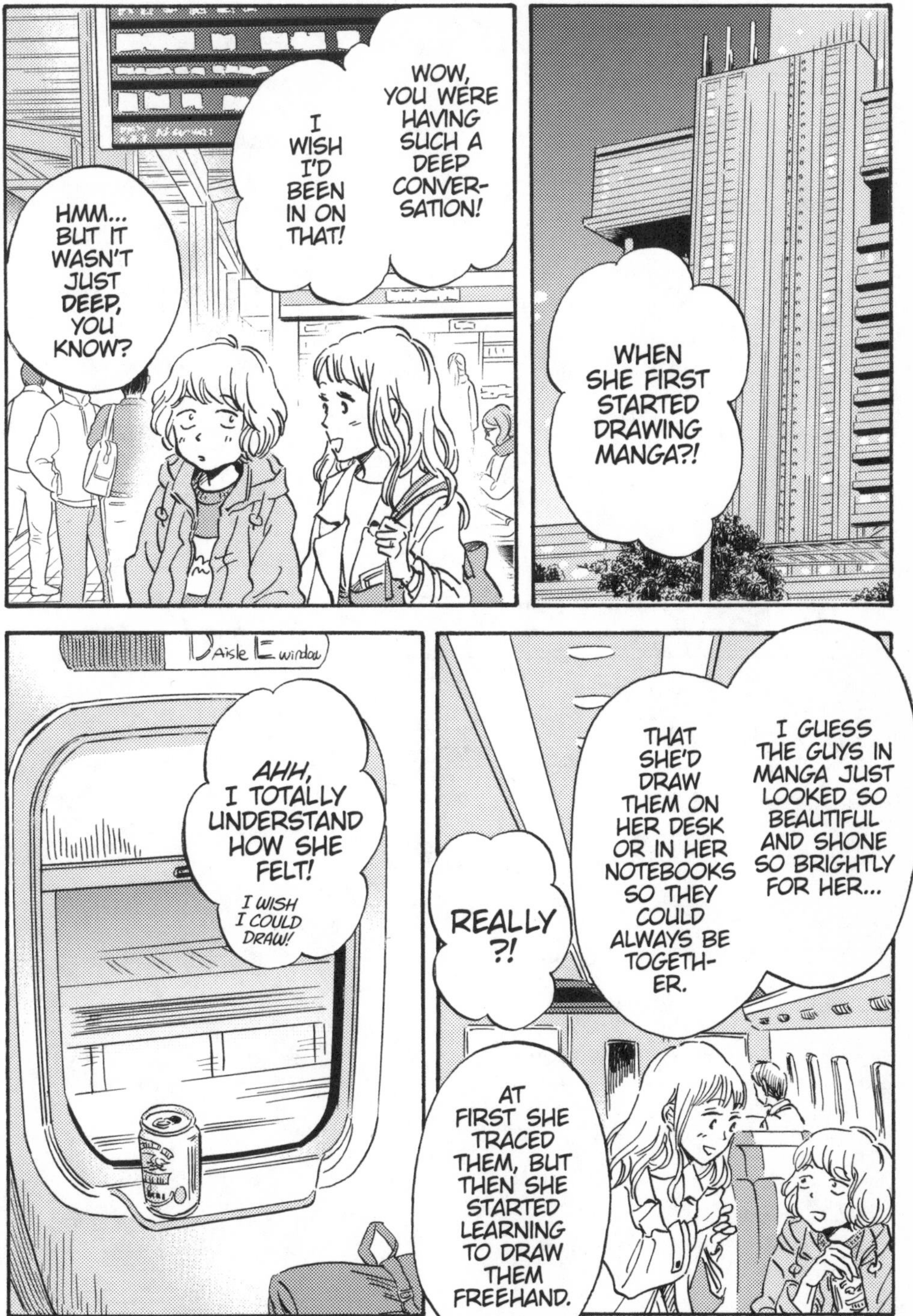
WHEN SHE FIRST STARTED DRAWING MANGA?!
WOW, YOU WERE HAVING SUCH A DEEP CONVER-SATION!
I WISH I'D BEEN IN ON THAT!
HMM... BUT IT WASN'T JUST DEEP, YOU KNOW?
I GUESS THE GUYS IN MANGA JUST LOOKED SO BEAUTIFUL AND SHONE SO BRIGHTLY FOR HER...
THAT SHE'D DRAW THEM ON HER DESK OR IN HER NOTEBOOKS SO THEY COULD ALWAYS BE TOGETH-ER.
REALLY ?!
AT FIRST SHE TRACED THEM, BUT THEN SHE STARTED LEARNING TO DRAW THEM FREEHAND.
D aisle E window
AHH, I TOTALLY UNDERSTAND HOW SHE FELT!
I WISH I COULD DRAW!

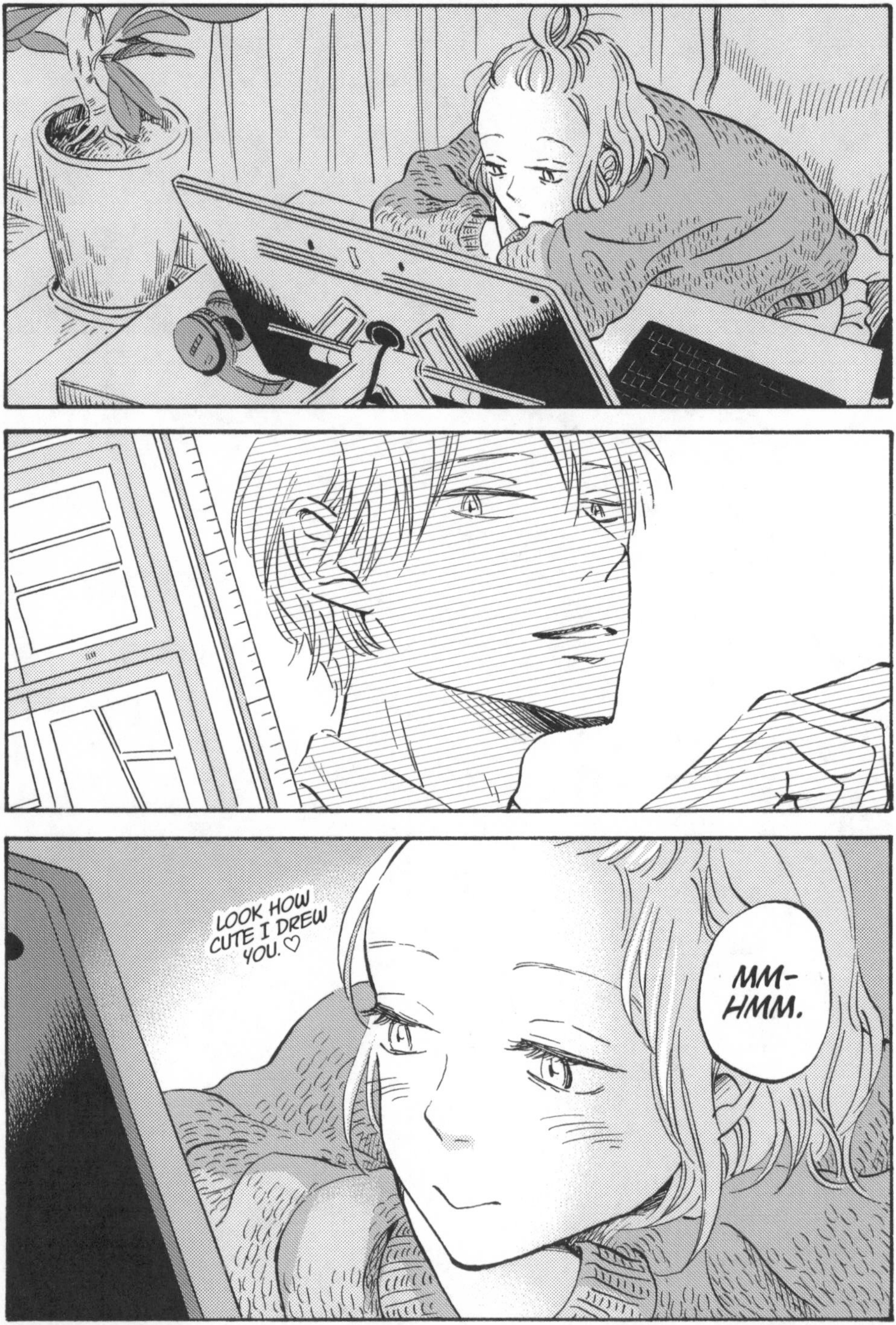
MM-HMM.
LOOK HOW CUTE I DREW YOU.♡

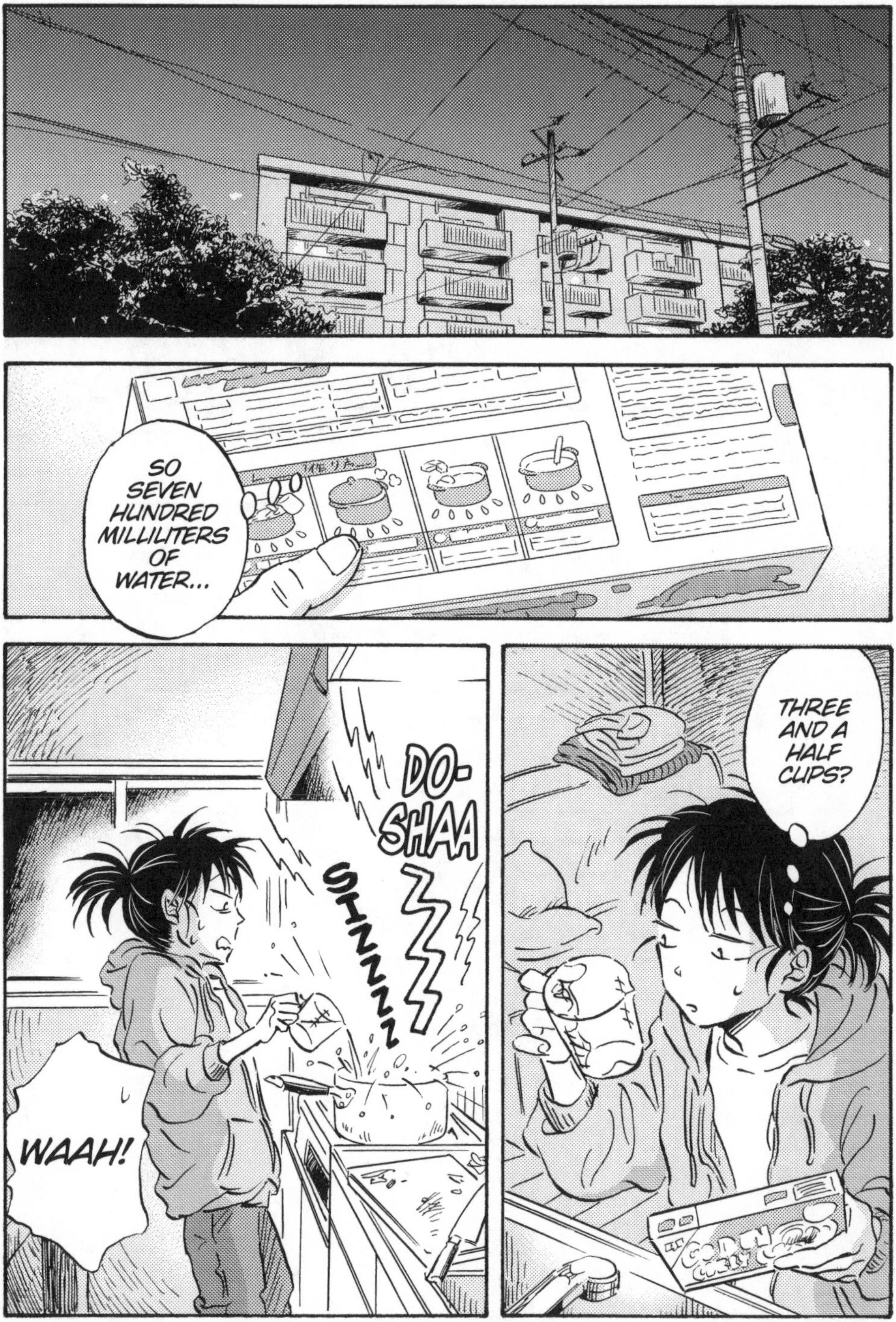
SO SEVEN HUNDRED MILLILITERS OF WATER...
THREE AND A HALF CUPS?
DO-SHAA
SIZZZZZ
WAAH!

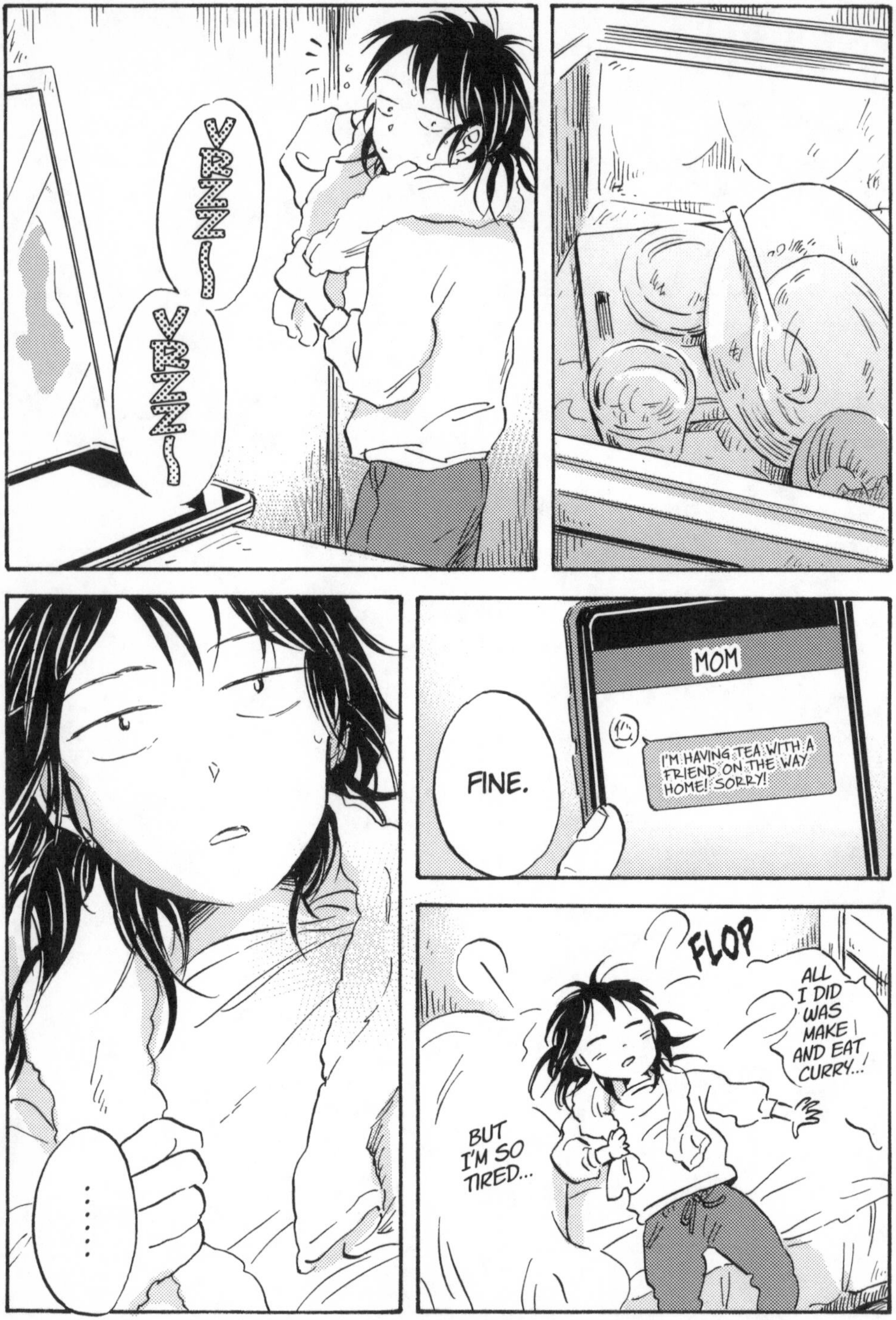
VRZZ!
VRZZ!
MOM
I'M HAVING TEA WITH A FRIEND ON THE WAY HOME! SORRY!
FINE.
FLOP
ALL I DID WAS MAKE AND EAT CURRY...!
BUT I'M SO TIRED...
......

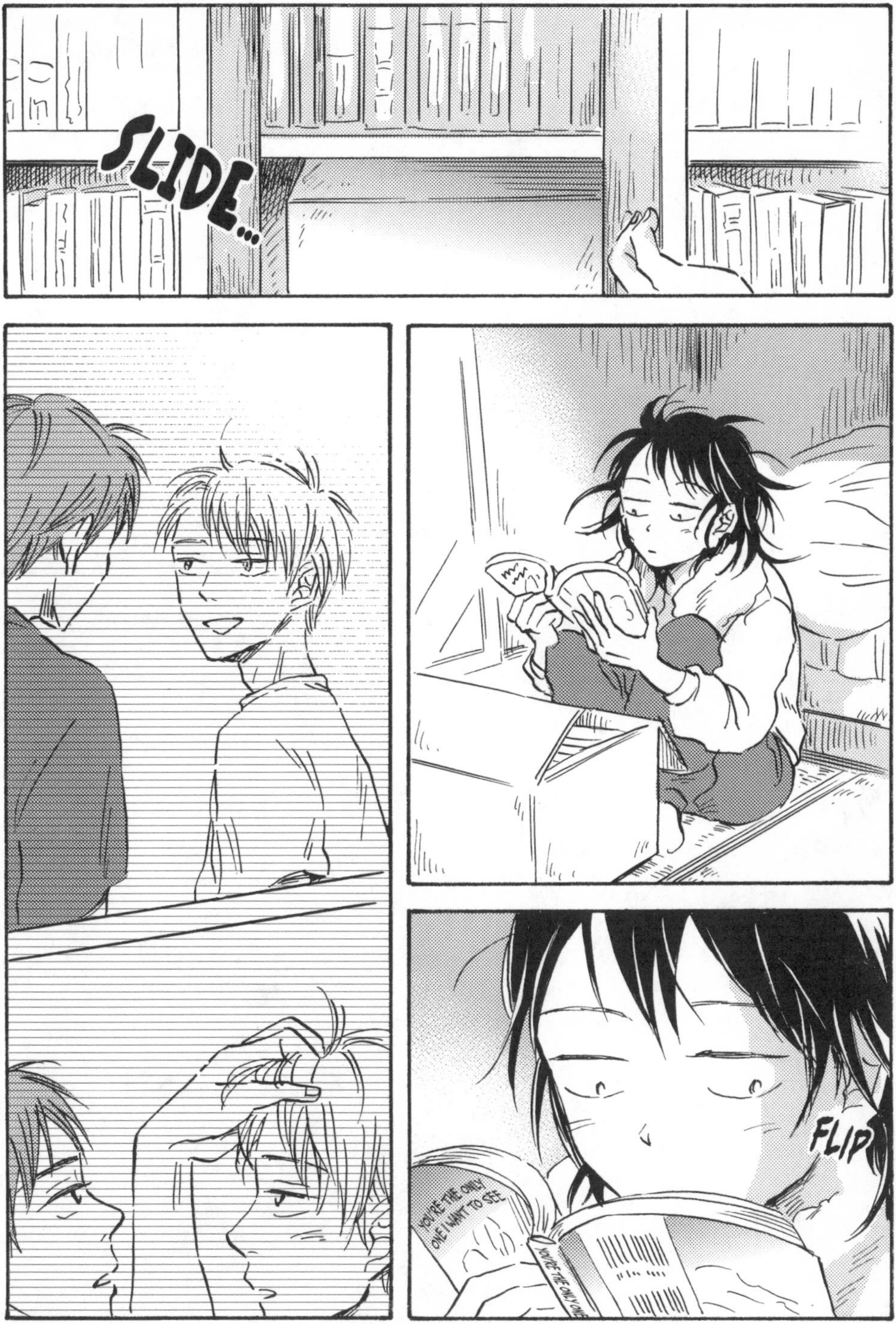
SLIDE...
FLIP
YOU'RE THE ONLY ONE
YOU'RE THE ONLY ONE I WANT TO SEE.

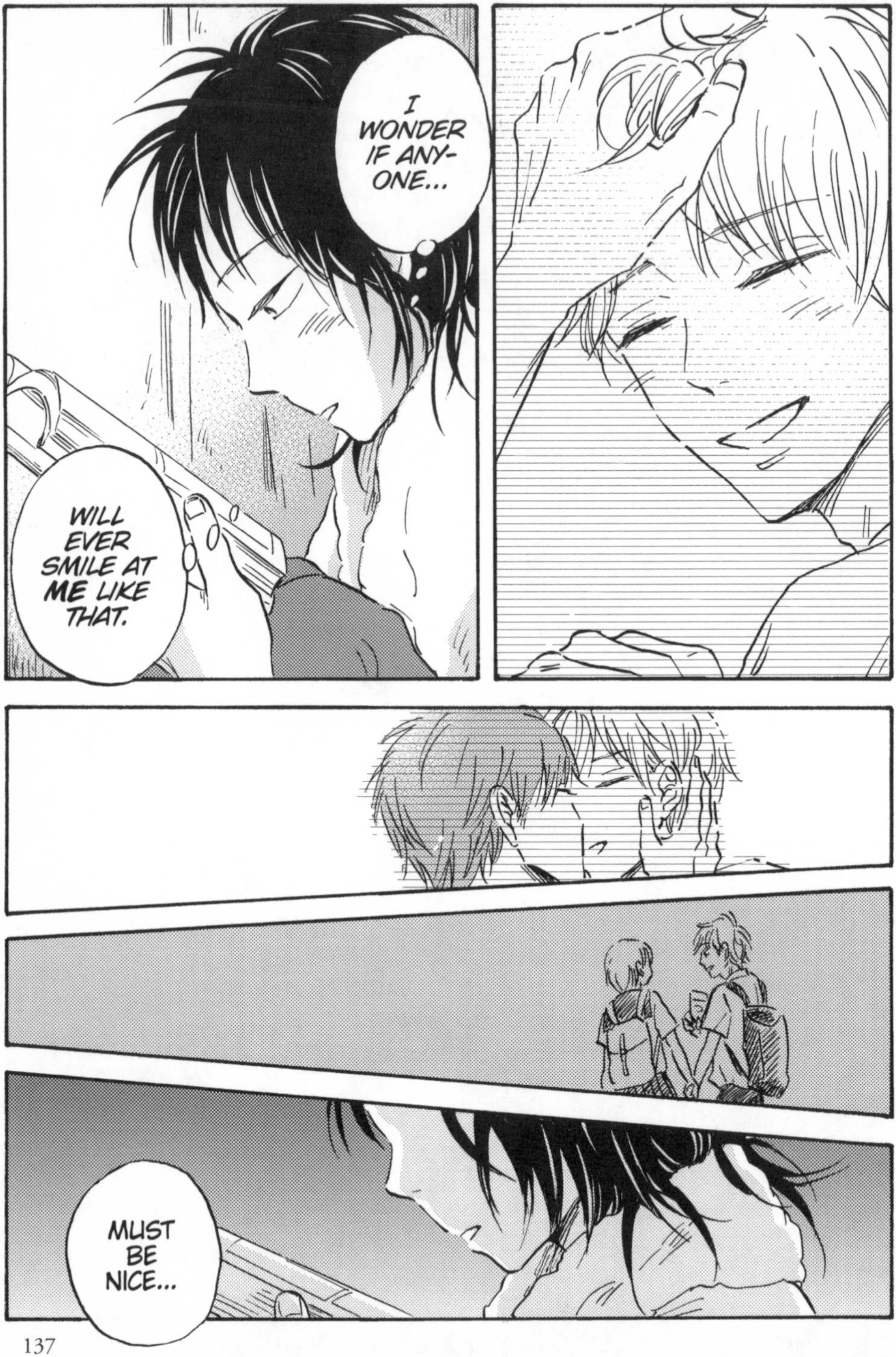
I WONDER IF ANY-ONE...
WILL EVER SMILE AT ME LIKE THAT.
MUST BE NICE...

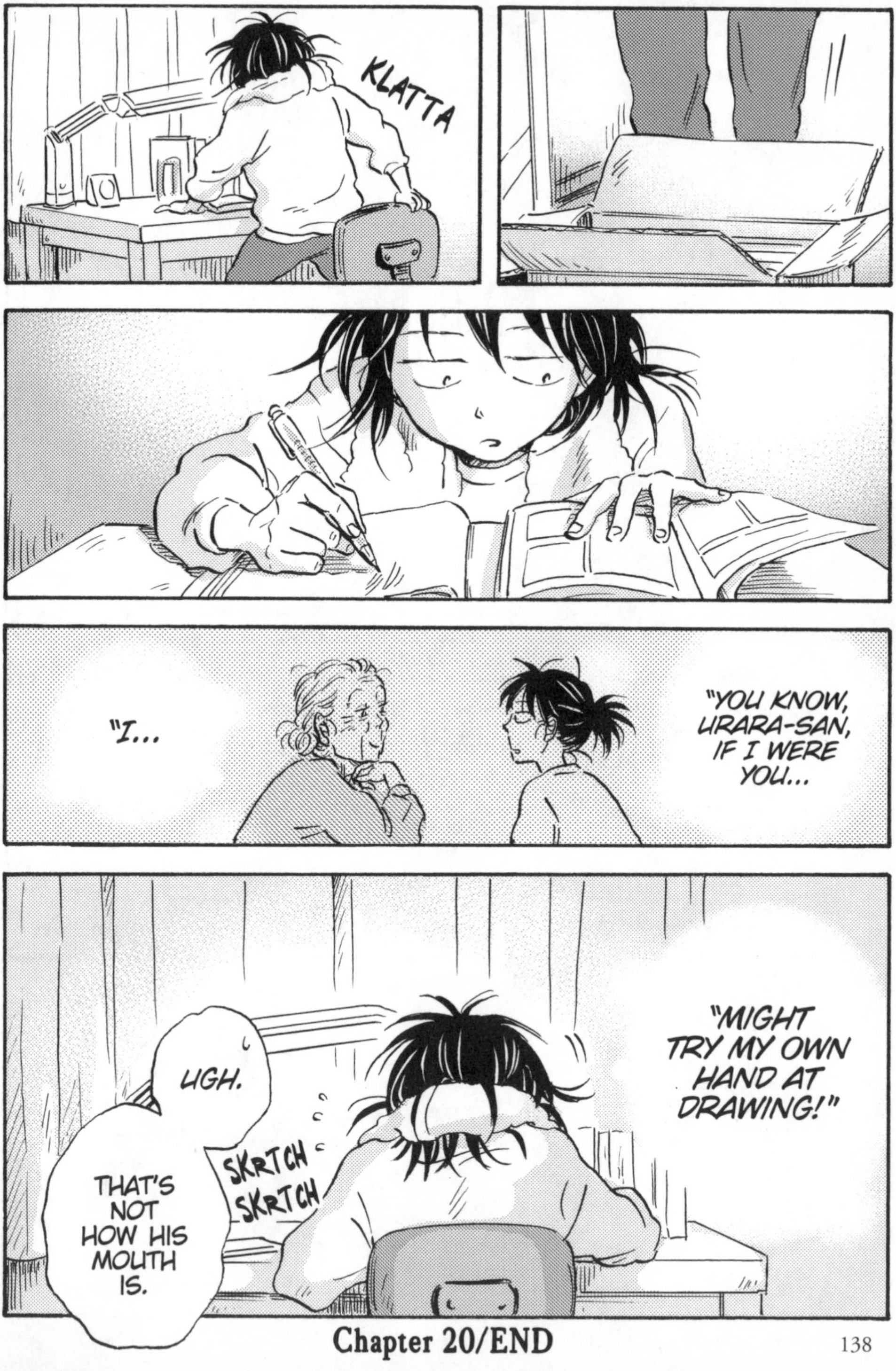
KLATTA
"YOU KNOW, URARA-SAN, IF I WERE YOU...
"I...
"MIGHT TRY MY OWN HAND AT DRAWING!"
UGH.
SKRTCH SKRTCH
THAT'S NOT HOW HIS MOUTH IS.

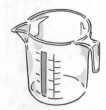

AFTERWORD

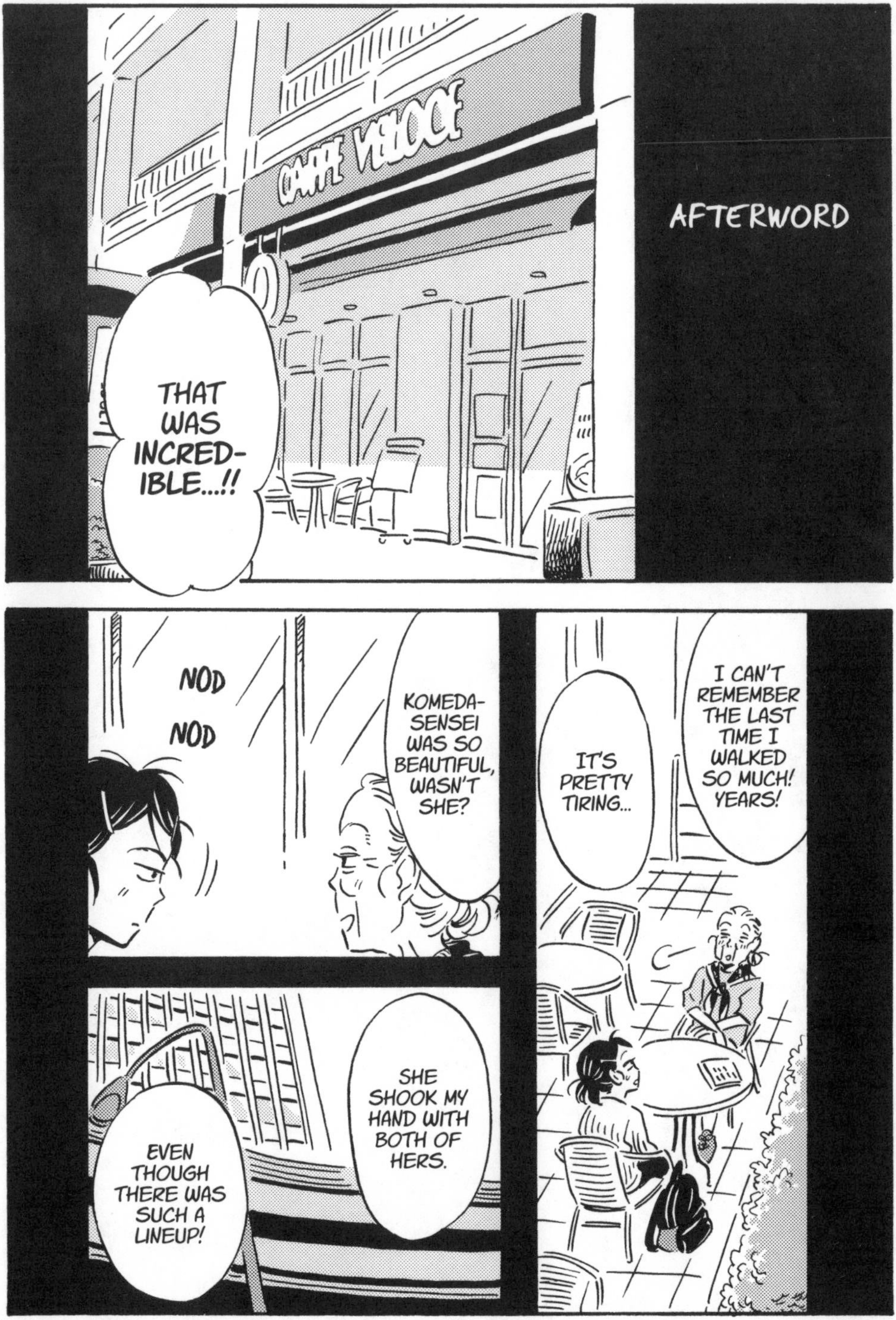
CAFFE VELOCE
THAT WAS INCREDIBLE...!!
I CAN'T REMEMBER THE LAST TIME I WALKED SO MUCH! YEARS!
IT'S PRETTY TIRING...
KOMEDA-SENSEI WAS SO BEAUTIFUL, WASN'T SHE?
NOD
NOD
SHE SHOOK MY HAND WITH BOTH OF HERS.
EVEN THOUGH THERE WAS SUCH A LINEUP!

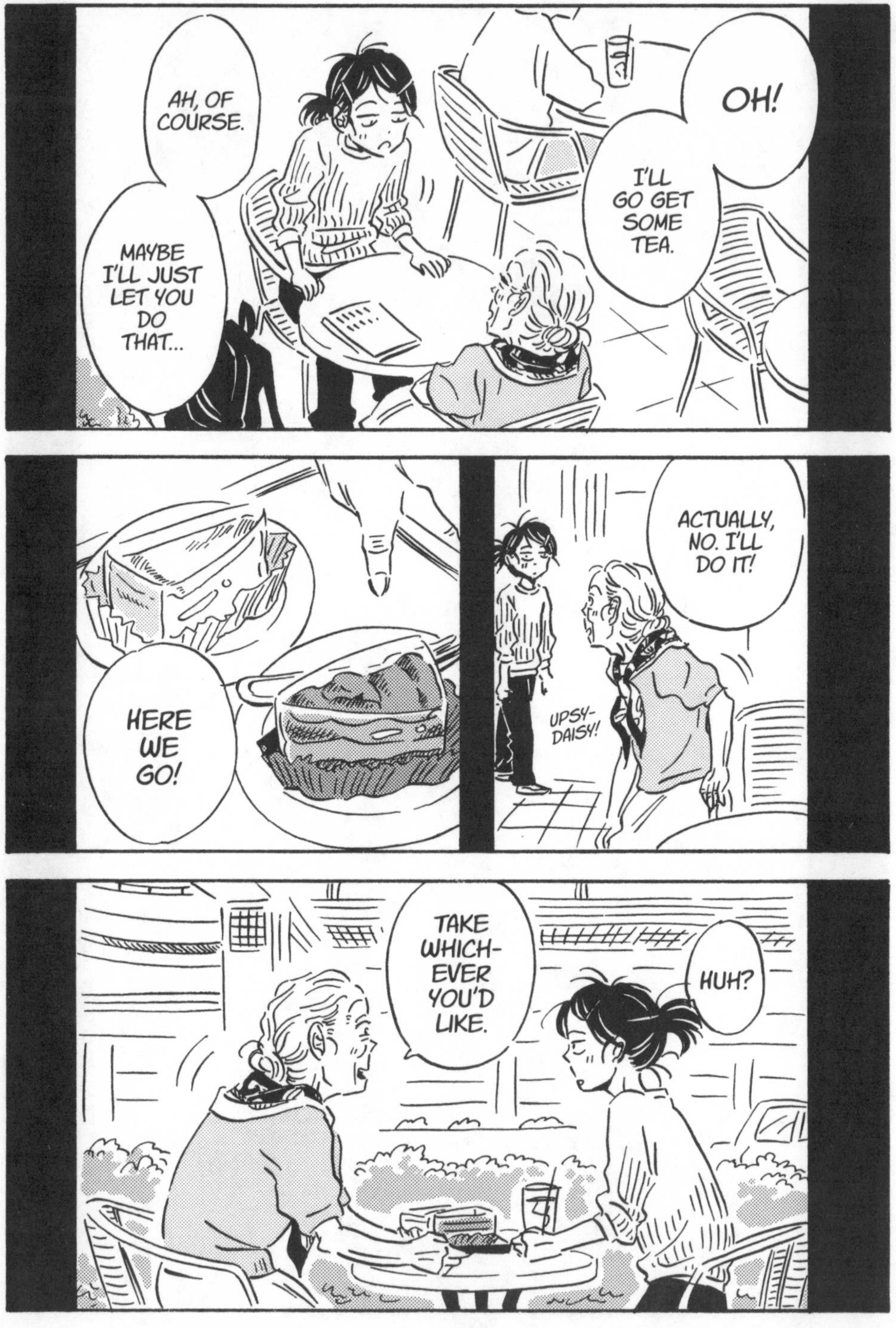
OH!
I'LL GO GET SOME TEA.
AH, OF COURSE.
MAYBE I'LL JUST LET YOU DO THAT...
ACTUALLY, NO. I'LL DO IT!
UPSY-DAISY!
HERE WE GO!
TAKE WHICH-EVER YOU'D LIKE.
HUH?

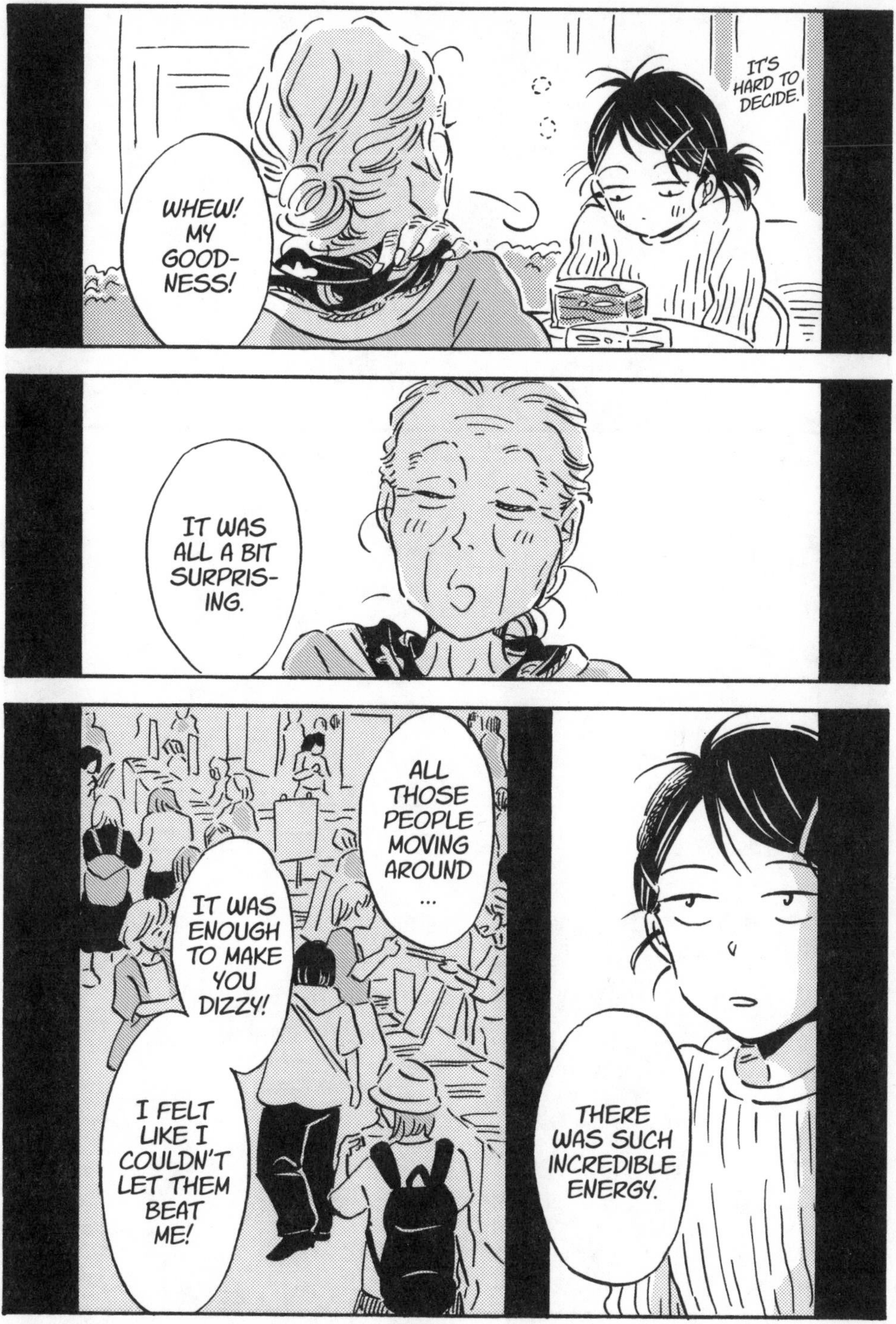
IT'S HARD TO DECIDE.
WHEW! MY GOODNESS!
IT WAS ALL A BIT SURPRISING.
THERE WAS SUCH INCREDIBLE ENERGY.
ALL THOSE PEOPLE MOVING AROUND ...
IT WAS ENOUGH TO MAKE YOU DIZZY!
I FELT LIKE I COULDN'T LET THEM BEAT ME!

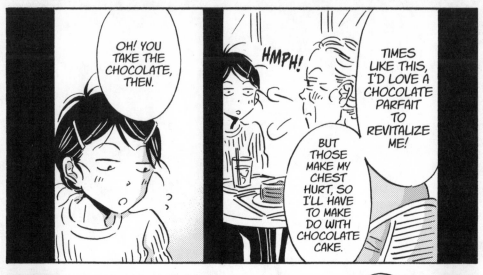

HMPH!
TIMES LIKE THIS, I'D LOVE A CHOCOLATE PARFAIT TO REVITALIZE ME!
BUT THOSE MAKE MY CHEST HURT, SO I'LL HAVE TO MAKE DO WITH CHOCOLATE CAKE.
OH! YOU TAKE THE CHOCOLATE, THEN.
OH DEAR! THAT'S NOT WHAT I WAS TRYING...
ER... ACTUALLY ...
YOU DON'T MIND?
NOPE, NOT AT ALL.

THANK YOU FOR PICKING UP VOLUME 2! I ONLY RECENTLY LEARNED THE WORD "AFTERPARTY," BUT IT SEEMS LIKE A BLESSED TIME.

KAORI TSURUTANI OCTOBER 2018

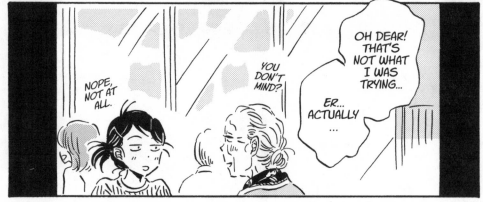

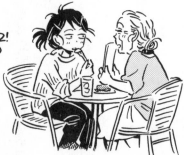

COVER DESIGN
Kohei Nawata Design Office

STAFF
Naomi Harada
Fumi Iwasaki
Keiko Nagatomo

EDITOR
Masayasu Noguchi

SPECIAL THANKS
Akane Kannari, ShuCream, Inc.
Natsuko Kanno
Morio Kobayashi
Konno Shoten
Shogaku Asagaya branch
nico salon

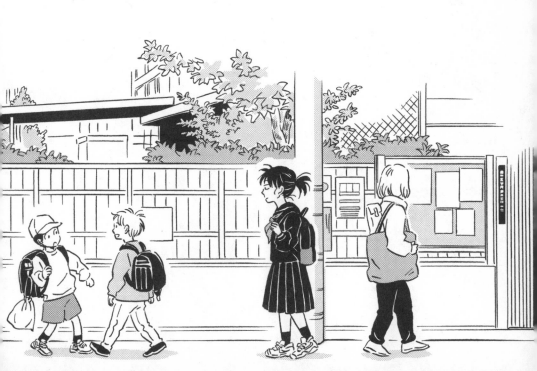

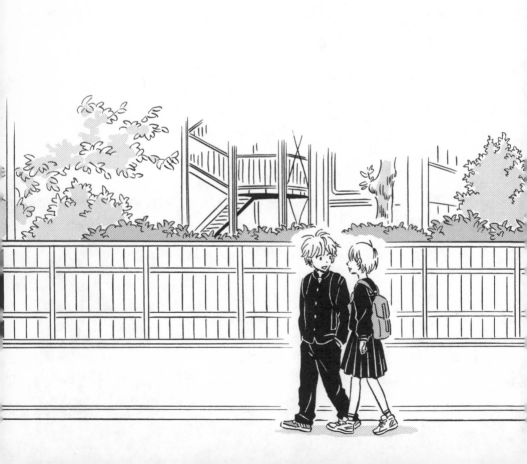

SEVEN SEAS ENTERTAINMENT PRESENTS

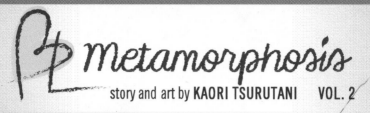

BL Metamorphosis

story and art by **KAORI TSURUTANI** VOL. 2

TRANSLATION
Jocelyne Allen

ADAPTATION
Ysabet MacFarlane

LETTERING
Ray Steeves

COVER DESIGN
Nicky Lim

LOGO DESIGN
Ki-oon

PROOFREADER
Danielle King

EDITOR
Jenn Grunigen

PREPRESS TECHNICIAN
Rhiannon Rasmussen-Silverstein

PRODUCTION MANAGER
Lissa Pattillo

MANAGING EDITOR
Julie Davis

ASSOCIATE PUBLISHER
Adam Arnold

PUBLISHER
Jason DeAngelis

METAMORPHOSE NO ENGAWA Vol. 2

First published in Japan in 2018 by KADOKAWA CORPORATION, Tokyo.
English translation rights reserved by Seven Seas Entertainment
under the license from KADOKAWA CORPORATION, Tokyo.

Seven Seas press and purchase enquiries can be sent to Marketing Manager Lianne Sentar at press@gomanga.com. Information regarding the distribution and purchase of digital editions is available from Digital Manager CK Russell at digital@gomanga.com.

ISBN: 978-1-64505-504-4

Printed in Canada

First Printing: July 2020

10 9 8 7 6 5 4 3 2 1

FOLLOW US ONLINE: ***www.sevenseasentertainment.com***

READING DIRECTIONS

This book reads from ***right to left***, Japanese style. If this is your first time reading manga, you start reading from the top right panel on each page and take it from there. If you get lost, just follow the numbered diagram here. It may seem backwards at first, but you'll get the hang of it! Have fun!!

1
2
3
4
5
6
7
8
9

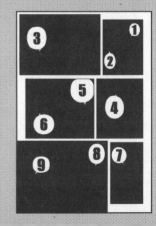